LINE

1935	1940	1945	1950	1955	1960	1965	1970	1975

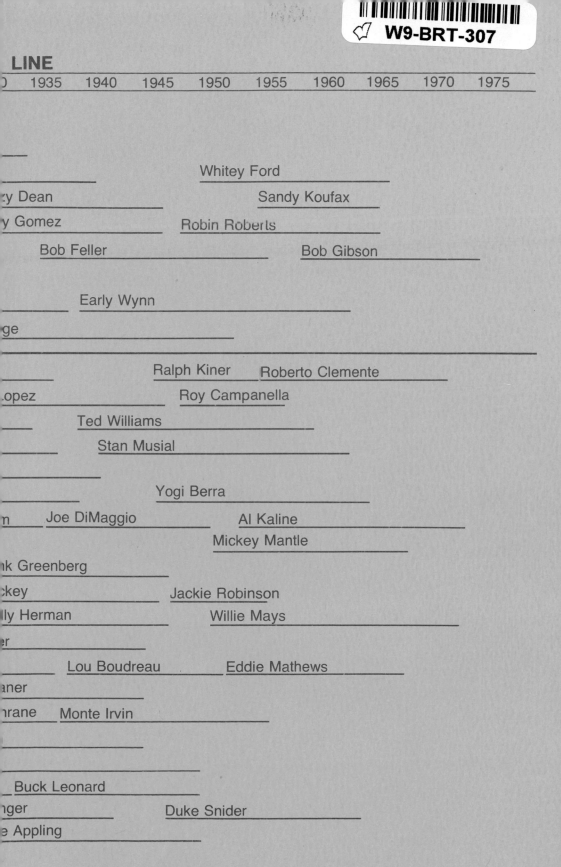

Whitey Ford

y Dean

Sandy Koufax

y Gomez

Robin Roberts

Bob Feller

Bob Gibson

Early Wynn

ge

Ralph Kiner   Roberto Clemente

opez

Roy Campanella

Ted Williams

Stan Musial

Yogi Berra

n   Joe DiMaggio   Al Kaline

Mickey Mantle

k Greenberg

key   Jackie Robinson

ly Herman   Willie Mays

er

Lou Boudreau   Eddie Mathews

aner

rane   Monte Irvin

Buck Leonard

ger   Duke Snider

e Appling

1983

To Dad

Merry Christmas

Red (George) + Dottie

Your "oldest Kids"

FOR THE LOVE OF IT

FOR THE LOVE OF IT

HALL OF FAMERS

TELL IT LIKE IT WAS

by Anthony J. Connor

MACMILLAN PUBLISHING CO., INC.

New York

Macmillan Publishing Co., Inc.
866 Third Avenue, New York, N.Y. 10022
Collier Macmillan Canada, Inc.

Library of Congress Cataloging in Publication Data
Main entry under title:
Baseball for the love of it.
Bibliography: p.
1. Baseball players—United States—Biography.
2. Baseball—United States—History. I. Connor,
Anthony J.
GV865.A1B34   796.357'092'2   [B]   81-23608
ISBN 0-02-527500-3   AACR2

10 9 8 7 6 5 4 3 2 1

Designed by Jack Meserole

Printed in the United States of America

Photo Credits

Boston Red Sox: pages 2, 24, 66, 254; New York Yankees: pages 4, 22 (inset), 25, 44, 50, 71 (inset), 86 (top and bottom), 97, 121, 129 (top and bottom), 139, 147 (top and bottom), 149, 150–51 (left, center, and right), 159, 180, 184, 196, 199, 201, 204, 215, 219, 231, 243, 248, 251, 292, 313 (left); Pittsburgh Pirates: pages 18 (left), 26, 54, 72 (left and right), 74, 96, 197; Detroit Tigers: pages 78, 80, 163; Texas Rangers: page 100; Atlanta Braves: page 100 (inset); Philadelphia Phillies: page 257; Timothy Connor: pages 7, 8, 13, 21, 22, 55, 63, 71, 83, 106, 107 (right), 122, 123, 191, 202, 227, 241, 260, 269, 271, 273 (left and right), 276, 279 (bottom), 306, 309, 310, 313 (right); Anthony Connor: pages 19, 59, 107 (left), 212 (left and right), 221, 266, 318; George Brace: pages 42, 112; Buck Leonard: page 206; Cool Papa Bell: page 211; The National League: pages 8 (inset), 30, 56, 76, 83, 133, 134, 148, 160, 178, 181, 189, 192, 217, 232, 262, 282; The Card Memorabilia Associates: pages 18 (right), 55 (inset), 89, 112 (inset), 221 (inset), 266 (inset); The National Baseball Hall of Fame: pages 127, 130, 136, 234, 279 (top), 294; *Baseball Bulletin*: pages 93, 120, 176; United States Navy: page 288.

For my parents who gave me so many priceless gifts
and for P.J. who's with me all the way.

Contents

Part Two THE STAR

Part Three THE OLD-TIMER

Foreword

Baseball, it has been said, is a game of inches. But even more, it is a game of innocence. It is a child holding tightly to his father's hand as he is taken to his first big league ballgame. Some twenty years later the scene is repeated—the child, now a man, has his own hand clasped just as tightly by *his* son as they approach the ballpark together for the first time.

The father, as his father before him, knows full well that baseball is as much business as sport. He also knows that the world is not just and that life is not fair. But, given the slightest encouragement, mind and heart keep to their separate orbits. As father and son pass through the turnstiles, walk side-by-side through the damp passageways under the stadium, and then suddenly emerge into the dazzling brightness—the vast green playing field laid out like a magic carpet before them—they share the excitement that today is something very special for both of them. The parent passes on the wonder and awe of his own youth to his children, and in so doing renews it within himself.

Anthony Connor has captured this transcendent quality of baseball in his marvelous book. The voices of the great players evoke poignant memories, reminding us that the game was indeed once played mainly for the love of it. And clearly, as their words reveal, it left as deep and lasting an impression on the players as on the fans.

It is especially good to have *Baseball for the Love of It* at this particular time, when owners and players seem blind to why baseball has become so tightly woven into the fabric of American life. As a symbol of joy and loyalty, a shared illusion that links generation to generation, baseball has grown from the fragile roots of trust, faith, allegiance, and make-believe that bind owners, players, and fans in a common fate.

Sportswriter Red Smith once observed that ninety feet between bases is the nearest thing to perfection that man has yet achieved. The game itself is so appealing, its rules and distances so consumately designed, that it prospers despite arrogant owners, greedy players, and disorderly spectators gnawing away at its vitals. As money grows more important than the game, the foundations that underlie the popularity of baseball are in danger of slowly disintegrating.

Baseball should heed its own heritage. Philosopher Jacques Barzun once said that "whoever wants to know the heart and mind of America had better learn baseball." The converse is equally true: whoever wants to know the essence of baseball had better learn the heart and mind of America.

The strongest thing baseball has going for it today is its yesterdays, which is what this book is all about.

LAWRENCE S. RITTER
1982

Preface

In writing *Baseball for the Love of It*, I was assembling a jigsaw puzzle. For two years I worked and played with the words of one hundred of the greatest players of baseball history—digging them up, dusting them off, poring over them, polishing them, trying them in different combinations—all the things you always do with the pieces of a jigsaw puzzle. As any puzzle person will affirm, the patience to sit alone in silence for hours, days, and months on end is a golden virtue. The puzzle had over twenty-five hundred pieces. Slowly the picture emerged—a huge mural of a century of baseball viewed from the inside.

Actually, the number twenty-five hundred represents a maximum. Ultimately, only about five hundred of the pieces fit the finished puzzle: The other two thousand make a most impressive heap on the cutting-room floor. The book's first draft was two hundred sixty thousand words. The more modest one-hundred-thousand-word volume you now hold is the product of three painful but necessary revisions. Please don't bother inspecting the pages for evidence of mayhem. All traces of blood have been scrubbed away.

Fifty-four thousand of the words come from thirty-four hours of taped interviews. This is the heart of the book, just as it was the most important (and most enjoyable) phase of its creation. The rest of the words come from various sources, which are enumerated in the Notes. I searched back in time through these supplementary sources primarily seeking the voices of important players long since dead, and I have juxtaposed those legendary old voices with those of the more recent stars in an attempt to capture some of the sweep of the long decades since the umpire wore a top hat and Kelly was "The King."

Mostly, I've left it to you, the reader, to draw your own conclusions from these juxtapositions, but for what it's worth, I'll inform you now of my chief bias. I've chosen to emphasize the historical continuities rather than the discontinuities, simply because I believe they are more significant. As much as society has grown and changed, and the world of baseball along with it, the nature of the individual remains eternally the same. The emotions of boyhood described by King Kelly in the 1880s (from "First Magic") could be those of any boy in the 1980s. Similarly, the physical decline described by Buck Leonard in "The Veteran" would be immediately recognizable to a player of any era. Thus my emphasis is on the timeless, the universal, and the human more than on the historical and social aspects of the baseball world, although these aspects too are treated. The voices change from passage to passage, but the perspective is always personal. The players speak here directly to you.

In ordering the passages I followed two imperatives—chronological and logical when possible, merely logical when necessary. For example, in "Changing Times," when Johnny Evers's prescient remarks on the reserve clause (from 1910) seemed particularly relevant to contemporary controversies, I felt free to sandwich them between the words of Sandy Koufax (from 1966) and Ralph Kiner (from 1980). Generally, though, chronology was respected, and when I did feel the need to flash forward or back, I clarified the move by labeling the passage appropriately.

Finally, in case you're wondering, Why only Hall of Famers? No, I'm not a snob. No, I wouldn't go so far as to label them a "control group." But I do value the few consistencies guaranteed by the artificial limitation. Every one of these men is a baseball insider. All have experienced "stardom." All possess the rich perspective of long service. All are old-timers, and generally they speak with the frankness and honesty I've learned to expect from that age group. (Few of them, I suspect, would have been quite as candid during their active playing days.)

But there's more, and here's where it becomes personal. On one very real level, in researching and writing *Baseball for the Love of It*, I was purely and simply a young man in search of wisdom. Stan Musial's words in "Wisdom for Rookies and Other Young" apply directly to my own experience. "I've always valued my older friends and respected their experience. When Ty Cobb came around to offer advice, I took it—and profited from it. Still do." Similarly, I've profited from the wisdom of Stan "The Man," as well as the others interviewed.

Many of these men were my boyhood idols, and naturally, I wanted to meet them as would any fan. But I desired more than just a brush with celebrity. I wanted to learn whether they are really any different from the rest of us, and if so, how. These men have risen to the pinnacle of their chosen profession. Why? Is it simply a matter of raw talent? What, if anything, makes these Hall of Famers special?

And now my searching and researching are done. In this sense, I'm a fan reporting back to my fellow fans. Contrary to media rumor, these "superstars" are not eight feet tall. Death will surely claim them as it will claim us all. In their youth all were admirable physical specimens, some were even awesome; but today, aside from their famous faces, they're indistinguishable from any other group of prosperous ex-jocks. As a rule, though intelligent and clearheaded, they are not particularly brilliant or notably complex.

Nevertheless, they *are* special men, men who had the faith and courage and, of course, the ability to pursue their youthful dreams to the limit. They were willing to commit themselves fully to that pursuit with all the risks and sacrifices thereby entailed, and I haven't known many in my life about whom I could make that statement so unequivocally. Thus to me they are romantic heroes, heroes in a limited sphere undoubtedly, but heroic nonetheless.

Baseball was not just a game to these men. It was a passion, a total challenge that evoked their finest efforts—physical, mental, *and* spiritual. Referring again to my friend Mr. Musial, he tells of his concentration at the plate, concentration so perfect that he didn't just think, he *knew* what pitch was coming next. And if Whitey Ford happened to be throwing that pitch, he claims that he can remember it fifteen years later along with every other pitch he ever threw. How many of us can make such statements about our work?

Nor were these men motivated primarily by money. I speak only of the men I met, but I maintain that their *ultimate* motivation, that inner drive that resulted in consistent excellence, season after season, came not so much from money as from a tremendous pride in performance and a need to excel against the very best competition. In Bill Dickey's words, "That competitive spirit means the difference between great and mediocre." Clearly, the ballplayers who speak in

Baseball for the Love of It come from the former, not the latter, category.

In summary, I maintain that the Hall of Famers I met and interviewed were as a group entirely worthy of the respect that is widely afforded them. I sincerely thank them for sharing their time and memories and for what they've taught me—about baseball and, more importantly, about the living of life.

New York City
1981

Acknowledgments

During the nearly three years between idea and its published realization, every possible disaster struck, all classic pitfalls were encountered, and numerous battles were lost. And yet the war was won, clearly won. I'm *delighted* with this publication. And to think that I once doubted the operation of God's grace in the world. Yes, I'd be a vain fool to try and hog the credit.

So . . . some acknowledging. In addition to the aforementioned Amazing Grace, there were people—many more than I'll ever even know—who contributed to the book's safe passage. Yes, I realize the list below is incomplete. (If I miss your name please holler: I'll send roses.)

Thanks to Barbara Tuchman—patroness of the New York Public Library's Wertheim study where I spent many many hours. Thanks to the PR people for photos and all-around helpfulness—Dick Bresciani and Bill Crowley of the Red Sox, Howard Starkman of the Blue Jays,

Mickey Morabito of the Athletics, Betsy Leesman of the Yankees, Dan Ewald and Bob Miller of the Tigers, Burton Hawkins and Dan Schimek of the Rangers, Wayne Minshew of the Braves, Jim Ferguson of the Reds, Arthur Richman of the Mets, Joe Safety and Sally O'Leary of the Pirates, Stu Smith of the Giants, Martin Appel of the Office of the Commissioner, Bob Fishel of the American League, and especially Katey Feeney of the National League.

Before I go any further I'd better thank an obvious group—the Hall of Famers, especially those willing to share time and talk with a friendly stranger, namely Messieurs Appling, Bell, Berra, Campanella, Cronin, Dickey, Feller, Ford, Gehringer, Grimes, Herman, Irving, Kaline, Kiner, Leonard, Lindstrom, Lopez, Mantle, Marquard, Mathews, Musial, Roberts, Roush, Sewell, Snider, (L.) Waner, and Williams—one hell of a bunch of guys. Extra thanks to Monte Irvin for the memorable afternoon at Baychester Diagnostic Reception Center in the Bronx.

Thanks also to the following: Larry Donald, editor and publisher of *Baseball Bulletin*, for photos; Mike Aronstein, President of TCMA and world class expert on baseball photos, for photos and photo advice; Cliff Kachline, historian at the National Baseball Hall of Fame, for early encouragement and several later consultations; and Andy Moursund, old friend and world class expert on rare books and baseball history. Who else would have had a copy of King Kelly's *Play Ball!*, copyright 1888, just floating around the living room?

Thanks also to my friends Dick Green and Eliza Hicks for help with photo selection. Eliza also did the dust jacket photo.

Thanks to Larry Ritter, idol and mentor, and Bob Weil, advisor, reader, critic, and friend. These last two are also baseball authors.

Thanks to Jane Cullen, my editor and friend at Macmillan, who maintained her humor and charm at all times. I think she's becoming a baseball fan. Thank you also to Julian Bach, my agent/guardian angel, and one of the best in the business.

Finally, special thanks to those members of my family who have taken a most active interest in the book to the extent that they've rolled up their sleeves when needed to pitch in—to Tim, advisor, second conscience, visual consultant, photographer (contributed twenty-eight photos), editor, brother, oldest friend; to Mother, reader, supporter, bottomless fountain of love; to Dad, critic, editor, teacher, fellow researcher, and the John J. McGraw of my teenage baseball career. And to P.J., all-around solid platinum Rolls-Royce of a mate and friend.

Written for the love of it,

Anthony J. Connor
New York City

The author thanks the following for permission to reprint passages of previously published material:

Robert Broeg for excerpts from *Stan Musial* by Stan Musial (as told to Bob Broeg). Copyright 1964 by Robert Broeg and Stan Musial; Liveright Publishing Corporation for excerpts from *My Thirty Years in Baseball* by John J. McGraw. Copyright 1923 by Boni and Liveright, Inc. Copyright renewed 1950 by John J. McGraw; Doubleday and Company, Inc. for excerpt from *My Life in Baseball* by Ty Cobb. Copyright 1961 by Trust Company of Georgia, executor of the Estate of Tyrus Cobb; Macmillan Publishing Company, Inc. for excerpts from *The Glory of Their Times* by Lawrence S. Ritter. Copyright 1966 by Lawrence S. Ritter; E. P. Dutton Publishing Company, Inc. for excerpts from *My Life In and Out of Baseball* by Willie Mays (as told to Charles Einstein). Copyright 1966 by Willie Mays. Also for adapted excerpt from *The Babe Ruth Story* by Babe Ruth (as told to Bob Considine). Copyright 1948 by George Herman Ruth; Random House, Inc. for excerpts from *Casey at the Bat: The Story of My Life in Baseball* by Casey Stengel (and Harry T. Paxton). Copyright 1962 by Casey Stengel and Harry T. Paxton; Viking Penguin Inc. for excerpts from *Koufax* by Sandy Koufax (with Ed Linn). Copyright 1966 by Sandy Koufax. Also for excerpts from *Whitey and Mickey* by Whitey Ford, Mickey Mantle, and Joseph Durso. Copyright 1977 by Whitey Ford, Mickey Mantle, and Joseph Durso.

When I was a boy, life was a
baseball game.
                    —AL KALINE in
                       1980

Part One

THE

BOY

The young Ted Williams

All I want out of life is that when I
walk down the street, folks will
say, "There goes the greatest hitter
who ever lived."
—TED WILLIAMS at
age twenty

DREAMS

Willie Mays in 1961

. . . every common sight
To me did seem
Apparell'd in celestial light,
The glory and freshness of a dream.
                            —WILLIAM
                    WORDSWORTH,
                    "Intimations of
                    Immortality"

1.

First Magic

Willie Mays
From the time I was less than two, my father started me with a ball. He was Kitty-Kat—that was his nickname, that's what the other players called him on the pickup semipro teams around Birmingham. And they called him that for a reason. He was the most graceful fielder, they said, that anybody ever saw.

Piper Davis [former manager of the Birmingham Black Barons] said to me, a couple of years back, "You get the greatest instinctive jump on a ball I ever saw, except for maybe Joe D. or his brother Vince. But you've got more range than either of them, and you field ground balls better. And you don't know how to look bad under a fly ball."

"Sounds like I'm pretty good," I said.

"Only one better," he said. "Your old man, Kitty-Kat. Lot of things you can do, he couldn't do. But *graceful?* Man he was a poem. Know the difference? You don't *pounce.* You're a grabber. The old man, though—that's why we called him Kitty-Kat—now, *he* knew how to *pounce!*"

And that was the game. When I was two years old my dad would roll the ball at me, easy, and I'd stop it and then take it in my right hand and throw it back. And that was it—no matter how bad I threw it, he'd catch it. Like Piper said, Kitty-Kat would *pounce*. Till I wanted to pounce too.[1]

King Kelly in 1888

I am a firm believer in the boys of America. If I could afford it, I would allow all the small boys to witness the ball games free of charge. The small boys are a tower of strength to the game of baseball. Perhaps the revenues of the club are not made rich by their presence at the league games. Perhaps they do go "junky" (that is, pick old waste paper and junk) during the morning hours, for the purpose of getting pennies enough to go on a shed roof to see a ball game; perhaps they do make life a burden to grown-up men, asking for pennies to take them in; perhaps they do pick out the favorite knotholes in the fence, and fight for their possession against bigger and stronger boys.

They do all these things. Yet, on the other hand, look at the great good they do. They know the names of almost every player in the league. The chances are that they know more about my season's record than I do myself. . . . They go home at night and talk baseball to their fathers, mothers, sisters, cousins, and aunts. They make veritable gods of their favorite players at home. The result is that the father has a strong curiosity to see these players. He may go alone, or he may take his wife or family. . . . If he is lucky he will take the small boy.

Why?

Because the small boy will learn him how to score a game, and assist him in numerous other ways. . . . He will tell him who the best batter is, who can pitch best, who can scoop in the high flies best, who can cover the bases in the quickest time, and one hundred and one other things which the parent would never hear of were it not for the bright, wide-awake, little fellow at his side. The parent begins to think more of his boy. He feels proud of the knowledge he possesses. He sighs to himself, observes, perhaps, that this is a progressive age, and thinks that at his age he never thought of baseball. He forgets that there wasn't a great baseball fever when he was a boy.[2]

Joe Cronin

I was born and reared in San Francisco. When I was growing up there back in the years around World War I, we never used to think of the major leagues. It was all the Pacific Coast League. San Francisco had *two* minor league teams in the same league, the Missions and the Seals. I mainly went to see the Seals. They had a lot of veteran

"*Magic—enough to stir any young boy.*"

ballplayers who had passed their peak and been sent down as well as the young players working their way up. The veteran players liked playing in the Coast League because they had every Monday off. And as you know the weather out there is so conducive to easy living.

My idol was Willie Kamm, the stylish third baseman who was sold from the Seals to the Chicago White Sox for one hundred thousand dollars in 1922, which was a record price at that time. Yeah, I idolized Willie—so did half my friends—and then years later I found myself playing in the major leagues against him.

So there was a lot of magic—enough to stir any young boy. Since I was seven years old I guess I always wanted to be a ballplayer. It was in my blood. Used to nip trucks to get to the ball park.

Funny thing about that. I learned that you could get into Recreation Park—that's where the Seals played, at the corner of Fifteenth and Valencia Street—if you went down there early and helped the man who was in charge of the turnstiles. So I went down bright and early one day and helped this fellow set up, and sure enough he let me in. I was the first person in the ball park, and I went out to the bleachers to watch the players warm up. Four Oakland players were the first ones to come out, and they started playing pepper out behind second base, hitting the ball toward where I was sitting in center field.

Well, the ball got by all three of the fielders; and in my anxiety to assist I jumped over the fence, got the ball, and rolled it back to them. Next thing I knew this cop was throwing me out of the ball park.

After dreaming all night long about how I was gonna get in free, I got myself kicked out before the game even started.

A few years later I come into the ball park as a member of the Pittsburgh Pirates, through the pass gate. I walk by the same cop and nod to him, and I'm thinking to myself, You don't know it, but you threw me out of this place one time.

Sandy Koufax

I was born in the Borough Park section of Brooklyn on December 30, 1935.

In my early years I was a street kid—"street," in this sense, meaning the school yard, the playground, the parks, the beaches, the community centers. I went where the games were.

The buildings in our neighborhood were single- and double-story wooden houses, with what we called "stoops" in Brooklyn, although they seem to be called porches everyplace else. Leading up to the stoops were three or four steps on which the younger kids would play stoopball—throwing the ball against the steps until somebody's mother came out and kicked you away.

The rules were very strict. The official ball, the only ball ever used, was a small hard pink rubber ball that would really fly if you could

Sandy Koufax in 1980. INSET: *with the Dodgers in the early 1960s.*

catch the edge of the step. Although it had the name "Spalding" plainly printed across its middle, it was known without fail—any group of kids, any neighborhood—as "a Spal-*deen*," with the last syllable hit as hard as possible. The pronunciation was important; it gave the game its special flavor and gave us players a special status. By hitting the last syllable so hard, we made it seem as if we were hard guys playing with a hard ball.

I still see small pink balls in variety stores and drugstores, and I always wonder whether the kids still call them spaldeens. If they don't they're not really playing the same game we played. They're just throwing a ball against some steps.

From stoopball you graduated into stickball and punchball. In punchball you stuck to the Spaldeen; in stickball you used an old tennis ball because the seams let you pretend it was really a baseball. Stickball and punchball are almost the same game except that in punchball you hit the ball from out of your own hand with your fist, while in stickball (when it is played in the street) the ball is served up to you on the bounce and you hit it with a small bat or broomstick.

In both games you had full teams if you had enough kids around. If you didn't you just did the best you could. The bases were probably the fender of a car on one side of the street and a hydrant on the other, with a sewer cover for second base. The ball, being fairly soft, could not be hit for any great distance, and if you hit one that covered two sewers, you were a man of distinction.

Mothers left you pretty much alone. You were now battling automobiles and cops.[3]

Ty Cobb

[My father's] academic mind searched for—but found nothing useful—in whacking a string ball around a cow pasture and then chasing madly about the bases while an opponent tried to retrieve said pill and sock you with it. That was one of the rules of town ball, the first bat-and-glove game I played. If the defensive fielder could hit the base runner with the ball, the latter was out. Also, a home run entitled the hitter to another turn at bat. If you kept on homering you could swing all day. In Carnesville, Georgia, first, and, later, when we moved to Royston, I hungered for competition. It wasn't that I gave baseball a second thought as a career—skinny ninety-pounder that I was. My overwhelming need was to prove myself a real man. In the classroom I was merely adequate—except for a flair for oratory, which brought me a few prizes, I couldn't hope to match my celebrated father for brains. In town ball—pitted at the age of fourteen against older boys and men—was the chance to become more than another schoolboy and the son of Professor Cobb.

The professor's attitude was "Quit fooling around and settle down to some serious work." At fourteen he felt I should have formed a definite lifetime plan.

I thought, He's my father and of course he's right. I felt guilty that some great ambition hadn't seized me beyond handling hard hoppers and line drives. Nevertheless, I tried out for the Royston Reds—composed mostly of husky eighteen- to twenty-five-year-olds. I wasn't yet fifteen and I was spindly. I guess I swung a bat with my hands spread a few inches apart from the very beginning. I wasn't strong enough to get around on the ball any other way. That grip was to arouse considerable curiosity later and answer many a major league hitting problem for me. But it began . . . from necessity.

I can't say that the Reds were overwhelmed at my arrival. I had sent away for "how to sprint" books advertised in the *Police Gazette* and spent hours practicing fast starts and pumping my knees high. Although I had plenty of speed I looked like a horsefly by comparison with those full-grown ball hawks who played for the "First Nine" of Royston. But they couldn't shoo me away. I was determined to earn one of those cardinal-red uniforms. . . .

My first position on the diamond was catcher. A pitch glanced off a bat and caught me in the eye. End of catching. I went out to shortstop and got in the way of the first hard clod-cutter—off the bat of a grown man—I'd ever tried to handle. It was smashed straight at me. I couldn't duck without dishonor . . . something kept me from pulling my head. . . .

I made the play and threw out the runner. . . .

Instinctively, I knew I was in the right place.

But my glove was a disgrace. It was just a tattered piece of leather I'd sewn together. Down at the dry-goods store was a model I couldn't live without. But I didn't dare ask my father to buy it.

Slipping into my father's library I selected two of his more expensive books, traded them for the glove, and complimented myself on a deal well made. It wasn't stealing, the way I saw it. The library contained books by the score. I had no glove. The exchange was merited. Anyway, who'd notice the volumes were missing?

Professor Cobb did. And he took another view of it. . . .

"Tyrus," he said in his quietly ominous way. "I want to talk to you." He led me into the library and shut the door.

Let us draw the curtain of mercy over the scene.[4]

Connie Mack

The first big adventure in my boyhood was that day in 1883 when we young ballplayers in East Brookfield, Massachusetts, made a daring venture. Our manager wrote a letter to Cap Anson, inviting him to bring his Chicago Colts to East Brookfield on their way back from a series in Boston.

"We'll guarantee you $100," our offer read.

What do you think happened? Cap Anson accepted. We couldn't have been more pleased or surprised if we had fallen heir to the Rockefeller fortune.

We went out and looked over our sandlot where Anson's Chicago Colts were to play an exhibition game. It was a vacant lot littered with what I once called Irish confetti: tin cans, plug-tobacco tags, and shoe-finding scraps.

Some of the others and I were working in the shoe factory at that time, and we used our lunch hours to dump the debris from the factory as far away as possible from what we called the diamond. We wanted to get it out of sight so that our Chicago visitors wouldn't stumble over it.

We had heard that the Colts were elaborate dressers, wearing white stockings and short dark Dutch pants; sometimes black tights, and loud-colored checkered bathrobes. One season they had appeared in dress suits with white-bosomed shirts, and they threw their spike-tailed coats as they walked onto the diamond. We also heard that they rode in state in open carriages, drawn by dapper white horses, four men in each carriage.

Imagine all that glamour coming to our little village of East Brook-field! Well, the players came, but left the glamour at home.

The gala day in East Brookfield found all the villagers trying to see the game. It was a bigger event to us than the inauguration of a president. We cheered ourselves hoarse as Anson and his Colts trotted onto our sandlot.

What a glorious sight it was! Anson played first base. A little fellow named Nicol played in right field. What a roar he got from us East Brookfielders when he ran up behind the great Anson and sneaked between his legs! Cap, who was a born showman, appeared to be sur-prised and bewildered. We nearly burst our buttons with laughter at the spectacle. . . .

When it was over, we passed the hat to raise the $100 guarantee for our visitors. Dimes, nickels, and pennies fell into it. When we counted these we found we had just enough.

With a rousing ovation from old East Brookfield, we waved our hats good-bye as Anson and his galloping Colts left our home town.[5]

Wahoo Sam Crawford

I grew up in Wahoo, Nebraska. "Wahoo Sam." I insisted they put that on my plaque at the Hall of Fame. That's my home town, and I'm proud of it. . . .

In those days baseball was a big thing in those little towns. The kids would be playing ball all the time. Nowadays basketball and football seem to be as popular among kids as baseball, maybe more so, but not then. And we didn't have radio, you know, or television, or automobiles. I guess, when you come to think of it, we spent most of our childhood playing ball.

Heck, we used to make our own baseballs. All the kids would gather string and yarn, and we'd get hold of a little rubber ball for the center. Then we'd get our mothers to sew a cover on the ball to hold it all together. We didn't use tape to tape up the outside, like kids did ten or twenty years later. We didn't see much tape in those days, about 1890 or so. Of course, they had tape then, electrical tape, but not much. . . .

Every town had its own town team in those days. I remember when I made my first baseball trip. A bunch of us from around Wahoo, all between sixteen and eighteen years old, made a trip overland in a wagon drawn by a team of horses. One of the boys got his father to let us take the wagon. It was a lumber wagon, with four wheels, the kind they used to haul the grain to the elevator, and was pulled by a team of two horses. It had room to seat all of us—I think there were eleven or twelve of us—and we just started out and went from town to town, playing their teams.

One of the boys was a cornet player, and when we'd come to a town he'd whip out that cornet and sound off. People would all come out to see what was going on, and we'd announce that we were the Wahoo team and were ready for a ball game. . . . We didn't have any uniforms or anything, just baseball shoes maybe, but we had a manager. I pitched and played the outfield both.

It wasn't easy to win those games, as you can imagine. Each of those towns had its own umpire, so you really had to go some to win. We played Freemont, and Dodge, and West Point, and lots of others in and around Nebraska. Challenged them all. Did pretty well, too.

We were gone three or four weeks. Lived on bread and beefsteak the whole time. We'd take up a collection at the games—pass the hat, you know—and that paid our expenses. Or some of them, anyway. One of the boys was the cook, but all he could cook was round steak. We'd get twelve pounds for a dollar and have a feast. We'd drive along the country roads, and if we came to a stream, we'd go swimming; if we came to an apple orchard, we'd fill up on apples. We'd sleep anywhere. Sometimes in a tent, lots of times on the ground, out in the open. If we were near some fairgrounds, we'd slip in there. If we were near a barn, well . . .[6]

Al Lopez

In 1925 a team of big leaguers came barnstorming through Tampa, right after the World Series, planning on playing each other or playing against a local pickup team. When they got to Tampa they thought it might be a good idea to get one of the local kids to play with them, to attract some customers. I was asked. I was only seventeen years old at

Al Lopez in 1980

the time and had caught just one season in the Florida State League, so you can imagine how scared and excited and delighted I was to play with big leaguers.

"Great," I said. "Who's pitching?"

"Walter Johnson," they said.

"Walter Johnson?" This was a little more than I'd expected.

"Do you think you can catch him?"

"I don't know," I said. "But I'll try."

So they advertised it: Walter Johnson pitching, Al Lopez catching. I thought that was pretty funny, me being an equal drawing card with Walter Johnson. But they figured it would attract a lot of people from over in Ybor City, where I lived.

Johnson was very nice. Just before we went out to warm up, he came over to me and said, "Look, I'm not going to really let out. I'm going to bear down on just two fellows—Ike Boone and Jack Fournier. They hit me pretty good, so I'm going to bear down on them. You be ready when they come up."

He bore down on them all right. He pitched just five innings that day, so he faced those guys twice each and he struck them out twice each. Johnson must have been around thirty-eight years old then, but still a great pitcher. He could still fire it when he wanted to. And you know, he was easy to catch. You could follow his ball, and he was always around the plate.

After it was over he told somebody, "That boy did real well back there. Handled himself fine." You can bet that made me feel good.[7]

Stan Musial

Back in the spring of 1938, I ran into Johnny Bunardzya, young sports editor of the Donora, Pennsylvania, *Herald*.

"How would you like to ride down to Pittsburgh with me and see the Pirates play the Giants?" he asked.

Even though Donora is only twenty-eight miles from Pittsburgh, I had never seen my favorite team play. . . . [T]he price was high for a kid who didn't have the money or, when he did, didn't have the time because of a summer job or ball game he was playing in himself. . . . The closest I'd come to Forbes Field before this had been in 1935. I'd saved up for the interurban trolley fare and the ticket to the ball game, but a friend had touched me for a loan and hadn't paid it back in time. So I missed seeing the one and only Babe Ruth make a grand exit with three home runs for the Boston Braves.

When Johnny Bunardzya offered three years later to take me to a big league game on his press pass, I played hooky from school.

Bunardzya remembers that I was bug-eyed when, from the upper tier behind first base, I got my first glimpse of the field.

"What a beautiful park!" I said then—and still do. To someone who has played on assorted hillside and river-front ball fields in the Monongahela Valley, any big league diamond is a jewel.

I don't remember too many details about that first big league game I saw, though I believe the Giants won, 5–3. A big New York left-hander, Cliff Melton, who was always tough on Pittsburgh, beat Pie Traynor, the Waner brothers, and the rest of my favorites.

I do remember, and so does Bunardzya, that after a few innings, I turned to him and said, "John, I think I can hit big league pitching."[8]

14   THE BOY / DREAMS

When I was a kid I felt baseball was
great for America. Always they
used to say Babe Ruth was the best
there ever was. But Babe Ruth was
an American. What we needed was
a Puerto Rican player they could
say that about, look up to, try to
equal. A country without idols is
nothing.　　　　　—ROBERTO
　　　　　　　　　　CLEMENTE

2.

Idols and Mentors

Babe Ruth

I spent most of the first seven years of my life living over my
father's saloon in Baltimore. When I wasn't living over it I was living in
it, studying the rough talk of the longshoremen, merchant sailors,
roustabouts, and waterfront bums. When I wasn't living in it I was
living in the neighborhood streets. I had a rotten start, and it took me a
long time to get my bearings. . . .

In 1902, when I was seven years old, my mother and father placed
me in St. Mary's Industrial School in Baltimore. It has since been called
an orphanage and a reform school. It was, in fact, a training school for
orphans, incorrigibles, delinquents, boys whose homes had been broken by divorce, runaways picked up on the streets of Baltimore, and
children of poor parents who had no other means of providing an education for them.

I was listed as an incorrigible, and I guess I was. Looking back on
my early boyhood, I honestly don't remember being aware of the differ-

ence between right and wrong. If my parents had something that I wanted very badly, I took it. I chewed tobacco when I was seven, not that I enjoyed it especially, but, from my observations around the saloon, it seemed the normal thing to do. . . .

I stayed in the school—learning to be a tailor and shirtmaker—until February 27, 1914. The last item in my "record" at St. Mary's was a single sentence which read: "He is going to join the Balt. Baseball Team. . . ."

It was at St. Mary's that I met and learned to love the greatest man I've ever known. His name was Matthias—Brother Matthias, of the Xaverian Brothers, a Catholic order which concentrates on work among underprivileged boys here and in Europe.

I saw some real he-men in my twenty-two years in organized baseball, but I never saw one who equaled Brother Matthias. He stood six feet six and weighed about two-fifty. It was all muscle. He seldom raised his voice, a sharp contrast to what I had known at home and in my neighborhood. But when he spoke he meant business. . . .

It wasn't that we were afraid of Brother Matthias. Some men just have an ability to command respect and love, and Brother Matthias was one of these. He could have been anything he wanted to be in life, for he was good-looking, talented, and dynamic. Yet he had taken vows of chastity and poverty and shut himself off from the world. I don't know why, but he singled me out when I first came to St. Mary's. It wasn't that I was his "pet." But he concentrated on me, probably because I needed it. He studied what few gifts I had, and drew these out of me. . . . He always built me.

Brother Matthias saw very early that I had some talent for catching and throwing a baseball. He used to back me into a corner of the big yard at St. Mary's and bunt a ball to me by the hour, correcting the mistakes I made with my hands and feet. When I was eight or nine I was playing with the twelve-year-old team. When I was twelve I was with the sixteen-year-olds, and when I was sixteen I played with the best team in school. All because of Brother Matthias. . . .

It was Brother Matthias who made me a pitcher. He did it to me to take me down a notch. I played a lot of baseball at St. Mary's, but I never had any hope of making a career of the game, and I guess I never would have played it professionally if Brother Matthias hadn't put me in my place one day and changed not only my position on the field but the course of my life. . . .

I was fourteen or fifteen at the time, and we were playing a game in which we were taking a terrific beating. One pitcher after another was being knocked out of the box, and finally it seemed funny to me. When our last pitcher began to be hit all over the lot, I burst out laughing at him. I guess I said a few things too.

Brother Matthias called time immediately and walked over.

"What are you laughing at, George?" he asked me in his strong but gentle way.

"That guy out there . . . getting his brains knocked out!" I howled, doubled over with laughter.

Brother Matthias looked at me a long time. "All right, George, you pitch," he said.

I stopped laughing. "I never pitched in my life," I said. "I can't pitch."

"Oh, you must know a lot about it," he said casually. "You know enough to know that your friend isn't any good. So go ahead out there and show us how it's done."

I knew he meant business. . . . I didn't even know how to stand on the rubber, or how to throw a curve, or even how to get the ball over the plate.

Yet, as I took the position, I felt a strange relationship between myself and that pitcher's mound. . . . It seemed to be the most natural thing in the world to start pitching—and to start striking out batters. I even tried a curve or two and, kidlike, curled my tongue to the corner of my mouth while doing it. It became a habit that I carried into the major leagues with me, and I couldn't break it until Bill Carrigan, my first big league manager, convinced me that I was "telegraphing" every curve with my tongue.

Brother Matthias saw to it that I didn't get far away from the pitcher's box during my last two seasons at St. Mary's. But he knew there was a time for play and a time for work. I could never duck a class to get to the ball field. . . . But baseball had won out. Through baseball, I got the second break of my life. The first break, it will always seem to me, was the fact that I met Brother Matthias. He was the father I needed.[1]

Lloyd Waner

Dad encouraged us to play ball. He sure did. Every chance he had he took us out to play catch. Now he was a good pitcher, and he took some pride in that, especially in the curveball he could throw, and it was a darned good one, too, very fast breaking. So when we went out to play catch he tried to take it easy because we were so small. . . . When he wanted to throw one of his great curveballs he'd tell us it was coming. Finally one day Paul [Lloyd's brother] said to him, "Throw anything you want. Don't make any different, curve or not." So Dad figured he'd teach us a lesson and started mixing those pitches up, curves and fastballs. But we surprised him.

Finally Dad stopped and put his hands on his hips.

"You fellows are all right," he said. "I'll swear, I'm throwing my

LEFT: *Lloyd Waner*. RIGHT: *Paul Waner*.

best curves and I can't even fool you. You fellows sure have quick little hands."

I was around eight years old at the time and Paul was eleven. . . .

Dad managed a local team for a while, and one day he put me into the game as a pinch hitter. I never will forget it. . . . I was so small that the other team thought Dad had put me in to try and work out a base on balls. But I hit at the first pitch I saw and poked it over the third baseman's head down the left-field line. We were playing in a cow pasture, and the ball rolled into some weeds and got lost. I started running, so excited I was shaking. When I got to third base they were still out in the weeds looking for the ball. I stood there and didn't know what to do. Gee, I thought, the ball is lost. So I ran out there to help them look for it, too excited to hear my dad yelling at me to come across the plate. Well, they finally found the ball, and whoever picked it up took one look at me and tagged me out. Dad never let me forget that one.

So you had that combination of things. The constant playing, the desire, the love for the game, the encouragement of good coaching from our dad; it all helped to develop what God-given abilities we had.[2]

Joe Cronin in 1980

Joe Cronin

Growing up in San Francisco, I was lucky in that I lived only half a block away from Excelsior Playground, which was part of the excellent playground sport program sponsored by the city in those days. There were teams in all sports for all age groups, and you'd grow up through the system. You'd travel all around town to play scheduled games at different playgrounds, and as a result, you'd meet all the athletes. I remember Tony Lazzeri lived across the street from Jackson Playground. He was a couple of years older than my gang. Excelsior was playing Jackson one time and we were ahead in the fifth inning, and they sent somebody over to knock on Tony's door and get him to come over and pitch them out of the jam. So he came and shut us out the rest of the way and hit the home run to win the ball game.

And in the winter, they'd have clinics and exhibitions featuring big league players. I can remember Ty Cobb coming to our playground—I think it was the winter of 1920—to give us some instruction in baseball fundamentals. And there were others—Willie Kamm, Lefty O'Doul, Lew Fonseca, Long George Kelly. We looked up to these guys and followed them around the sandlots of San Francisco. So we were in a great baseball—a great *sports*—environment, thanks in part to the playground department.

We had tennis tournaments. I never had the price of a pair of tennis shoes; but one year when I was fourteen, Stella Harris, our playground director, bought me my first pair out of her own pocket. I won the city-wide playground tennis championship in those shoes.

Speaking of Stella Harris, she became my lifelong friend; and later she became the director of North Beach Playground where Joe DiMaggio played when he was a boy. When I saw her one winter—this was *years* later—she told me about this fine young boy. She said, "He's just like you were, Joe, always playing baseball. His name is Joe DiMaggio."

There's a footnote on DiMaggio, still a few years later. The San Francisco Seals used to have Saturday morning workouts for kids— tryouts really. And they'd have different big leaguers come down and talk to them about aspects of the game, proper attitude, life in the big leagues, and that kind of thing. Kind of like the playground clinics I mentioned earlier. So one Saturday they asked me to come down. I didn't know it of course, but Joe told me later he was in that group. And, incidentally, he did sign with the Seals.

Bob Feller

My first glove was a Rogers Hornsby glove, the old three-fingered glove. Used it for years. Every two years I'd buy a new one. Wish I'd saved at least one of them. It'd be a real collector's item today. Hornsby was my first idol because we could get the Cubs games on our radio out on the farm in Iowa. I even took up second base as my first position because that was where he played.

Years later I met him, in fact, I pitched to him and struck him out. Of course, he was forty-one years old at the time. It was my second year in 1937 when he was still managing the Browns. He was the toughest right-handed hitter I ever pitched to, as a matter of fact. DiMaggio gave me more trouble, but if you compare their two records, Hornsby was the best. He had very strong theories about training—wouldn't even go to movies because he thought they were bad for his eyes. You can't disprove him. He batted .358 lifetime. So I picked a pretty good hitter for a boyhood idol, wouldn't you agree?

Ted Williams

I grew up in San Diego, and the closest big league baseball at that time was played in St. Louis. Hell, that was two thousand miles away and pretty near seemed like the end of the world. But I did read the sports pages, and when I was at as impressionable an age as can be, say twelve or thirteen, the names of certain big leaguers were in my mind. Hornsby and Ruth were over the hill, but Paul Waner was right at the top of his game. Lou Gehrig was certainly on top. But for some reason,

Bill Terry's name was the name that hit me a little bit in a special way. I'd be playing, or just swinging a bat, and I'd say to myself, "Bill Terry's up, last of the ninth, bases loaded, 3-and-2 count." You know how kids announce their own games. "Here's the pitch. Terry swings. . . ."

Actually though, Charles Lindbergh, at that time, was my greatest single idol. Oh yeah. Oh boy, I used to draw pictures of Lindbergh, his face, his helmet, and his goggles. And his plane, the *Spirit of St. Louis*. I never drew a picture of Ruth or Terry or any ballplayer. But I drew pictures of Lindbergh—and George Washington, and Napoleon. Those three guys.

"At as impressionable an age as can be . . ."

Ralph Kiner

I first got hooked into following big league baseball in 1934. The Detroit Tigers happened to be winning the American League pennant that year, and I guess for that reason they became my team. Love at first sight I guess. Hank Greenberg, Charlie Gehringer, Mickey Cochrane, Goose Goslin, Jo-Jo White, Rogell at shortstop. Bridges, Auker, and Schoolboy Rowe on the mound. I can still rattle off the whole lineup. And the funny thing is I never saw them play. I was way out in southern California then, and of course there was no TV. It just goes to show what an eleven-year-old boy can do with a newspaper box score and a good imagination.

Bob Feller

My father never played ball when he was young, but from very early in my life he took a strong interest in my development as a player. His dad died when he was nine years old, and he was left with three sisters and his mother and an Iowa farm to run. He'd had a brother, but his

Bob Feller in 1980. INSET: *with the Indians in the late 1940s.*

brother had died when he was very, very young. So my dad was the only man in the family, and working the land was his life. But he had great dreams for me. And I don't think he ever doubted that I'd eventually play professional ball.

We played baseball together constantly while I was growing up. He pitched batting practice to me, even built me a batting cage out of leftover lumber and chicken wire. Later, he caught me when I pitched. This was every night practically, after our farm chores were done. During cold or rainy weather, we'd play in the barn. He'd have me pitching under game conditions with a dummy batter and everything.

He bought me proper equipment too: uniform, spikes, a good glove always, and official league balls, not the nickel rocket variety that a lot of my friends had to use.

And we talked and talked about baseball, studied books on the fine points of the game, sitting around our big warm kitchen. It was my father who persuaded me to specialize in pitching, though it took me a while to accept not playing every game.

But probably the greatest thing he did for me was when I was twelve, we built a complete ball field on our farm. We called it Oakview 'cause it was up a hill overlooking the Raccoon River and a beautiful view of a grove of oak trees. That lasted four years. We had a complete diamond with an outfield fence and scoreboard and even a grandstand behind first base.

We charged a small admission to cover our expenses—my father transported the players and my mother fed them. We never made any money, although some of the neighbors were sure we did. But mainly we had a great old time. Our team of farm boys played teams from as far west as Omaha, some pretty fast teams too. We drew some pretty fair-sized crowds on certain weekends. I was the only real "kid" on our team, but I did just fine.

Oakview Park was my incubator as a pitcher. Looking back on it now I have to be pretty thankful that my father was the man he was.

Duke Snider

I grew up in southern California, and there wasn't any major league baseball out there, but I followed the Pacific Coast League which was a very good league. We used to go to games at Wrigley Field in Los Angeles and watch the Angels play the Hollywood Stars, San Diego Padres, San Francisco Seals, teams like that.

I heard big league games on the radio, and the 1941 Dodgers stood out in my mind, especially two names—Pee Wee Reese and Pete Reiser. Little did I know that someday I'd be their teammate on those same Dodgers. Actually, it was mainly because of these feelings that I signed with the Dodgers from among the several offers I received. The Dodgers lost the World Series that year if you recall. Hugh Casey was pitching, and the ball got by Mickey Owen on a third strike, and every baseball fan knows the rest. . . .

Another early idol of mine was Lou Gehrig. I always considered that record for consecutive games to be just phenomenal. I was pretty broken up when he died.

When that movie *Pride of the Yankees* came out with Gary Cooper playing Lou Gehrig, I saw it maybe fifteen times. In fact, my family today has a videotape of it that we still show every once in a while, and I still get tears in my eyes watching that show.

When I first reported to the Dodger ball club in 1947, John Griffin, the clubhouse man, asked me what number uniform I'd like, and I asked, "What numbers are available?" He mentioned number 4. . . . That was Gehrig's number. So I asked for 4, and I wore it for my whole career.

Ted Williams

Nobody taught me about hitting. I learned.

Someone asked me recently, Do the young players today listen to instruction? Do they come up and seek advice? As a matter of fact, I'm surprised that more of them don't. But they are listening, and I know that they're listening because I'll hear them repeating things I've said.

I never had anyone directly tell me, "You oughta do this or that." I did overhear older players talking on the sandlots—and we had damn good sandlot ball in southern California. And I'd hear some of the better hitters say, "Good wrist action." Well, I don't believe in that part of it really, *but* these things all registered in my thinking. I remember one day one of the better sandlot hitters, after I'd been batting one of those old taped-up balls around—and I must've had good ears 'cause I don't think he meant me to hear it—he said, "That Ted's got good wrist action." Well, today as I look back with what I know about hitting, I don't say "good wrist action." I say "good hip action." But anyway, that encouraged me. I said, "If this guy thinks I've got good wrist action now, wait'll he sees me next time."

So that's the kind of thing that stimulated me, not what somebody told me. As a matter of fact, everyplace I ever went where I thought there was a good hitter, especially *professional* hitters, I'd try to learn something mainly by keeping my eyes and ears open. The first guy I ever asked for advice was Lefty O'Doul. He'd been batting champion

"I know that they're listening because I'll hear them repeating things I've said." Ted Williams with Jack Brohamer, spring training, 1980.

with the Giants, and he was a hell of a hitter. Boy, did he look good up there! So I went up and asked him, "What do I have to do to become a great hitter?"

He said, "Kid, I've seen you in batting practice. . . ." Now this is the great Lefty O'Doul, and I'm just barely eighteen years old. He says, "You just keep doing exactly what you're doing and don't let anyone change you." Now that lifted me to the *heights!*

And nobody ever did try to change me. Nobody!

Mickey Mantle

The idol of my early days was definitely my dad. He was the bravest man I ever knew. He never complained, and he never acted scared even when he was dying of Hodgkin's disease in 1951 and 1952. No boy ever loved his dad more than I did. I'd do anything to make that man happy. All it took from him was a sharp look, and I knew what was right and what was wrong.

His real name was Elvin, but they called him Mutt. He was a damned good ballplayer, but he had to work in the mines all his life to support our family during the Depression in one of the poorest parts of the country—in dust bowl country out in Oklahoma. I know that's why he felt so strongly about my making good in baseball. And that's why I'm glad he had a chance to see me play with the Yankees before he died.

Elvin Mantle, Cliff Mapes, and Mickey Mantle, Commerce, Oklahoma, 1951

"A long, skinny Irish lad with hatrack shoulder blades . . ." Connie Mack.

I was about seventeen then. I
remember I had trouble sleeping at
night. I used to get up and walk
through that little town—had
about twenty-four thousand people
in it—walk all night, look up at
the stars, and burn with a desire to
get away. I felt I was being held in
some sort of bondage. I just had to
get out of that town. It was about
that time I decided I would become
a ballplayer.   —TY COBB

Decision

Connie Mack

My father died when I was in my teens. I consoled my mother, who
by that time had a big family of growing youngsters to feed, with the
fact that I would support the family. This placed the responsibility on
me, a long, skinny Irish lad with hat-rack shoulder blades. . . .

When I was twenty-one I went into conference with my mother and
told her I could be of greater help to the family if I went somewhere
else where I could make more money. I argued that the other boys were
now getting big enough to help her at home. . . .

I told her I wanted to become a big league baseball player. . . .
Nothing could dissuade me. . . . The idea had been part of me ever since
I was nine years old. The love of baseball had grown with me.

"I've got a chance to sign up with a professional team," I explained. "I don't want to spend my life in a factory."

When my mother realized that my heart was so set, she reluctantly
consented.

"Promise me one thing," she said. "Promise me that you won't let them get you into bad habits. I've brought you up to be a good boy. Promise me that you won't drink."

I promised her, and that promise I shall keep to the end of my life.

When I told them at the factory of my decision, they were greatly upset, not that I was so valuable to them, but because they thought I would never make good, that I'd be a failure. I knew they really expected me to come back, hat in hand, and ask for my old job again.

When I walked out of my old home town in 1884, my sole worldly possessions were a pair of buckskin gloves with their fingers cut off to make catcher's mitts. I was on my way to fulfill my promise to myself. I was going to try to make the big leagues, and to make my dreams come true. For this was America, the land of opportunity.[1]

Ty Cobb in 1914

Parents, as a rule, object strongly when a boy proposes to go into pro ball. This objection, however, is not as prevalent now as it was ten years ago when I was making my decision. My father kicked worse than Clark Griffith does on a close call against him when I broke the news to him that I had a chance to go with the newly organized professional club in Augusta.

"You won't be gallivanting around the country playing ball," he said. "You'll go along to school and then, when you graduate, do some real work."

We argued until three o'clock in the morning before I finally wore him down. He agreed to let me try it for one season.

So I went with Augusta at age seventeen and even got a home run in the opening game of the 1904 season, but two days later they canned me.

I have found out since that my father made it his duty to journey in from home to watch that first game. . . . Maybe that's why he was sore when I called him with the news that I'd been released.

He asked, "Well, what are you going to do?"

I told him I had an offer to go to Anniston in the Tennessee-Alabama League for very much less money.

"So long as you're in it now, you've got to stick long enough to show them they were wrong, Tyrus. Go after it," he said. "And one more thing—don't come home a failure!"[2]

And in 1961

I had the shivers when I hung up. In giving me his blessing, in my hour of defeat, my father put more determination in me than even he knew.[3]

Rube Marquard

I told my parents I wanted to be a ballplayer, but Dad would never listen. "Ballplayers are no good," he'd say, "and they never will be any good."

And with that he'd slam the door and go outside and sit on the porch, and not talk to me for the rest of the evening.

One of my friends was a catcher named Howard Wakefield. He was about five years older than I was. In 1906 he was playing for the Waterloo club in the Iowa State League, and that summer—when I was only sixteen—I got a letter from him.

"We can use a good left-handed pitcher," the letter said, "and if you want to come to Waterloo I'll recommend you to the manager."

I wrote Howard that my dad didn't want me to play ball, so I didn't think he'd give me the money to go. . . . Now if they could possibly arrange to send me some money for transportation . . .

Well, pretty soon I got a telegram from the Waterloo manager. He said: "You've been recommended very highly by Howard Wakefield. I'd like you to come out here and try out with us. If you make good, then we'll reimburse you for your transportation and give you a contract."

Of course, that wasn't much of an improvement over Howard's letter. So I went upstairs to my room and closed the door and wrote back a long letter to the manager, explaining that I didn't have any money for transportation. But if he sent me an advance right now for transportation, then I'd take the next train to Waterloo and he could take it off my salary later on, after I made good. I didn't have the slightest doubt that I would make good. And, of course, I didn't mention that I was only sixteen years old.

I mailed the letter to Iowa, and then I waited on pins and needles for an answer. Every day I had to be the first one to get at the mail. . . . So every day I waited for the first sight of the mailman and tried to get to him before he reached the house.

As it turned out, I could have saved myself a lot of worrying. Because no letter ever came. Three weeks passed and still no answer. . . .

Finally, I just couldn't stand it anymore. I gave some excuse to my folks about where I was going—like on an overnight camping trip with the Boy Scouts—and I took off for Waterloo, Iowa, on my own.

From Cleveland, Ohio, I bummed my way to Waterloo, Iowa. . . . It took me five days and five nights, riding freight trains, sleeping in open fields, hitching rides any way I could. My money ran out on the third day and after that I ate when and how I could.

Finally, though, I arrived at my destination. It was early in the evening of the fifth day. The freight slowly drew into the Illinois Central station at Waterloo, Iowa, and just before it stopped I jumped off and went head over heels right in front of the passenger house. I hardly had time to pick myself up off the ground before the stationmaster grabbed me.

"What do you think you're doing?" he growled. "Come on, get out of here before I run you in."

"No, I said, "I'm reporting to the Waterloo ball club."

"You're what?" he says. "My God, did you ever wash your face?"

"Yes I did," I said, "but I've been traveling five days and five nights, and I'm anxious to get to the ball park. Where do the ballplayers hang around?"

"At the Smoke Shop," he said, "down the street about half a mile. If you walk down there probably whoever you're looking for will be there."

So I thanked him and told him I'd see that he got a free pass to the ball game as soon as I got settled, and started off for the Smoke Shop. It turned out that two brothers owned the Smoke Shop, and they also owned the ball club. One of them was behind the counter when I walked in. He took one look at me and let out a roar.

"What are you doing in here?" he yelled. "This is a respectable place. Get out of here."

"Wait a minute," I said. "I've got a telegram from the manager of the ball club to report here, and if I make good I'll get a contract."

"Are you kidding?" he said. "Who in the world ever recommended you?"

Rube Marquard in his prime

"Howard Wakefield did."

"Well," he said, "Wakefield is in back shooting billiards. We'll soon settle this!"

"I'd like to go back and see him," I said.

"Don't go back there," he shouted. "You'll drive everybody out. Did you ever take a bath?"

"Of course I did," I said, "but I've bummed my way here and I haven't had a chance to clean up yet."

So he called to the back and in a minute out came Howard. "Holy Cripes!" he said. "What happened to you?"

I was explaining it to him when in came Mr. Frisbee, the manager, and I was introduced to him. "I received your telegram," I said. "I didn't have enough money to come first class or anything like that, but here I am."

"Keokuk is here tomorrow," he said, "and we'll pitch you."

"Tomorrow? You don't want me to pitch tomorrow, after what I've been through?"

"Tomorrow or never, young fellow!"

"All right," I said. "But could I have five dollars in advance so I can get a clean shirt or something?"

"After the game tomorrow," he said, and walked away.

So Howard took me to his rooming house, and I cleaned up there and had something to eat, and they let me sleep on an extra cot they had.

The next day we went out to the ball park, and I was introduced to the players and given a uniform that was too small for me. The Keokuk team was shagging balls while I warmed up, and they kept making comments about green rookies and bushers and how they'd knock me out of the box in the first inning. Oh, I felt terrible. I had an awful headache and I was exhausted. But I was determined to show them that I could make good, and I went out there and won that game, 6–1.

With that I felt sure I'd be offered a contract. So after the game I went to Mr. Frisbee and said, "Well, I showed you I could deliver the goods. Can we talk about a contract now?"

"Oh," he said, "Keokuk is in last place. Wait until Oskaloosa comes in this weekend. They're in second place. They're a tough team, and if you can beat them then we'll talk."

"Can't I get any money, any advance money, on my contract?" I asked him.

"You haven't got a contract," he said.

"All right," I said, and I didn't say another word.

That evening I didn't say anything to anybody. But when it got dark I went down to the railroad station, and the same stationmaster was there.

"Hey," he said, "you pitched a fine game today. I was there and you did a great job. What are you doing back here? . . ."

I said, "I'm going back home to Cleveland, and I want to know what time a freight passes by." And I explained to him everything that had happened.

He was very nice to me, and after we talked awhile he said, "Look, this train comes in at one o'clock in the morning, and the engine unhooks and goes down to the water tower. When it does, you sneak into the baggage compartment, and meanwhile I'll talk to the baggage man before the engine gets hooked up again. Then when the train pulls out and is about five miles out of town he'll open the baggage door and let you out."

So that all happened, and when we were five miles out of town the door opened and the baggage man appeared. I talked with him all the way to Chicago, and as we got close to the yards he said to me, "OK, you better get ready to jump now. There are a lot of detectives around here, and if you're not careful they'll grab you and throw you in jail. So once you get on the ground, don't hesitate. Beat it away from here as fast as you can."

The baggage man must have told the engineer about me because we slowed down to a crawl just before we approached the Chicago yards, and off I jumped. I got out of there quick and took off down the street. . . . It was the middle of the morning, and I had hardly slept a wink the night before.

I'd walked about three or four blocks when I passed by a fire engine house. Evidently all the firemen were out at a fire because the place was empty. I was tired, so I went in and sat down. Well, they had a big-bellied iron stove in there, and it was warm, and I guess I must have fallen asleep, because the next thing I knew a couple of firemen were shaking me and doing everything they could to wake me up. They called me a bum, and a lot of other names, and told me to get out of there or they'd have me thrown in jail.

"I'm no bum," I said, "I'm a ballplayer."

"What, you a ballplayer! Where did you ever play?"

So . . . I told them all about it.

They still didn't really believe me. They asked me did I know Three-Fingered Brown, Tinker, Evers, Chance, and all those fellows.

"No," I said, "I don't know them. But someday I'll be playing with them, or against them, because I'm going to get in the big leagues."

"Where are you going now?" they asked me.

"Back home to Cleveland."

"Have you got any money?"

"No."

So they got up a little pool of about five dollars and said, "Well, on your way. And use this to get something to eat."

I thanked them, and as I left I told them that someday I'd be back. "When I get to the big leagues," I said, "I'm coming out to visit you when we get to Chicago."

And home I went.[4]

[Marquard did return to that firehouse in Chicago—many times—during a long and successful big league career.]

Stanley Coveleski

I was born in 1890 in Shamokin, Pennsylvania. That's anthracite country, about halfway between Scranton and Harrisburg. When I was twelve years old I was working in the mines from seven in the morning to seven at night, six days a week. Which means a seventy-two-hour week, if you care to figure it up. For those seventy-two hours I got $3.75. About five cents an hour. There was nothing strange in those days about a twelve-year-old Polish kid in the mines for seventy-two hours a week at a nickel an hour.

What *was* strange was that I ever got out of there. . . .

I never played much baseball in those days. I couldn't. Never saw the sunlight. Most of the year I went to work in the dark and came home in the dark. I would have been a natural for night baseball. Never knew the sun came up any day but Sunday.

But every evening after I got home I'd throw stones at tin cans. I don't know why. Just for something to do, I guess. Heck, we didn't have any television then, or radio, or automobiles, or even a telephone or electric lights. Had to do *something*. So I threw stones. I'd put a tin can on a log, or tie it to a tree, and stand maybe forty or fifty feet away and throw stones at it. Did that every night till it was time to go to bed. I did that for so many years I could hit one of those things blindfolded.

Well, the semipro team in town heard about me being so good throwing stones at tin cans, and they asked me if I'd like to pitch for them. That was in 1908, when I was eighteen. Then, before I knew what hit me, I was signed to a contract with Lancaster, and I was out of those damn mines for good.[5]

Edd Roush

Winters can be *awful* cold in Indiana and winter mornings awful dark. I grew up on a farm, and one of my chores was to milk the cows, which meant getting up before dawn and going out to that dark cold barn. I guess I minded it more than the cows, and I began to feel like I had to get away.

I was playing ball on the town team and doing pretty well, so one cold dark winter morning I said to myself, "I'll be a ballplayer."

I didn't expect to ever make it all the way to the big leagues, but I didn't care. I just had to get away from them damn cows.

Babe Ruth in 1928

When I was eighteen, Brother Gilbert wrote a letter to Jack Dunn, manager of the Baltimore Orioles, telling him about me and asking Jack to come around and see for himself. . . .

I'll never forget the day Brother Gilbert called me over and introduced me to Jack. I was flabbergasted. I hadn't known about the letter, and the idea of shaking hands with a real professional baseball man was almost too much. Jack was mighty good to me and talked for quite a while about baseball. Finally he got me into a uniform and out in the yard. He had me pitch to him . . . and at the end of a half hour Dunn called a halt and went into the office with Brother Gilbert.

In about a half hour they called me in, and Brother Gilbert explained that Mr. Dunn thought I would make a ballplayer and wanted me to sign a contract with the Orioles. Since I wasn't yet of age, Brother Gilbert explained, Mr. Dunn would take out papers as my guardian and would be responsible for me when I was away from the school.

"How about it, young man," Dunn asked me, "do you want to play baseball?"

I guess I must have come near falling over in my excitement. Did I want to play baseball? Does a fish like to swim? . . .

"Sure," I said, "I'll play. When do I start?"

But Brother Gilbert stopped me.

"Wait a minute, George," he said, "this is a serious business. Boys play baseball for fun, but you're a man now and you're taking a man's job. You know playing professional baseball isn't like playing on the sandlots. . . . It won't be easy. Besides," he added, "I want you to understand all the arrangements. Mr. Dunn has agreed to pay you six hundred dollars for the six-months season. That's approximately twenty-five dollars a week. Will you be satisfied with that?"

Looking back now, of course, six hundred dollars doesn't look like much money. But that day, there in the school office, it sounded like a fortune. And twenty-five dollars a week! I'd be as rich as Rockefeller! And for playing baseball! I never even hesitated. If Brother Gilbert expected me to do any serious thinking he sure got a disappointment that day.

"Sure, I'd like it," I said, and said it fast too, for fear Dunn might change his mind. And so it was arranged. A contract was drawn up, and I signed it. Then I beat it out of doors to tell the rest of the boys . . . that I was signed to a contract—a real honest-to-goodness professional baseball player!

Less than two years ago I sat in Colonel Ruppert's private office in New York and signed my name again—this time to a three-year contract calling for seventy thousand dollars a year. The newspaper boys were on hand, and the photographers, and the whole baseball world made a great ado about this signing. But honestly, that new contract for the largest salary ever paid a ballplayer didn't give me half the kick I got that afternoon back in 1914 when I signed with Jack Dunn to play ball with the Baltimore Orioles at twenty-five dollars a week.[6]

Paul Waner

I went to State Teacher's College at Ada, Oklahoma, for three years, although I didn't really intend to be a teacher. Maybe for a little while, but not forever. What I wanted to be was a lawyer, and I figured sooner or later I'd go to law school

But all at once baseball came up, and that changed everything. Of course, I was playing ball on amateur and semipro teams all the while I was in high school and college. In those days, you know, every town that had a thousand people in it had a baseball team. . . . There were so many teams along there in the Middle States, and so few scouts, that the chances of a good player being "discovered" and getting a chance to go into organized ball were one in a million. Good young players were a dime a dozen all over the country then.

How did they find me? Well, they found me because a scout went on a drunk. Yes, that's right, because a scout went on a bender. He was a scout for the San Francisco Seals of the Pacific Coast League, and he was in Muskogee looking over a player by the name of Flaskamper.

He looked him over and sent a recommendation—that was late in the summer of 1922—and then he went out on a drunk for about ten days. They never heard a thing from him all this while, didn't know anything about him or where the heck he was.

He finally got in shape to go back to the Coast, but on the way back a train conductor by the name of Burns . . . found out that this fellow was a baseball scout. Well, it so happened that I went with this conductor's daughter—Lady Burns—at school. So naturally—me going with his daughter and all—what the heck—he couldn't wait to tell this scout how great I was. How I could pitch and hit and run and do just about everything. He was such a convincing talker, and this scout needed an excuse so bad for where he'd been those ten days, that the scout—Dick Williams was his name—decided, "Doggone it, I've got something here."

When he got back to San Francisco, of course they wanted to know where the heck he'd been and what had happened. "Well," he said, "I've been looking over a ballplayer at Ada, Oklahoma. His name is Paul Waner, and he's only nineteen years old, and I think he's really going to make it big. I've watched him for ten days and I don't see how he can miss."

Then Dick quickly wrote me a letter. He said, "I've just talked to the Frisco ball club about you. I heard about you through the conductor, Burns. I told them that I saw you and all that, and I want you to write me a letter and send it to my home. Don't send it to the ball club, send it to my home. Tell me all about yourself, your height, your weight, whether you're left-handed or right-handed, how fast you run the hundred, and all that. So I'll know, see, really know."

So I wrote him the letter he wanted, not really thinking too much about it at the time. But the next spring, darned if they didn't send me a contract. However, I sent it right back, 'cause my dad always wanted me to go to school. He didn't want me to quit college. My father was a farmer, and he wanted his sons to get a good education.

But they sent the contract right back and even upped the ante some. So I said, "Dad, I'll ask them for five hundred dollars a month, and if they give it to me will you let me go?"

He thought about it awhile and finally said, "Well, if they'll give you five hundred dollars starting off, and if you'll promise me that if you don't make good you'll come right back and finish college, then it's OK with me."

"Why surely, I'll do that," I said.

So I told the Frisco club about those conditions. But it didn't make any difference to them. Because they could offer you any salary at all and look you over, and if you weren't really good they could just let you go and they'd only be out expenses. They had nothing to lose.

So out I went to San Francisco for spring training. That was in 1923.[7]

Cool Papa Bell

When I was seventeen years old, my mother sent me to St. Louis to get a better education than I could get back home in Starkwood, Mississippi. I had four older brothers and an older sister already living there, see, and I could stay with them. Well, I never did go to school. Instead I got me a job at the packing house and played ball on weekends. My four brothers all played on a sandlot semipro team called the Compton Hill Cubs, and I joined up with them too, as a pitcher. That's right, I was a left-handed pitcher then and a *good* pitcher.

In 1922 I pitched against the St. Louis Stars in a game over in East St. Louis. They beat me but I struck out eight, mostly with my knuckleball; and I guess they liked me, because a few days later they offered me a contract to play professional baseball full time.

My brother advised me to sign that contract, just to say I played pro ball. Said, "We made a mistake by not going for it. Don't you make the same mistake."

My sister didn't want me to sign. She wrote my mother back in Starkwood. Said, "He's gonna leave us. We'll never see him no more."

My brother said, "Pay no mind. Stay with me. You won't have to pay a nickel or a dime for room and board. Just so you can say you played professional baseball. You can work winters in the packing house when they're killing the hogs and they need more workers. They'll save you a job. But in the summer, play ball!"

So I signed that contract for ninety dollars a month, but I didn't sign it for no money. It was 'cause my big brother told me to and I knew he was right.

That was my first season, and I played baseball practically straight through, *summers and winters*, till 1950. Twenty-nine summer seasons and twenty-one winter seasons of baseball.

Charlie Gehringer

I was born and raised on a Michigan farm, and knowing firsthand how much back-breaking work that involved, I decided pretty early what I *didn't* want. I figured maybe baseball would have shorter hours and easier work, so I figured I'd go after that.

When I was a student at the University of Michigan, I got my big break through Bobby Veach, the old Tiger star. He used to come up around Fowlerville near our farm and hunt pheasant, and he heard about me from another hunter, a local man named Floyd Smith who'd seen me play. So Veach elected to bring me down to Navin Field to work out for a week and show the Tigers what I could do.

I was nervous at first, but it worked out very favorably. Ty Cobb was the manager, and I guess I caught his eye. I'd hit with the pitchers and the rookies, and then I'd go out and get lost among the outfielders. Well, he made me come back in and hit among the regulars. They hated that in those days—to have a bush leaguer come in—and I felt uncomfortable, but that was Cobb. This was Cobb too: After watching me hit and field out at second base, he climbed up to Mr. Navin's office—this was with his uniform and spikes on—and got Mr. Navin down to watch me. Well, to get right to the point, they signed me up. Very simple. No big bonus, just a generous contract with their London club in the Michigan-Ontario League. And some free advice from Cobb on stock market investments, which didn't do me much good because I didn't have any money to invest.

My thinking when I signed the contract was that even if I didn't make it to the big leagues, I could be a coach. I knew I could at least make it in the minors. An old-time umpire told me once, "If you don't make it to the big leagues in three years, you might as well forget it." Well, I made it in two.

It was a gamble, and I won. When you first see those big league players they look like superstars, but after you play with them, you realize, "I can play as well as these fellows. I can do *better* than some of them." So you get over that in a hurry. It looks much harder when you're watching from the stands. After a week down on the field with those Tigers, I felt confident that I had a good chance to make their ball club.

Billy Herman

I never played first-string baseball in high school. It wasn't because the coach didn't know talent either. I just wasn't any good.

But I fiercely wanted to play ball, and I begged my way in. Signed for nothing. Would have paid to get that contract with the Louisville Colonels back in 1928 when they signed me. I still wasn't any good.

They farmed me out to Decatur, Illinois, a Class B team. Decatur sent me back to Louisville after just a few days. When I got there the Colonels were on the road. I hung around there a week until Cap Neal got back in town, and Cap Neal the manager sent me to Vicksburg—a Class D town, as low as you can be sent.

They didn't even like me at Vicksburg, and I don't blame them. I was lousy. They wired Cap that I wasn't good enough to make their team and that I was being returned.

It was as low as you can go, and I couldn't make it. Then Cap Neal saved my career—got me another chance—by telling a lie—well I guess it was a lie because it certainly wasn't the truth. He wired Vicksburg back that no wonder I didn't look good because they had been playing me at shortstop and my regular position was second base. The truth of the matter was that I had never played second base in my life. I had been only a substitute third baseman and shortstop in high school.

Anyway that little white lie got me a second and last chance—as a second baseman now.

I didn't go great, but I must have done well enough because I stuck with them at second. So if Cap hadn't misled them about my true position, I'd have been sent home because Class D is the end of the line. I'd have dropped out of baseball. Instead, I stuck with second base for the next twenty years.[8]

Bob Feller

I signed for one dollar and an autographed baseball. It wasn't even a new baseball.

I was pitching American Legion ball in Des Moines, Iowa, about twenty miles from my home town of Van Meter at the time. One of the Legion umpires was a bird dog for the Indians, and he kept bugging Cy Slapnicka until Slapnicka agreed to give me a look at the same time he was scouting Claude Passeau, who was also pitching in the area. Well, he never did see Passeau. But he did sign me on a page of stationery from the Chamberlain Hotel in Des Moines. Actually the agreement was signed with my father; I was only sixteen at the time.

I'm glad I didn't receive a big bonus. I believe you should get paid after you do your job, not before. I was very confident that I'd make good, and opportunity was more important to me than security.

Yogi Berra

Before they made this draft rule you could go with any club you wanted. Maybe that's why the Yankees were such a legend. With Lou Gehrig and Babe Ruth and Joe DiMaggio, everybody wanted to be a Yankee. But it's a funny thing—I wanted to be in St. Louis, which was my home town. But the Cardinals wouldn't give me the bonus I wanted and neither would the Browns. I wouldn't sign for less than five hundred dollars because that's what my pal Joey Garagiola got.

We were both recommended to the Cardinals; but Mr. Rickey, who was their general manager then, said OK to giving Joey the bonus but nothing for me. He finally offered me two hundred fifty dollars to sign, but I said, "No, I want the same as Joey's getting." I didn't care about monthly salary or anything else, just that bonus, because I thought I was as good a ballplayer as Joey was.

The Browns wouldn't give me my five hundred dollars either. They'd give me a job with one of their farm clubs, but no bonus. I couldn't understand it, and it hurt my feelings.

A friend of mine who did some bird-dog scouting for various teams sent a letter then to George Weiss, who was general manager of the Yankees at that time. He told him that all I wanted was five hundred dollars to sign, and I'd take any salary they offered. So they scouted me and offered me my five hundred dollars and ninety dollars a month to play with Norfolk, Virginia, the next summer in the Piedmont League. Naturally, I agreed. Later I found out that the five hundred dollars was only if I finished out the season with the club, but then it was too late to argue. Well, I did finish out the season, and I had myself a start in pro ball.

Robin Roberts

As a kid I was mainly a third baseman and played some first base and a little outfield. I never pitched seriously until I was in college at Michigan State. I was actually there on a basketball scholarship, a six-foot-one forward—nowadays they don't even let you in the gym if you're that short—unless you can really motor. So anyway, they knew I could play basketball, but they were surprised when the spring rolled around and I went out for the baseball team. They asked me, "Well, what do you play?"

And I said, "What do you need?"

And they said, "Pitchers."

So I said, "Well, I'm a pitcher."

And I didn't realize at the time how right I was. Two years later I was pitching in the big leagues.

Jackie Robinson

I promised Rachel I wouldn't stay in baseball long. "All I want to do," I told her, "is make some money. They're going to pay me a hundred dollars a week. I've got to help my mother out, and I don't know anywhere else I can make that kind of money starting off."

Rachel understood, but she didn't like it. She wanted me to get a job in Los Angeles.

So I went with the Monarchs, strictly for the money. I never dreamed of sticking with a career in baseball. All the time I was playing I was looking around for something else. I didn't like the bouncing buses, the cheap hotels, and the constant night games. . . .

After I joined the Monarchs, Rachel went to New York to do graduate work. I kept playing ball and wondering if I was going to lose my girl.

The solution to our problem came later in August of that season.

We were playing the Chicago American Giants at Comiskey Park, and just before the game a man leaned over the rail near our dugout and introduced himself to me.

"I'm Clyde Sukeforth," he said. "I represent the Brooklyn Dodgers. I came out here today to see you play."

I shook his hand and said I was glad to meet him. Actually, I was neither impressed nor elated. Down through the years an athlete meets a lot of people. Some of them are exactly who they say they are, but there are others who assume names and titles just as a matter of convenience. . . .

Consequently, when Clyde Sukeforth said he represented the Brooklyn Dodgers I almost laughed in his face. I was sure that this fellow standing before me was just another crackpot.

Sukeforth here to scout me for the Brooklyn Dodgers of the National League? No one could tell me that. As far as I was concerned neither the Dodgers nor any other major league team was thinking of signing a Negro player any more than of signing a member of a girls' softball team. . . .

When I left Sukeforth and sat down in the dugout with the rest of the Kansas City players, one of them asked, "Who's the white fellow you were talking with, Jackie?"

"I don't know," I said. "He says he's scouting me for the Brooklyn Dodgers."

Everyone on the bench laughed, including me. One of the players jumped up and saluted me. "I'm a scout, too," he said, standing very erect. "I'm from Moose Face Troop No. 60, and if I pass my Eagle test next week, I'm gonna fly away."

We all got a great kick out of it, and by the time the game started I had practically forgotten Sukeforth.

But when it was over and I came out of the dressing room, he was standing there. I nodded and started to walk past him. I wanted to get to the Grand Hotel on the South Side and get my dinner. But Sukey—as I came to call him later—stopped me. I wanted to tell him to leave me alone. But he was so courteous and soft-spoken that I just couldn't.

As we walked along the street, he talked to me. "Mr. Rickey wants me to bring you to Brooklyn," he said. "He wants to have a talk with you."

"When?" I asked, almost disdainfully.

"He wants to see you tomorrow, if possible," Sukeforth said. "He's really anxious to talk with you."

I said, "Come on now, stop kidding. What the devil do you want? I'm hungry. I want to go eat."

Sukeforth shook his head as though he considered me a hopeless case. But he didn't give up. "I'm telling you the truth," he said. "Now you get yourself together and come on like you have some sense in that head of yours."

His commanding voice was not insulting. I stopped walking suddenly and looked at him. "You mean that you're taking me to Brooklyn yourself to see Mr. Rickey?" I asked.

"Yes," he said. "He wants to see you, and I'm acting under instructions to take you to him right away." . . .

"Listen," I said. "I'm making one hundred dollars each and every week with the Kansas City Monarchs. If I go to Brooklyn tonight and don't show up here for tomorrow's game, I'll get fired."

Sukeforth smiled. "Don't worry about that," he said. "I think you've seen your last days with Kansas City."

I didn't know what to do. We started walking again. I wanted to go someplace and sit down and think, but I couldn't tell him to leave me alone. He was being too nice and too patient.

Suddenly I became disgusted with myself. Why the reluctance? Why the hesitancy? After all, it was a gamble; you don't get anyplace in life if you don't take a risk once in a while. If I did go to Brooklyn and this all turned out to be a hoax, I could probably get a job with some other team. Maybe Kansas City wouldn't fire me. . . .

I knew that if I did go to Brooklyn it wouldn't take me long to find out what was going on. I knew that after I had talked with Mr. Rickey ten minutes, I'd know what the future held in store for me. Kansas City, I reasoned, couldn't find a new shortstop that quickly.

Sukeforth interrupted my thoughts. "You'd better hurry and make up your mind," he said. "We don't have much time."

He was right. I'd have to pack, eat, and get to the station in less than an hour. "Okay," I said, "I'll go. I don't know if I'm doing the right thing, but it's worth a gamble." [9]

Christy Mathewson

A young ballplayer looks on his
first spring-training trip as a
stagestruck young woman regards
the theater. She can think only of
the lobster suppers and the
applause and the colored lights.
—CHRISTY
      MATHEWSON in
      1914, *Pitching in
      a Pinch*

PROMISE

The greatest right-handed pitcher ever—Walter Johnson

> On opening day, the world is all
> future, no past.
>
> —LOU BOUDREAU, in 1948
> *Player-Manager*

4.

Opening Day

Ty Cobb

On August 2, 1907, I encountered the most threatening sight I ever saw on a ball field.

He was only a rookie, and we licked our lips as we warmed up for the first game of a doubleheader in Washington. Evidently, manager Pongo Joe Cantillon of the Nats had picked a rube out of the cornfields of the deepest bushes to pitch against us. The new boy was making his big league debut that day.

He was a tall, shambling galoot of about twenty with arms so long they hung far out of his sleeves and with a side-arm delivery that looked unimpressive at first glance. We began to ride him as the game opened.

One of the Tigers imitated a cow mooing, and we hollered at Cantillon: "Get the pitchfork, ready, Joe—your hayseed's on his way back to the barn!"

The sandy-haired youngster paid no attention at all. The first time I faced him I watched him take that easy windup—and then something went past me that made me flinch.

The thing just hissed with danger. We couldn't touch him, and so we waited, expecting the kid to turn wild and start issuing walks. But after four innings he hadn't thrown more than a dozen balls.

We were most respectful now—in fact, awed—and there was only one answer left to his incredible, overpowering speed. We bunted. Sure enough, the boy hadn't handled many bunts, and I beat one out, then advanced to third on his wild throw, following another bunt, and scored a moment later.

Scrambling all the way we finally beat young Walter Johnson, 3–2, but every one of us knew we'd met the most powerful arm ever turned loose in a ball park.[1]

Wahoo Sam Crawford

We were after the pennant that year, our first pennant, and we needed that game badly. Big Joe Cantillon was managing Washington at the time, and before the game Joe came over to the Detroit bench and said, "Well boys, I've got a great apple knocker I'm going to pitch against you guys today. Better watch out, he's plenty fast. He's got a swift."

And here comes Walter, just a string of a kid, only about eighteen or nineteen years old. Tall, lanky, from Idaho or somewhere. Didn't even have a curve. Just that fastball. That's all he pitched, just fastballs. He didn't need any curve.

He had such an easy motion it looked like he was just playing catch. That's what threw you off. He threw so nice and easy—and then swoosh, and it was by you![2]

Walter Johnson

That first game the Tigers really showed me something. Ty Cobb and Sam Crawford bunted me all over the infield. I fell all over myself . . . and the people in the stands laughed themselves sick. I was so confused I even missed the bus back to the hotel . . . and was walking there in my uniform when some fans gave me a lift.[3]

I was the greenest rookie that ever was. Do you know that the evening after the first game I ever pitched in Washington, I was standing out on the sidewalk when a man approached and said, "You're famous already, kid. See? They've named a hotel for you."

I looked across the street and, sure enough, there was a big illuminated sign that said "Johnson Hotel." Well, do you know that I was so green that I actually believed the man?[4]

Christy Mathewson

The great question which confronts every big league manager is how to break a valuable young pitcher into the game. Rube Marquard came to the Giants in the fall of 1908 out of the American Association, heralded as a world-beater.

When the club was fighting for the pennant at that time, McGraw was up against it for pitchers.

"Don't you think Marquard would win? Can't you put him in?" Mr. Brush, the owner of the club, asked McGraw one day when they were discussing the pitching situation.

"I don't know," answered McGraw. "If he wins his first time out in the big leagues, he'll be a world-beater, and if he loses, it may cost us a good pitcher." But Mr. Brush was insistent. Here a big price had been paid for a pitcher with a record, and pitchers were what the club needed. The newspapers declared that the fans should get a look at this "eleven-thousand-dollar beauty" in action. A doubleheader was scheduled with the Cincinnati club, and the pitching staff was gone. McGraw glanced over his collection of crippled and worked-out twirlers. Then he saw Rube Marquard, big and fresh.

"Go in and pitch," he ordered after Marquard had warmed up.

McGraw always does things that way, makes up his mind about the most important matters in a minute and then stands by his judgment. Marquard went into the box, but he didn't pitch much. He has told me about it since.

"When I saw that crowd, Matty," he said, "I didn't know where I was. It looked so big to me, and they were all wondering what I was going to do, and all thinking that McGraw had paid eleven thousand dollars for me, and now they were to find out whether he had picked up a goldbrick with the plating on it very thin. I was wondering, myself."

What Marquard did that day is a matter of record. Kane, the right fielder on the Cincinnati club, was the first man up, and although he was one of the smallest targets in the league, Marquard hit him. He promptly stole second, which worried Rube some more. Up came Lobert, the man who broke Marquard's heart.

"Now we'll see," said Lobert as he advanced to the plate, "whether you're a busher." Then Lobert whacked out a triple to the far outfield and stopped at third with a mocking smile on his face.

"You're identified," said Hans; "you're a busher."

Some fan shouted the fatal "Take him out." Marquard was gone. . . . Marquard was two years recovering from the shock of that beating. McGraw had put him into the game against his better judgment, and he paid for it dearly.[5]

Casey Stengel

I remember my first time at bat against the Chicago Cubs. Their catcher, Jimmy Archer, looked up and said, "So you're the new star of Brooklyn, huh? Well, I hope you get on and try to steal."

Well, I did get on and got the green light.

I took off for second. I was twenty feet from the bag when I saw Johnny Evers with the ball. I tried to slide around him, but it was no use. He really crowned me. As I was laying there he pulled up one pant leg, "Oh, trying to spike me! Why you big busher, you! Next time you come down here you better wear a tin helmet because I'm gonna slam that ball right down your throat!"

And for a while there I didn't get along too good with Mr. Johnny Evers.[6]

Mickey Cochrane

The A's arrived at Shibe Park for the opening game of 1925. Boston was the rival, and Cy Perkins was behind the bat for us. Came the eighth inning and the Red Sox had tied the score. In our turn at bat the bases were loaded when it came Cy's turn to hit, and Connie Mack commenced to look for a hitter. On the mound, working for the Sox, was Rudy Kallio; and Rudy had been something of a "cousin" of mine on the Coast in 1924.

When Connie looked over the bench for a pinch hitter, I remarked: "Give me a bat, I can hit that guy."

"All right, son," said Connie, "go up there if you think you can."

I went up and singled to left, driving in the winning run. Cy took off his catching equipment just as the man crossed the plate, the boys on the bench told me much later, and said, "There goes Perkins's job on that base hit." I caught 135 games that season.[7]

Al Lopez

In 1928 Brooklyn called me up in the fall of the year after my minor league season at Macon, Georgia, had ended. So I went up there and sat around on the bench for two and a half weeks. Finally, Wilbert Robinson put me in the last two days of the season, a doubleheader on Saturday and a game on Sunday. It was a great experience, but I did *not* get a hit. We were playing the Pirates, and they had Glenn Wright, who was a great shortstop, and Pie Traynor on third. Well, I was a pull hitter, and I hit some hard shots to the left side, but every ball was either to Wright or Traynor. I was hitting the ball *good*, and I thought I had hits several times, but each time I'd see that ball flying into the first baseman's mitt. I'd never seen infielding like that at Macon, and it was kind of discouraging. I went home to Florida for the winter, thinking to myself, What've you got to do to get a base hit in this league?

Joe Cronin

My first game in the big leagues, I subbed for Glenn Wright against the Reds. Threw one ten feet over the first baseman's head. Booted a grounder.

To tell you the truth, I'd rather remember my first big day against the Yankees. We had a doubleheader, and I hit six for eight with three triples that day. Hit them all three to right center. I can still hear their manager, Miller Huggins, yelling from their bench with his high squeaky voice, "Coive him. Coive the busher." And I just dug in harder and thought to myself, Go ahead. Give me your best! That was in the fall of that year, 1928; and I think those two games had a lot to do with them looking me over pretty good in 1929.

Bob Feller

The first time I pitched against big league hitters was against the Gashouse Gang in an exhibition game in Cleveland. They had fellows like Frankie Frisch, the Dean brothers, Joe Medwick, Pepper Martin, Leo Durocher, Terry Moore, and Ripper Collins—a tough club. Steve O'Neill, our manager, who had once been a good catcher for the Indians, decided he'd pitch me the middle three innings and catch me himself.

I was only seventeen, but I wouldn't say I was particularly nervous. If anyone was nervous, it was the Cardinals. See, I was a little wild back in those days, and that day I was as fast as I've ever been. The first batter up was Leo Durocher. I threw one ball over his head, two behind him, and got two in the strike zone. Then O'Neill said to him, "You'd better watch yourself Leo. This kid hasn't got the best control in the world."

So Leo dropped his bat, ran into the dugout, and hid behind the water cooler.

Everybody was laughing except for Cal Hubbard the umpire and me, of course.

Hubbard said, "Get back out here and hit. You're making a travesty out of this game. You still have one strike left."

Leo said, "You take it, Cal. I don't want it." Finally, he came back and stood in the back of the box and waved at one. That was my first big league strikeout.

I pitched my full three innings and struck out eight of the nine. Gave up two hits and allowed one run, which was actually unearned.

There's a story that circulated at the time that a photographer asked Dizzy Dean to pose with me after the game and Dean said, "After what he did today, you'd better ask him if he'll pose with me."

Whitey Ford as a Yankee pitching coach

Ted Williams

I'll never forget my first game. It was against the Yankees in Yankee Stadium. I'd been asking everyone about all the pitchers, and one of the veterans on the team, Jack Wilson—a hell of a good pitcher and a hell of a guy—was needling me a little bit about being cocky and nervous, which I was. Red Ruffing was the Yankee pitcher, a big guy with an easy motion but his ball used to . . . in the last six feet it kind of ooomed, built up on you, and was right by you. Ruffing was past his peak but was still a hell of a pitcher. Won twenty games that year. Anyway, first time up, he struck me out on three pitches. Second time up—same thing.

Well, this Wilson was an old agitator. I'm sitting there boiling, and he came over to me and leaned close and said, "What do ya think of the major leagues now, bush?" And I said, "Screw you." I said, "I know I can hit this guy."

Well it just so happened I did hit Ruffing the very next time up. I hit him real good, and after that, old Wilson stopped agitating me.

Stan Musial

The first pitch I ever saw in the majors was the first knuckleball I'd ever seen in my life. Jim Tobin of the Braves was the pitcher, and his ball seemed to just float up there, but it *danced*. My first swing I was off stride, and I hit an easy pop fly to third base.

Next time up, still against Tobin, there were two on and two out, and I doubled and drove in two runs. I was thrilled. Here I was doing what I'd dreamed of ever since I was a youngster . . .

But I *still* hate those knuckleball pitchers.

Duke Snider

My first game in the big leagues was the Dodgers' season opener in 1947. That was the first game Jackie Robinson ever played in too, and of course he got all the ink. I pinch-hit for Dixie Walker in the late innings and got a base hit to right. The next day the whole story was about Jackie and the Dodgers' winning and finally a last little sentence that said, "Duke Snider got his first major league hit." I sent the clipping home to my mother and wrote her that Jackie got all the ink, but I was outhitting him. I was batting 1.000.

Whitey Ford

When I first reported to the Yankees, the team was in Boston. I arrived at seven in the morning, and the first thing I did was call Billy Martin, whom I'd known in the minors. I woke him up, in fact, but Billy didn't mind; he said, "I've got two girls who are going to have breakfast with us." And, sure enough, when we went downstairs, there were these two girls in the lobby. One of them had been living near Billy in New Jersey, and she knew some of the ballplayers. But it looked pretty funny, a couple of rookies walking into the Kenmore Hotel dining room at breakfast time with two blondes, and we took a bit of heat from the rest of the players for that little entrance.

Later that day, I made my entrance with the Yankees as a pitcher, and it wasn't as splashy as breakfast with Billy's blondes. Tommy Byrne started the game against the Red Sox, and by the fourth inning, we were losing something like 11–2, so Casey took a "big chance" and brought me into the game. Vern Stephens was on third base, Walt Dropo was on first, and the batter was Bobby Doerr, who singled for another run. And that was my long-looked-for debut. I gave them seven hits, six walks, five runs, and even one wild pitch in four or five innings, and I think we ended up losing 17–4, something tidy like that.

What I remember most about that game was that their first-base coach kept hollering something at all their batters. Finally Tommy Henrich came over to me from first base and said, "That coach is calling every pitch you're throwing." The next day Jim Turner, our pitching coach, had me throwing in the bull pen, and we found out why. I was twisting my elbow whenever I cranked up for a curveball.[8]

Al Kaline

My first big league game was the same day I signed—right out of high school. My dad and I signed in Baltimore, and then we took a train with the scout over to Philadelphia where the Tigers were playing.

I sat on the bench keeping my mouth shut until the seventh inning when Freddie Hutchinson, the manager, who I don't think even knew my name, said, "Kid, come over and grab a bat. You're hitting for the pitcher." I grabbed a bat—didn't even know whose it was—ran up to the plate, swung at the first pitch, flew out to center field, and I was *so* happy. Happy just to get it over with and get back inside the dugout. I was scared to death; I'm sure I was white as a sheet.

The next night I went in the outfield as a defensive player. I was still nervous, but once I'd had a chance to do everything—bat, play the field, run the bases—then it wasn't really as bad.

Still, I wasn't sure I belonged there. I was skinny as a rail, really weak-looking, and I wasn't sure I could hit major league pitching. The one thing I had going for me as a hitter was that I never struck out. Even as an eighteen year old in the majors, there were very few pitchers that I didn't at least make contact with the ball. And I could *run*, so I did get on base.

In the field, it was different. The first time I went out to play with the outfielders I said, "Hey, I'm as good as any of these guys. I can throw better than anybody here, and I can go get the ball with any of them." I might've been raw, but I did know from the very first day that I was a major league fielder.

I can remember a reporter asking
for a quote, and I didn't know what
a quote was. I thought it was some
kind of a soft drink.
                              —JOE DIMAGGIO

5.

The Rookie

Ty Cobb

I came to Detroit with the reputation of being a fresh busher. In truth, my only wish was to make good. Instead of cooperating, though, the older men tried to make my life miserable. They didn't confine themselves to cutting remarks. They also played tricks on me. Broke my bats and worse. They seemed determined to get me off the club. I made up my mind they wouldn't succeed. I was learning fast that the manners my family had taught me had no place in baseball. I knew I'd have to forget being a gentleman and show them that I was rougher and tougher than any of them.[1]

Burleigh Grimes

In the fall of 1916 after my minor league season with Birmingham, Alabama, ended, I went up to finish out the season with the Pirates in the National League, which was the first time I ever came in contact with big leaguers. The Pittsburgh Pirates with Honus Wagner, Babe

*Honus Wagner, the greatest
shortstop ever*

Adams, Max Carey, Home Run Frank Schulte. I won a couple of games
for them that September.

Honus Wagner was a wonderful fellow. Always having fun. Never
too serious. He loved to tell whoppers. He was forty-two then but still
covered his position at shortstop. I remember the first game I ever
pitched against Brooklyn at Ebbets Field. It was a tight spot, about the
seventh inning, score tied 1–1, a man on first base. Wagner came over
to the mound from shortstop and said, "Make him hit it to me, Kid."
Well, I didn't *make* him do it, but the guy did hit a hard grounder right
to short. Perfect double-play ball. I was proud of myself and figured old
Honus had to be impressed. Well, the ball bounced off Wagner's foot
out into left-center, the runner scored, and the batter wound up on
third. Old Honus came over to me with his head down, looking kind of
annoyed. He said, "Those damn big feet have *always* been in my way."

Joe Sewell

I finished the University of Alabama in the spring of 1920, intending to go on and become a doctor like my father before me. That
summer I had an offer to play professional ball down in New Orleans,
and I took it, still intending to study medicine in the fall. Well, I was

going along pretty good down there playing shortstop, when all of a sudden I got a call from the Cleveland Indians. It was as a result of one of the worst tragedies ever in baseball. Ray Chapman, the Cleveland shortstop, got killed by a pitch that hit him in the head. I can remember hearing the news, and I was shocked by it like everyone else. But I never *dreamed* I was the man fate intended to fill that position. I'd only been playing professional ball for a month and a half, and I got the call to go to Cleveland. I'd never even *seen* a major league ball game, but there out of the blue I was right in the middle of a red-hot three-way pennant race—White Sox, Indians, and Yankees. Cleveland was about two games out in front when I come to town.

The second day I was there, Tris Speaker, the manager, told me he was putting me in the lineup. The boy they had in there playing for Chapman was a good fielder, but he couldn't hit. I guess they thought I could. I wasn't quite so sure.

But I did all right. Stayed there eleven years.

And we did win the pennant that year and the World Series. And I never went to medical school. And I have no regrets. I wouldn't trade my thirteen years in the big leagues for anything.

So it all began with tragedy. But for me personally the story had a happy ending.

Joe Sewell in 1980. INSET: *with the Yankees in the early 1930s.*

Billy Herman

I came up to the Chicago Cubs at the end of the 1931 season from Louisville in the American Association. Breaking in was rougher back in those days than it is today. The veterans resented you, because you were after their jobs; and the coaches ignored you unless you made a mistake. There was very little instruction back then. They figured you'd had a good seasoning in the minors and left you on your own. If you couldn't cut it there was always somebody else to take your place. At least that's how it felt to me. Maybe it felt even more that way because of who I broke in under—Rogers Hornsby.

He was a real hard-nosed guy. He ran the clubhouse like a gestapo camp. You couldn't smoke, drink a soft drink, eat a sandwich. Couldn't read a paper. When you walked in the clubhouse, you put your uniform on and got ready to play. That was *it!* No more kidding around, no joking, no laughing. He was dedicated to the game and made sure you were too. A very serious person. Tough guy to play for, especially for a young kid like me. I was scared to death to start with, and he scared me more. Very cold man. He was liable to go a month and never even say hello to you. Walk right by you, look right through you, and keep going. A very odd person. When you *would* hear from him is if you made a play he didn't think was quite up to his standards. It still burns me up just a little bit to remember some of his sarcastic remarks.

"A real hard-nosed guy." Rogers Hornsby.

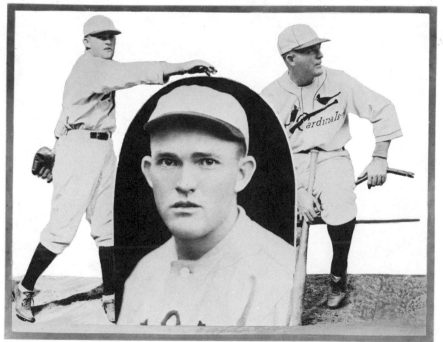

Actually, it was even worse for me than for the others because I was taking *his* position. He still wanted to play second base, but the club had spent a lot of money for me, and they wanted me to play. So as manager he had to play me. So it was a little tough at times on both of us. He didn't play at all as a regular after I got there.

I will say this for Hornsby, though. He knew baseball, and he did a *good* job running the ball game. I'll also say that he was a fair-minded guy. And I'll also say that in later years he mellowed. When he was working for the Mets, thirty years later, I'd run into him in a hotel lobby or someplace, and he'd be very friendly and sit down and talk. But believe me when I first met him back in my rookie year, he didn't talk to anybody. A real hard-nose!

Ted Williams

Hitting was everything. I thought always in terms of hitting against those pitchers that were getting better all the time as I progressed up the ladder from the Coast League to the Association and finally to the American League. The Coast League was a *good* league, but they didn't have the young hard throwers that the Association had. Boy, those guys impressed me immensely. I said to myself when I saw a young Trout or a young Benton, "Jesus, I don't know why *he* ain't in the big leagues!" Of course, they ended up in the American League, and I had the pleasure of facing them for many years. But at the time, despite my high batting average, I didn't know if it was for real. I've never really said this before; but hell, I'd never seen a big league game; how did I know how the hell good they really were up there? Here I was seeing some guys who were plenty tough for me and *they* hadn't made it.

I guess that insecurity was the reason why I was so brash when I first came up. It was a defense mechanism. I may sound braggadocious, but I'm not really a braggative person. I'm a little loud and I'm a little quick and energetic and I might impress people as conceited, but that really isn't the way I *feel* about it. Some of those older guys did give me a little needling now and then, but hell, I look back on all those guys and I love them. Because there was nobody who didn't appreciate my enthusiasm. And I think most of them understood that I was nervous.

But after I'd played in the American League one round, one series against each team, I said—and you know I wasn't hitting that good, only about .260—but I said, "I don't see no blinding fastballs or exploding curves." And I knew after that one round that I could hit in the big leagues. And from July 4 on that season, I hit .380.

Joe Cronin

When he first came up, Williams set some pretty high goals for himself. He was a perfectionist. Williams was absolutely a perfectionist. He could take a camera apart and put it right back together. He went into the Naval Air Corps in World War II, jumped right in, and became a great flier. Today he's probably the number one sport fisherman in the country. And of course, he was a perfectionist at the bat. The only thing he didn't do . . . he didn't become a great fielder. He was adequate, just adequate. I guess if he had to do it over again, he'd work on his fielding a lot more. But that would have required taking time away from his batting practice. And he was out there from six in the morning to six at night working on his batting. And when he wasn't swinging a bat, he was talking hitting. Oh yeah, and doing push-ups. Ted was a great fellow for fingertip push-ups. Or he'd pick up a chair with one hand and walk around the clubhouse with it. He kept his wrists and his arms *strong*.

So he had great determination. And he had *confidence*. He told me when he first came down to spring training, "Joe, I want to be recognized with Ruth and Gehrig and the very greatest hitters of all time." Well . . .

The season started, 1939. The first time around the league, the first western trip we made, he might've struck out ten times in the four towns, and his average was pretty low. But he kept saying, "Don't worry. Don't worry. I'll hit these guys." He kept his confidence. "I'll hit 'em!"

He knew what he wanted, and he knew he was gonna do it. Wasn't any *doubt* about it.

Stan Musial

I started the 1941 season as a dead-armed pitcher in Class D and ended it as a Cardinal outfielder (with a batting average of .426 in twelve games). In a leap that long, you know there's luck involved.

I injured my arm late in 1940, and at spring training in '41, they gave me one last chance as a pitcher. As a matter of fact, my next-to-last outing ever as a pitcher was against the Cardinals themselves in an exhibition game in Georgia. They knocked me around pretty good, and it was right afterwards that management decided to try me as an outfielder. Which was fine with me. I'd already realized I'd never be another Carl Hubbell. As a matter of fact, I *always* had more confidence in my hitting than in my pitching.

Well, that season, 1941, I hit so well, they kept advancing me right up the ladder, from D to C, from C to Triple A, and finally to the top—all in one summer. Like I said, there was *luck* involved. Enos Slaughter hurt his shoulder and Terry Moore got beaned, and they were short of outfielders, and of course they were in a hot pennant fight with the Dodgers. So they called me from Rochester to St. Louis.

After a day or so Billy Southworth, the manager, put me in the lineup, and I got a couple of hits. So he kept putting me in, and I got

Stan Musial in 1980

more hits, and I had a hot hand there for a couple of weeks right to the end.

That was a big turning point for me because the next spring I got off to a very slow start, and I'm sure they'd have farmed me out if they didn't remember that hot hitting September of 1941.

I have a good memory from that first fall, a lot of good memories, but one in particular! When I first joined the club I was like most rookies, afraid to talk to the veterans. That's the way it was and probably always will be. But after a week of playing regular and hitting the ball well, I felt more like I belonged. We were on the train from Philadelphia to Pittsburgh, and we had a long session one evening in the dining car. I was talking with Terry Moore, saying how much had changed since spring training when I pitched against the Cards in Georgia, and he'd hit a home run off me. It seemed just unbelievable to be playing next to him in the outfield and all that.

He looked at me, amazed, and said, "You're that kid lefty who pitched against us?"

I nodded, and he called John Mize over. John had also hit a homer off me in that game. "Hey John. You remember that left-handed kid we hit those long home runs off in Georgia last April? That kid was Stan Musial."

Ralph Kiner

I had a good offer to go with the Yankees, but I signed with the Pirates in late 1940 because Sloppy Thurston, the scout who signed me, convinced me that I'd make it to the big leagues a lot faster through the Pittsburgh farm system. Never dreaming that World War II would come along . . .

When I got out of the Navy in December 1945, I began preparing for spring training, which was only a couple of months away, and I got myself into just sensational shape.

Sure enough, I had a spring training like no one's *ever* had. I learned that I was ticketed to report to the Hollywood Stars, the Pirates' top farm club; but I was *determined* to stick with the big club. I'd waited long enough. And I just tore it up. Hit about a dozen home runs and hustled from morning to night. They had no choice but to keep me. In fact, I started the season for them in center field.

The first series was in St. Louis, and then we took a train home to Pittsburgh. It was the first time I'd ever been there, and I'll *never* forget my first impressions because they were so upsetting. The train arrived at the station about ten in the morning, and it was like midnight. The sky was just black with pollution from that soft coal they used to burn. I'd never seen anything like it. Then we drove out to take a look at the ball park. Well, the old Pirate ball park, Forbes Field, was probably the biggest park in the majors—365 feet down the left-field line and 457 in left-center. This was where I planned to hit my home runs? I said, "My God, let me out of here!" I was terribly discouraged.

That was the start of a very tough year for me. I was really a little over my head, especially after my long layoff in the service. But Frankie Frisch, who was manager that year, stuck with me and encouraged me in his rough gruff way, and I got it going a little bit by the end.

In fact, I ended up with twenty-three home runs, which led the league that year.

[That year, 1946, was the first of seven straight years Ralph Kiner led the league in home runs.]

Jackie Robinson

Less than a week after I became number 42 on the Brooklyn club, I played my first game. I did a miserable job. . . . I was in a slump. I went to plate twenty times without one base hit.

As my slump deepened I appreciated Manager Shotton's patience. I knew the pressure was on him to take me out of the lineup. People began recalling Bob Feller's analysis of me. I was "good field, no hit." There were others who doubted that I could field and some who hoped I would flunk out and thus establish that blacks weren't ready for the majors. Shotton, however, continued to encourage me.

Early in the season the Phillies came to Ebbets Field for a three-game series. I was still in my slump, and events of the opening game certainly didn't help. Starting to the plate in the first inning, I could scarcely believe my ears. Almost as if it had been synchronized by some master conductor, hate poured forth from the Phillies dugout.

"Hey, nigger, why don't you go back to the cotton field where you belong?"

"They're waiting for you in the jungles, black boy!"

"Hey, snowflake, which one of those white boys' wives are you dating tonight?"

"We don't want you here, nigger."

"Go back to the bushes!"

I have to admit that this day, of all the unpleasant days in my life, brought me nearer to cracking up than I ever had been. The abuse coming out of the Phillies dugout was being directed by the team's manager, Ben Chapman, a southerner. I felt tortured, and I tried just to play ball and ignore the insults. But it was really getting to me. What did the Phillies want from me? What did Mr. Rickey expect of me? . . . What was I doing here turning the other cheek as though I weren't a man? In college days I had had a reputation as a black man who never tolerated affronts to his dignity. I had defied prejudice in the army. How could I have thought that barriers would fall, that my talent could triumph over bigotry?

For one wild and rage-crazed minute I thought, "To hell with Mr. Rickey's 'noble experiment.' It's clear it won't succeed. My best isn't enough for them." I thought what a glorious, cleansing thing it would be to let go. To hell with the image of the patient black. . . . I could throw down my bat, stride over to that Phillies dugout, grab one of those white sons of bitches, and smash his teeth in with my despised black fist. Then I could walk away from it all. I'd never become a sports star. But my son could tell his son someday what his daddy could have been if he hadn't been too much of a man.

Then I thought of Mr. Rickey—how his family and friends had begged him not to fight for me and my people. I thought of all his predictions, which had come true. Mr. Rickey had come to a crossroads and made a lonely decision. I was at a crossroads. I would make mine. I would stay.[2]

Duke Snider

One guy who really helped Jackie a lot was Pee Wee [Reese]. I remember one time in Boston early in that rookie season—it was my first year as well as Jackie's—some of the Braves players began to heckle Pee Wee about being a southerner and playing ball with a Negro. Pee Wee didn't answer them or even look at them. He just walked over to Jackie and put his hand on his shoulder and began to talk to him. That shut the Braves right up.

Pee Wee also helped me many times. I remember one time . . . I only had three bats to my name, and I wanted to save them in case I got in a game. So I used any other bats I could get my hands on during batting practice. One time I picked up a bat of Eddie Stanky's and went into the batting cage. Well, he jumped in there after me and grabbed his bat and began to berate me. Pee Wee stepped in at that point and politely told Stanky to get lost.

Pee Wee was our team leader, and he touched every one of us. You could go to any one of the old Dodgers today and ask about Pee Wee and they'd tell you, "Without Pee Wee I'd never have become the player I became." That's why Pee Wee Reese belongs in the Hall of Fame. Those intangibles don't show up in a player's individual statistics, but they show up in the won-lost record of the ball club. Pee Wee was a winner. And, incidentally, so was Jackie Robinson.

Robin Roberts

I'll tell you a story that's kind of funny in a way. It was back in the early fifties. We were playing a series in Brooklyn, and one day I went early to Ebbets Field to watch the Dodgers take batting practice. There was this left-hander pitching who could obviously throw very hard. But he was very erratic. In fact, he was missing the cage with some of his pitches. So I happened to say to Carl Furillo, who was standing near me, I said, "Carl, who's that?"

He said, "Some Jew kid who'll never learn to pitch as long as he has a hole in his ass." And you know who it was of course. Sandy Koufax.

I remember Al Kaline . . . we were coming north from spring training in 1953. Al had just signed with the Tigers for a nice bonus, and I think he was eighteen, maybe nineteen. He was *very* young. See he never went to the minors. Al Kaline came right to the Tigers from high school. And they played him. And the games we saw him in, he didn't look like he could get the bat around. I mean we'd just *jam* him. Cause he's only eighteen. And we're *popping* the ball, banging it in there. And he'd hit the softest little pop flies, and everybody was laughing like mad. "Can you imagine giving a bonus to this kid?" So this year they picked him for the Hall of Fame.

Clemente. I don't know if you ever saw Roberto play, but he was the most unorthodox good ballplayer I ever saw. Most good ballplayers are smooth. They do things with rhythm. Well, Roberto had his own rhythm. He looked like he was falling apart when he ran. Looked like he was coming apart when he threw. His stance at the plate was ridiculous. When he swung he'd lunge and hit bad balls. There was no way he could hit the ball like that. But no one told Roberto that.

The first time I ever saw him, he came up to hit, and I turned to someone and said, "*Who* is *this?*" That was back when the Pirates were first bringing up a lot of different young guys, back in the early fifties with their youth movement. They even tried Tony Bartirome, their trainer, at first base one year. And it looked like Roberto was another one of these kind of guys. Especially with his terrible-looking unorthodox style. He really looked less like a ballplayer than anyone I've ever seen. It was a crazy thing. The only thing that made him look sensational was the results. And they *were* sensational. But everything he did was an effort. Nothing was graceful or smooth. But . . . course he's in the Hall of Fame too.

Now Willie Mays was the opposite. He came into Philly for the first time with the Giants in 1951 with a lot of publicity. He'd been hitting about .470 for Minneapolis. So I went out early the first day to see him in batting practice. And he hit about five balls in the upper deck. Then he went out in the outfield, and he could just run like the wind and throw like hell. And I remember thinking, This has to be as good-looking a baseball player as I ever saw. And it turned out he *was* the best player I ever saw.

Henry [Aaron] was the same way. When we first saw him in 1954, we knew right away it was just a matter of time. He just had to learn the strike zone. At first, you know, he'd swing at anything you threw up there. But we knew as soon as he got it down a little bit, he was gonna be murder. And he was.

Yeah, Henry and Willie were obvious talents. But Roberto and Sandy and Kaline weren't obvious at all, not at first anyway.

Bobby Winkles and Al Kaline, Cooperstown, New York, August, 1980

Al Kaline

My first manager, Freddie Hutchinson, took a good liking to me right off and treated me very well. He assigned me to sit next to Johnny Pesky on the bench every day so Johnny could explain the ins and outs of every situation that came up. Except for late-inning defensive substitution and occasional pinch-hitting, I spent the whole season on the bench.

Surprisingly, most of the older players liked me. Here I was a young guy just out of high school who was gonna take somebody's job away from him. In fact, one of the guys who treated me best was Pat Mullin, the outfielder whose job I *did* eventually take, forcing him to retire. I guess they liked me 'cause I kept my mouth shut. And I came out to the park early and shagged for them. I'd rather do that than sit in my hotel room. Certainly they'd earned a little seniority, and I was willing to go along with it, especially, as I say, 'cause it got me out of my hotel room. That rookie year was a lonely and difficult time for me because I really had never spent any time away from home before. Luckily there were some veteran ballplayers staying in the same hotel in Detroit, and although they wouldn't call me every night to go to dinner, they were around if I really needed them. And we'd go out to the park together, usually early. I looked forward to getting to the ball park and getting my uniform on. Then I didn't feel so lonely.

Everyone who makes the big leagues has been a baseball standout all his life. Even so, from a big league viewpoint, he has everything to learn. It's unbelievable how much you don't know about the game you've been playing all your life.

—MICKEY MANTLE,
The Quality of Courage

6.

Learning the Ropes

Babe Ruth in 1928

Take the average country kid rookie who goes south in the spring. He's green. He's unaccustomed to city life. He's embarrassed in the hotel dining room. But baseball is a great teacher. And after two or three seasons of play he's polished, capable of holding his own in most any company. And that isn't bunk. It actually happens.[1]

Harry Hooper

Babe Ruth joined us on the Red Sox in the middle of 1914, a nineteen-year-old kid. . . . He had never been anywhere, didn't know anything about manners or how to behave among people—just a big overgrown green pea. You probably remember him with that big belly he got later on. But that wasn't there in 1914. Babe was six foot two and weighed 198 pounds, all of it muscle. He had a slim waist, huge biceps, no self-discipline, and not much education—not so very different from a lot of other nineteen-year-old would-be ballplayers. Except for two

"Just a big overgrown green pea." The young Babe Ruth.

things: He could eat more than anyone else, and he could hit a baseball further.

Lord, he ate too much. He'd stop along the road when we were traveling and order half a dozen hot dogs and as many bottles of soda pop, stuff them in, one after the other, give a few big belches, and then roar, "OK, boys, let's go." That would hold Babe for a couple of hours, and then he'd be at it again. A nineteen-year-old youngster, mind you!

He was such a rube that he got more than his share of teasing, some of it not too pleasant. "The Big Baboon" some of them used to call him behind his back, and then a few got up enough nerve to ridicule him to his face. This started to get under his skin, and when they didn't let up he finally challenged the whole ball club. Nobody was so dumb as to take him up on it, so that put an end to that.

You know, I saw it all happen, from beginning to end. But sometimes I still can't believe what I saw: this nineteen-year-old kid, crude, poorly educated, only lightly brushed by the social veneer we call civilization, gradually transformed into the idol of American youth and the symbol of baseball the world over—a man loved by more people and with an intensity of feeling that perhaps has never been equaled before or since. I saw a man transformed from a human being into something pretty close to a god. If somebody had predicted that back on the Boston Red Sox in 1914, he would have been thrown into a lunatic asylum.[2]

Burleigh Grimes

They used to take the old catchers and put them together with the young pitchers and the old pitchers and the young catchers. Did you ever notice how many old catchers make pitching coaches later, or managers? Fellows like Uncle Robbie [Wilbert Robinson] . . .

You start with a muscle man and try to help him progress to a point where he can put his mind together with his muscle. A young pitcher back then had to learn above all to pace himself so he could go a full nine innings; because, of course, they didn't have much in the way of relief pitching. He also had to learn the hitters. That still helps, I guess, and always will.

Getting beat made the difference for me. I learned something new every time I lost a ball game, and I lost sixteen of them that first year I was up. But I learned how to pitch.

The second year I was traded to Brooklyn and won eighteen or nineteen for Uncle Robbie and lost only nine. Robbie taught me a lot. Besides the things I already mentioned, I guess the other main thing I learned was that control was more important than throwing hard. Though some days it makes no difference at all. You put the ball exactly where you wanted it, and they hit you regardless. It's just the percentage. And when you learn that, you've learned another valuable thing.

Al Lopez

I learned a lot about catching by observing. As a kid in Tampa, I used to go over to the spring-training camp of the Senators and watch Muddy Ruel behind the plate. He knew a lot of good tricks.

Later, when the Dodgers brought me up to the big league, I learned from Wilbert Robinson—we called him Uncle Robbie. He'd been a well-respected catcher back in the nineties with the famous Baltimore Orioles. I think I learned the most, though, from the veteran pitchers. You have to learn to think like a pitcher, how to set the batters up, and keep them off balance. I caught Dolf Luque at the end of his career, and that was an education, let me tell you. To me, he was the smartest pitcher I ever caught. He could spot the ball wherever he wanted, any kind of pitch, and he knew every hitter in the league. He'd shake me off until I knew exactly what to signal for. After a while I was thinking just like he was. Sometimes I'd have to signal him to pretend to shake me off, just to keep them guessing. We'd also sit together on the bench when our team was batting. So we had a perfect understanding. I learned that that was a big part of catching—getting the pitcher's confidence. If you have that understanding and that confidence, and, of course, if you can call a good game—you need that to maintain the confidence—you're a great asset to a pitcher. He doesn't have to worry about thinking then. He just takes the sign, and if he's comfortable with it, he pitches. He can concentrate on putting that ball in the mitt.

Duke Snider

I wouldn't have become the ballplayer I became if it weren't for Branch Rickey. Lots of people saw potential in me, but Mr. Rickey knew what to do about it. He was a man who could look at a raw young player and see that same player five years in the future. One day in 1947, my first year, he called Gil Hodges and me into his office and told us that someday we were gonna be the right- and left-handed power on the Dodgers. Gil was a third-string catcher then, and I was the sixth outfielder on the squad. We looked at each other in bewilderment, both wondering, What does he know that *we* don't know? We can't even crack the lineup.

The next year he moved Gil to first base, and he went on to become one of the greats at that position—*and* the right-handed power for our club.

With me, he decided to teach me the strike zone. See, in those days, any pitch that came within reach looked good to me, and I had a whack at it. In the dirt. Over my head. So I missed a lot. Mr. Rickey's remedy was to put me in the batting cage for three to four hours every morning with a pitcher and catcher and umpire. George Sisler, our batting instructor, supervised, and Mr. Rickey himself was there every day watching my progress. My assignment was simply to watch pitches go by, all morning long. I was not allowed to swing. I was just supposed to call every pitch, ball or strike. It was *amazing* how wrong I was. But I learned.

Willie Mays

I can remember the third or fourth game I was with the Giants. I had come down the clubhouse steps at the Polo Grounds and was on my way to the bench for the start of batting practice before a game when I heard a voice behind me.

"Hey, Hubbell!"

I turned around. It was Leo Durocher.

I said, "What'd you call me?"

"Hubbell," The Skip said.

"Carl Hubbell?"

"That's right."

"What for?"

"Because of the way you wear your pants," Durocher said. And it was true. I had the habit of wearing my baseball pants long and low, the legs going down well past the knees, the way Hubbell wore his.

Well, I laughed a little and started walking to the dugout again. But again I heard Leo's voice behind me.

"Hey, Hubbell."

"What now?" I said.

"Pull the pants higher. Get the legs up."

"What for?" I said.

"Shorten your strike zone," Leo said.

And he was right, of course. The strike zone is between the shoulder and the knee. A guy who wears his pants so low you can't tell where the knees are may find an umpire calling a strike on a low pitch.

But would *you* have thought of something like that?[3]

Mickey Mantle

It was July of my rookie year, and I was hitting some homers and knocking in some runs, but I was striking out too much, and I was getting mad and losing my confidence, hitting water coolers and all. Casey [Stengel] called me in and said he was going to send me back to the minors. Of course, I started crying, and he started crying. You know, he was like my dad by that time. He felt like he had took me in and brought me up. I felt like I could play because I had signs of being a "phenom" like they were saying, but I just wasn't doing it like I thought I was going to, and I was losing my confidence. So Casey *had* to send me back.

I went back to the minors and joined Kansas City, and the first time up, I bunted. George Selkirk was the manager at Kansas City then, and he called me over after the inning and said, "Look, we know you can bunt; we didn't send you down here to learn how to bunt. We want you to get your confidence back and start hitting the ball again."

But I didn't get another hit in my next twenty-two times at bat, and that's when I called my dad and said, "I don't think I can play ball anymore."

He was working in the mines in Oklahoma and he came to Kansas City the next day, and he came right into my hotel room and I thought he was going to say, "Geez, you're all right." But instead, he walked in and got my suitcase and started throwing the stuff into the suitcase. I said, "What's the matter?" And he said, "Hell, you ain't got no guts. I thought I raised a man. You're nothing but a goddamned baby." And I said, "What're you doing?" And he said, "Packing! You're going home. You're going to work in the mines, that's what we'll do, you can work back down there."

He had tears in his eyes; he was really hot. And when he said he thought he'd raised a man and all he had was a baby—well, that really curdled my guts.

Then he just threw the stuff down and said, "Get your ass on the ball. Shit, you ain't no baby, you can do it." And he just turned and walked out.

He stayed for the game that night, and I got a couple of hits, and then I wound up hitting something like .360 for Kansas City—drove in a lot of runs, hit a lot of home runs. And the Yankees called me back up.

I think that speech my dad gave me really did it. . . . It was the turning point in my whole life.[4]

Bill Dickey

Gehrig was a big help to me when I was a rookie. I'd been a good hitter in the minors, but I was having trouble with big league pitching and was beginning to wonder. In fact, to be honest with you, I was getting scared.

Now Lou was a big star already by that time [1928], but one day he took me aside and said, "I think I can help you with your hitting." This really surprised me. It was very unusual in those days for a veteran to take such an interest: Most of them just ignored you. If you got help it was from the coaches. But Lou worked with me for several days—I was uppercutting on the ball—and he straightened me out. Well, that was my first introduction to what a great fellow Gehrig was, and later on we became roommates and very good buddies. But who knows what might've happened to me if Gehrig hadn't taken that interest.

Yogi Berra in 1949, at the Yankee spring-training camp in Florida

Bill Dickey is learning me all his experiences.

And in 1980

Bill helped me out tremendously. He gave me a lot of tips about catching, placing my feet, gripping the ball. And especially how to *throw*. And he gave me a lot of encouragement. Built up my confidence. He was a very hard worker and a very good teacher.

Bill Dickey in 1949

Right now, Berra does about everything wrong, but Casey warned me about that. The main thing is he has speed and agility behind the plate and a strong enough arm. He just needs to be taught to throw properly. I know he can hit. I'd say Berra has the makings of a good catcher, I won't say great, but certainly a good one.

And in 1980

Yogi was a great kid and a good learner. He was very shy, I remember, and quiet, but he listened real well. It was really my job to work with him and make a judgment whether he should catch or play the outfield.

The Yankee staff would hold a meeting every week and talk about the ball club, and every week they'd ask me, "You gonna make a

Bill Dickey in 1980. INSET: *coaching for the Yankees in the 1950s.*

catcher out of Berra?" And I kept putting them off because I hadn't seen enough of him. Finally I gave them their answer. "I think he ought to make a pretty good catcher." And a pretty good decision that was! I think most of the others thought he should play the outfield, but he convinced me that he could handle catching. And I think Berra improved more as a defensive catcher, not just that spring but over the next few years too, than any catcher I ever saw. He became one of the truly all-time great catchers of baseball history.

Ralph Kiner

When I first played in the Pirates' farm system, I really got very little coaching. Maybe an occasional mental session with the manager or a veteran ballplayer, but as far as hitting, the understanding was "Do it yourself or not at all." I did an awful lot of reading and . . . I remember back in 1941 or 1942, I obtained a filmstrip of Babe Ruth's swing, broken down frame by frame, which I copied carefully and practiced whenever I got the chance.

Later, on the Pirates, Hank Greenberg changed my style. That was certainly one of the great turning points of my career. Hank came over to Pittsburgh in his last year as a player, and for some reason, they roomed us together on the road. Which was my good fortune. He'd been one of my early boyhood idols, and now that we were on the same team, he took a liking to me. Hank had a great propensity for work. He would take *hours* of extra batting practice, and he started inviting me along, till it became a regular thing. We'd shag for each other and have different people pitch to us. His philosophy was "work," and he passed it along to me.

LEFT: *The veteran—Hank Greenberg.* RIGHT: *The kid—Ralph Kiner.*

Like Yogi said when they got Bill Dickey to instruct him in catching, Hank "learned me his experience." He sure shortened up my learning time anyway. Hank's a very astute man, I think the brightest man I've ever known. He changed my stance and my whole approach to hitting—taught me to pull for power—and I jumped from twenty-three home runs in 1946 to fifty-one in 1947, the year he came. That's another story.

In '47, I got off to a horrendous start. Billy Herman was our manager that year—his first year as a manager—and he wanted to send me back to the minors. Greenberg went to the owner of the club, McKinney, and he said, "Don't send him out. He's got a great swing and a great attitude, and he's just on the verge of breaking through." I had hit just three home runs through the month of May, which was *nothing*. From June first to the end of the season, I hit forty-eight more. In about 110 games, I hit forty-eight home runs.

I'll never forget this: The day before I broke out on the streak was the low point of my major league career. Hank Borowy of the Cubs struck me out four times, and I was really down. It looked like the end of the line. But Greenberg encouraged me. "Stay with it," he said. "The fundamentals are there, and it is going to work." You know, it's hard to convince someone who's struggling so much, but he never gave up on me.

I have to credit Greenberg with another thing. That team was a disaster. Billy Herman had been brought over to be a player-manager with the Pirates, and he never played a game. But he acted as much like a player as a manager. He never drew that line of demarcation, and there was no discipline. No rules even. With the type of club we had in 1947, it didn't work. We had a lot of ballplayers who'd been kicked off other clubs for bad acting, and we *needed* discipline. As you might guess there were factions—the men who were serious versus the ones who just wanted to have a good time. So we had no team spirit. No *team* really.

This is where Hank comes in again. I could very easily have fallen in with the guys who loved their nights out. It's always easier to have a good time than it is to work. But Greenberg was very disciplined, and he passed that discipline on to me—helped keep me on the straight and narrow all that year. So I have to say my biggest break in baseball was meeting Hank Greenberg.

I still see Hank every chance I get. In fact, I consider him my best friend to this day.

Billy Herman

That was the worst year I ever had in baseball. I'd never managed before, and the team was struggling. It was a *bad* team, and I didn't know what I was doing. I didn't enjoy that year at all.

Kiner and Greenberg were two of the *very few* bright spots. Hank came over to the National League from the American League, which at that time was the stronger league, and he was a big star there; so he was a little bit on the cocky side. And he had some big deal with the owners, so I didn't have much control over him, but I didn't *have* to control *him*. He lived clean, worked hard, and did his job. And he worked with Kiner a lot on his hitting.

"That was the worst year I ever had in baseball." Billy Herman in 1947.

Kiner? He was just a young kid, and most young kids are easy to manage. It's the older guys who've been in the league eight to ten years who often get to be the wise guys. Those were the guys who ruined that year for me. But Kiner was like 99 percent of the young kids—eager to learn the ropes.

When a ballplayer's in his prime
years of life—from about twenty-
five to thirty-five—those are
the happy days.

—STAN MUSIAL at
age fifty-nine

Part Two

THE

STAR

Boston Beaneaters, 1892. King Kelly is sitting at the right hand of manager Bill Dahlen.

Every baseball club must have a
star, just as a dramatic company
must have a leading man; and as in
the theater, no star can shine
without the help of his supporting
cast.   —KING KELLY in
            1888, *Play Ball!*

THE SUPPORTING

CAST

Ty Cobb as a grizzled Tiger veteran

LEFTY GOMEZ, when asked what he considered his greatest asset as a pitcher:
"Fast outfielders."

7.

Teammates

Ty Cobb in 1914

Most managers appreciate the psychology of crowds now and play on the feelings of the spectators to help keep their teams at a high pitch. For instance, it used to be customary for big league players on opposing clubs to mix up in the practice before games and act friendly. Several smart leaders have laid down the law that none of their men is to speak or shake hands with a member of an opposing team while in uniform. Frank Chance was the most insistent. . . .

"You're ballplayers and not society dancers at a pink tea," I heard Chance remark to one of his men last season after the latter had come over to our side of the field to "mitt" a Detroit player. "You're paid to come out here and play ball, and you've been doing very little of it lately. I want to see some fight in you and not this social stuff. That handshake will cost you ten dollars. . . ."

Nor does the crowd like to see the opposing teams hobnobbing. It always enjoys watching players at loggerheads. Nearly all the big league managers are opposed to the brotherly love actions now.[1]

Wahoo Sam Crawford

I played in the same outfield with Cobb for thirteen years, from 1905 to 1917. Cobb was a great ballplayer, no doubt about it. But he sure wasn't easy to get along with. He wasn't a friendly, good-natured guy, like Wagner was, or Walter Johnson, or Babe Ruth. Did you ever read Cobb's book? He wrote an autobiography, you know, and he spends a lot of time in there telling how terrible he was treated when he first came up to Detroit, as a rookie, in 1905. About how we weren't fair to him, and how we tried to "get" him.

But you have to look at the other side, too. We weren't cannibals or heathens. We were all ballplayers together, trying to get along. Every rookie gets a little hazing, but most of them just take it and laugh. Cobb took it the wrong way. He came up with an antagonistic attitude, which in his mind turned any little razzing into a life-or-death struggle. He always figured everybody was ganging up against him. He came up from the South, you know, and he was still fighting the Civil War. As far as he was concerned, we were all damn Yankees before he even met us. Well, who knows, maybe if he hadn't had that persecution complex he never would have been the great ballplayer he was. He was always trying to prove he was the best, on the field and off. And maybe he was, at that.

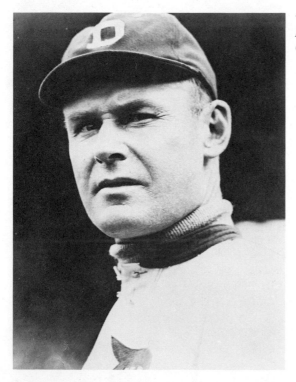

"We weren't cannibals or heathens." Tiger veteran Sam Crawford.

One thing that really used to get Ty's goat was when I'd have a good day and he didn't. Oh, would he ever moan then. Walter Johnson and I were very good friends, and once in a while Walter would sort of "give" me a hit or two, just for old-time's sake. But when Ty came up there Walter always bore down all the harder. There was nothing he enjoyed more than fanning Ty Cobb.

You see, Walter always liked my model bat. Somehow he got the idea that my bats were lucky for him. So very often when the Senators came to Detroit, Walter would come into our clubhouse and quietly ask me if I could spare a bat for him.

"Sure, Walter," I'd say, "go take any one you want."

He'd go over to my locker, look them over, pick one out, and quietly leave. Well, whenever the occasion arose when it wouldn't affect a game, Walter would let up a bit on me and I'd have a picnic at the plate—like, if Washington had a good lead and it was late in the game. I'd come up to bat and Gabby Street, Walter's catcher, would whisper, "Walter likes you today, Sam."

That was the cue that the next pitch would be a nice half-speed fastball. So I'd dig in and belt it. Of course, if it was a close game all that was out the window. The friendship deal was off then. Cobb never did figure out why I did so well against Walter, while he couldn't hit him with a ten-foot pole.[2]

Burleigh Grimes

Yeah, I played with a lot of the great ones. Just take a look at the list of the fellows in the Hall of Fame, and you'll see a lot of my old teammates. I played nineteen years and got traded nine times, so I played *with* most of them and *against* most of them. I'd spend my time with the players on my own team, whatever team that happened to be at the moment. Some teams didn't speak, like the Dodgers and Giants. So when I was a Dodger, I didn't talk to Giants; and after I was traded over to the Giants, I didn't talk to the Dodgers anymore. Sound complicated?

Hall of Fame teammates? Sure! Just take it year by year and team by team. Look it up in your *Baseball Encyclopedia*. Nineteen sixteen and 1917 I was with Pittsburgh. Honus Wagner, Max Carey. Both belong in there, no question. Nineteen eighteen to 1926 with Brooklyn. Zack Wheat. Rube Marquard. I roomed with Rube. Great roommate, cause he was so easygoing. He was always one of Uncle Robbie's favorites. Rube died this year, poor fellow. Dazzy Vance. Rabbit Maranville. Great ballplayer. Had a big wrinkle on the back of his neck and people'd say, "That's from drinking out of a bottle." He quit drinking though, went to the minors, and finally made enough money to start again.

Nineteen twenty-seven over to the Giants. Bill Terry. *Smart* guy.

Used to hold out all the time. Later on he was a *very* good manager. Today he owns a bunch of land down there in Florida, and he's got a pisspot full of dough. Rogers Hornsby. Never bothered anyone. Never alibied. Told you exactly what he thought. I liked the guy. Fred Lindstrom. Edd Roush. Mel Ott. Real quiet boy. Nice boy, Mel.

Nineteen twenty-eight over to Pittsburgh. Pie Traynor and the Waner brothers. Paul was the freewheeler. Never cared what the count was, he was just swinging. He was the better hitter, but Lloyd was the better runner. He'd run that average up high with leg hits. I believe he'd hit .400 today with that artificial turf. Once in Pittsburgh after I'd been traded away from the Pirates, he hit four bounders off me, and beat them all out. Two of them, we didn't make a throw.

In 1930 I was traded to the Braves, and then traded again to the Cards. On the Braves we had George Sisler, he's on my all-time team on first base.

Over in St. Louis, we had a *strong* club. Won the pennant that year, you know, and the next. We had Sunny Jim Bottomley, Chick Hafey, Jesse Haines. And Frankie Frisch. Frisch was a wonderful ballplayer. I put Hornsby on my all-time all-star team because he hit the ball farther, but Frisch could do everything.

The next year, I got lucky. I was traded to another team that turned around and won the pennant—the Cubs. We had Gabby Hartnett, Kiki Cuyler, Billy Herman. Gabby deserved his nickname. He kept that chatter going. Wonderful fellow and great catcher. Had as good an arm as ever hung on a man. [Billy] Herman was just breaking in then, just a little fellow but a *smart* ballplayer. McGraw wouldn't sign him to a contract with the Giants, 'cause he only weighed 155. So he came to the Cubs and became as good a second baseman as anyone in the National League. He could really handle that bat and ball.

In 1933, I went back to St. Louis, where I found myself playing with two more great Hall of Fame ballplayers—Ducky Medwick and Dizzy Dean. Dean was a character. There ain't enough time to say it all about Diz. I was there when he started. Pitched his first game in a pair of my shoes. Diz never changed even when he got famous. He was loud and cocky right from the start, but you can't call it just brag; he backed his words up. I recall a game in St. Louis one time, he walked into the Cubs' clubhouse meeting and said, "No need to have a meeting, boys. I'm pitching today, and I'm giving ya my hard one." They were a team of high-ball hitters, but he pitched them high and set them down. He showed them who was boss.

The next year they sent me over to Pittsburgh, and then toward the end of that season, I got traded over to my last team, the Yankees.

The Yankees didn't win the pennant that year, but they had some big names—Ruth I guess was the biggest of all. They also had [Lou] Gehrig, [Bill] Dickey, and [Earl] Combs, and [Red] Ruffing and [Lefty]

Burleigh Grimes in 1980. INSET: *with the Cardinals in the early 1930s.*

Gomez on the pitching staff. Gomez reminded me of Dean. He'd tell you a joke and then throw his fastball right by you. I could never do that. I'm talking about the fastballs, not the jokes. I always had to rely on control and staying one step ahead of the batters. But I tried not to be envious.

So all told I guess you could put together a pretty good all-time all-star team from just my former teammates. Fine players and a fine bunch of fellows. Wonderful memories.

Billy Herman

Burleigh [Grimes] was a little bit like Hornsby—real hard-nosed. The day he'd pitch, he didn't want anyone even *looking* at him. Son of a gun, he was mean on the mound. I remember when he was on Brooklyn, he hit Mel Ott on the head, last day of the season. I think Brooklyn was in last place and the Giants were about third, but Burleigh got mad—I guess Ott hit a home run off him—and he beaned the guy. That's the way he played.

I never will forget . . . he didn't like young players playing behind him. One day, Burleigh was pitching a game in Chicago in Stanley Hack's rookie year, and they hit two or three balls past Hack at third. He was just a young kid, and he was fighting the balls and probably should have stopped some of them. Well, Stanley was a real quiet kind of guy; and so finally after about the third one went by him, he snapped his fingers. Goddamn—he knew he should've had it. So Hornsby came out of the dugout to give Burleigh the hook, and Burleigh said, "Don't take *me* out. Take out that goddamn kid over there who snaps his fingers at the ball."

He was mad. He meant it. I liked him, though, and he liked me. In fact, we're still good friends. But he's *still* a rough old guy. . . .

Another great pitcher and good friend was my old teammate Diz [Dean]. A real character. All the stories you hear and read about him are true. He and I and Augie Galan and Hank Leiber used to be a foursome when we were on the Cubs together. We used to play cards *all the time*, even before breakfast. Diz'd do anything in the world to *win*. Playing for a penny, he'd cheat you. You'd catch him cheating, and he'd laugh with a big haw haw you could hear for half a mile. Nice big easygoing country boy, he didn't care. Next hand he'd be peeking at your cards—anything to win.

Joe Sewell

There'll never be another team like those old Yankees from the days of Ruth and Gehrig. What a collection of winners! We didn't need a manager. *You* could've managed that team. We kept each other bearing down on the field and had a good old time together off the field. Ruth. Gehrig. Dickey. Combs. We were good friends as well as teammates, and when there *was* a little rivalry, like the tension between Ruth and Gehrig towards the end, we didn't let it affect us on the field. I'm proud to have shared the field with such teammates.

Babe Ruth in 1928

Lou Gehrig would rather fish than eat. Most any day in winter you'll find him out on the banks after cod. This college kid is one of the queerest ballplayers I ever knew. It seems he never feels the cold weather. The coldest day in winter he'll come swinging down Broadway without an overcoat, his coat open and no vest. Never wears gloves and half the time goes bareheaded. Some of the boys claim he never had an overcoat on his shoulders until he joined the Yankees.

Lou is a great eel fisherman too, and in the summer after the ball game he'll take his mother in his car and go shooting down to Long Island to spear eels. His mother pickles them, and now and then she'll send a big jar of pickled eels around to the clubhouse. Last year when the boys struck a big hitting stride they got the idea that the pickled eels were responsible for their hitting, and for weeks they wouldn't go into a ball game until they all had taken a couple of bites of pickled eel.[3]

Bill Dickey

Lou [Gehrig] and I roomed together for a long time, and we were very good buddies. In fact, I'd say we were more like brothers.

The saddest thing I ever experienced was Lou's sickness, which as you know led to his death. It was almost impossible to believe that something like that was happening to someone so strong and healthy. One of the strongest fellows that ever lived. But something was obviously wrong. After all Lou was only thirty-five, and he'd always taken perfect care of himself. But he was falling down and muffing easy plays and had no power at the plate. Finally, he asked Joe McCarthy to bench him for the good of the team.

After that—this was in 1939—Lou went out to the Mayo Clinic, and they told him what disease he had and told him that he would reach a low before he would begin to come back. A lot of people thought Lou didn't know he was gonna die. Well, the first year he stayed with the ball club and continued rooming with me. The second year, of course, he was too sick to travel. But I remember once during that first year, we were on the train, going to Washington to play the Senators the following day. It was late in the afternoon. Lou and I were the last players to get off the train. And there were a bunch of kids waiting for us, so we stood out there and signed autographs for twenty or thirty minutes. Finally, we got into a cab, and this was the only time I ever saw that Lou knew that he didn't have too much longer. He said, "Look at all the happy kids, and here I am dying."

"One of the strongest fellows that ever lived." Lou Gehrig in his prime with the Yankees.

Seven future Hall of Famers at the 1937 All Star game—Gehrig, Cronin, Dickey, DiMaggio, Gehringer, Foxx, and Greenberg. A.L. won 8–3.

Immediately, he passed it off and got to kidding and laughing again; but after that I knew that he knew.

Roy Campanella

The Dodgers always had a family feeling. We were the first to have an integrated team, and we all stayed together for so many years and won so many times. Do you know the first ten years I played with the Dodgers, we won five pennants? My goodness, how many ballplayers play in the big leagues ten years and are in five World Series? Unbelievable!

We spent so much time together off the field. We used to have a good fishing group between Gil Hodges, Carl Furillo, Carl Erskine, Rube Walker, and myself. And Preacher Roe was quite a fisher too. Then there was a card-playing group—Pee Wee [Reese], Jackie [Robinson], Russ Meyer, Billy Loes, Durocher. Preacher also played cards. They played a lot of poker, whist, and *bridge*. You talk about *ladies'* bridge clubs. My goodness, they had a *league* of bridge players.

I remember Pee Wee and Duke [Snider] and Jackie used to play golf together all the time.

And at other times we would *all* be together. I remember one night pretty near the whole team went out to see Johnny Unitas play his first game with the Baltimore Colts.

We'd always go in a group. I'll never forget one night in Chicago after a day game with the Cubs. We'd heard of this Women's Softball League, and we said, "Let's go over and see how these women play." Well, somebody found out that we were in the stands, and the next thing we knew, they wanted Duke to come up to bat against their star pitcher. She could really throw the ball underhand! Do you know, Duke couldn't hit her! No, he couldn't. He couldn't even foul the ball. That's a short distance, and the way she could throw, and under the lights too. . . . I'll never forget that. I'm just glad they didn't call on me. The ladies were hitting her, but Duke could *not* hit that ball.

So we were more than just a team of individuals. We were like brothers. If someone was having a problem we didn't leave it to the manager. We'd get together, talk about it, work on it as a team.

Duke Snider

That old Dodger club *was* very close. The professional jealousy just wasn't there. Most of us had been together for a number of years, and when we'd gather in the clubhouse that first day of spring training, it was like when you were a kid going back to school in the fall with all your school friends. We could hardly wait.

Our wives once in a while got a little jealous because we spent so much time together. Lots of times after a road game, ten or fifteen of us would go out and spend the evenings together.

And we'd always sit around the clubhouse before and after the games. Sometimes we'd still be there an hour and a half after the last out. Talk about the game. Have a couple of beers, and a lot of laughs.

Pee Wee and I used to drive to the park together all the time. We'd get there an hour or two early and get ready to beat someone.

Campy'd come strolling in with a cigar and a panama hat and say, "The same team that won yesterday is going to win today."

This went on *year* after *year*.

I guess we weren't typical. More often, especially nowadays, it seems like a race to see who's the first one out of the clubhouse. We used to see the players from the other club go by in their street clothes, and we'd still be sitting around in our sweaty uniforms.

Erskine, Hodges, Jackie, Pee Wee, Campy—I was lucky to play with men like these. I'd seen Jackie play as a college athlete out in California—football, basketball, *and* baseball. He was seven years older than I was, but because of the color thing, he didn't start with the Dodgers until he was twenty-eight, and we were rookies together.

And as we became close friends I grew to admire and respect him as a *person* more even than as an *athlete*. What he had to go through as the first black player was unbelievable. I don't think people today really appreciate it. I know I wouldn't have been able to handle it. It was an unbearable situation. But he stuck it out and developed into the greatest competitor I've ever seen.

Jackie could not only beat you with the bat, ball, and glove, and his feet: I saw him win a game in Chicago one day with his *mouth*. Sam Jones was pitching for the Cubs, and Jackie got him *mad*. It was the ninth inning, tie score, and Jackie was yelling at him from the on-deck circle. Now, you just don't see that. *Terrible* things he was saying. I was the batter, and I heard someone yelling these obscene things at Sam, and I turned around, thinking it was coming from the stands. It was Jackie. I popped out, and Jackie got up there, and he was still hollering at him. "I'm gonna beat you, Sam. You got no guts, Sam!" Sam got so mad he hit him in the ribs and Jackie got to first. Then he was dancing off first—he could do it so well—and Sam kept trying to pick him off. Finally Sam threw one away, and Jackie got all the way to third on it. There he was, dancing off third, hollering, "I got you now, you so and so." Kept on needling him. On the third pitch, Sam bounced one in the dirt, the ball went all the way to the screen, and Jackie scored the winning run. That was Jackie.

Some of the others. Pee Wee. You know, Jackie admitted that without Pee Wee he might not have made it that first year. I think you'll find that if you talk to *any* person who ever played with Pee Wee they'll thank him for making them a better person. He was our captain and our leader, and the guts of our ball club. It makes me sick that he hasn't been chosen for the Hall of Fame.

"When we'd gather in the clubhouse that first day of spring training, it was like when you were a kid going back to school in the fall with all your school friends. We could hardly wait." The 1955 World Champion Dodgers.

And finally—Campy. He was the stabilizer on the team. He kept us loose. He and his roommate [Don] Newcombe. There are *many* stories I can tell about them, believe me. And all true.

One little story. Campy and Newk had an outstanding year one year and won every award possible.

The following spring we were in Cincinnati. Campy was batting about .125 and Newk was about zero and five.

The year before they'd go into hotels on the road, and the phones'd ring all the time until they finally had to tell the operators, "We don't want any phone calls unless they're long distance or emergency."

The next year they're off to this bad start. One day Newk gets on the bus and says loud enough for everyone to hear, "Hey, roomie, you remember last year, we were getting all those calls, and we had to call down and tell the operator not to put 'em through?"

Campy said, "Sure, roomie, I remember."

Newk said, "This year, we can't even get a wake-up call."

Mickey Mantle

If I miss anything today it's the atmosphere of the clubhouse. You live with those guys for eight months every year; and when you've finally got to leave them, a part of you dies.[4]

A fellow bossing a big league ball
club is busier than a one-armed
paperhanger with the flying hives.

> —TY COBB in 1914,
> *Bustin' Em and
> Other Big League
> Stories*

8.

Managers

Johnny Evers in 1910

The good manager is gifted with the power to rule men as well as to
lead them in battle, and his duties upon the field are the lightest part of
his work. . . .

The crowd which cheers the players has little conception of the
trials and tribulations of the manager who crouches unseen and forgotten . . . in the corner of the bench. The public does not realize that he is
dealing with twenty-two ultra-independent athletes, vulgarly healthy,
frankly outspoken, and unawed by any authority or pomp. Only persons who have one child, which possesses four grandparents, and
twenty or thirty aunts all trying to spoil it, can understand in full the
difficulties of the manager's job.

Ballplayers are about as spoiled, unreasonable, and pampered as a
matinee idol, and are worse because they are usually young and have
not even the saving grace of experience to guide them. The average
major league player is a youth who has jumped from small wages to a

comfortable income in a few weeks, from the criticism of the home crowd of a few dozen persons to the applause and cheers of perhaps twenty thousand persons. He is sought after, flattered, and pampered. He meets men and women of high standing who thoughtlessly praise him. The surprising thing is that ballplayers who succeed are not worse spoiled.

The young ballplayer has a brilliant day; he is exalted. He has a bad day, and the excited abuse heaped upon him by the crowd burns his sensitive soul. . . . He has all the day except a short time in the afternoon and perhaps an hour in the morning to exult over his triumphs or mourn over his errors, and in his bitterness he loses faith both in friends and enemies.

That stage requires several years to wear away. In about five seasons the player realizes that the public is fickle, that it does not mean its applause any more than it means its abuse. He begins to understand that in its excitement the crowd is "cussing the cards, not the players." . . .

It is small wonder that the major league players become spoiled. The hotel arrangements all are made for them; their baggage is checked, the train connections, berths, and carriages are all arranged for by the manager or secretary. The player is told when to go, where to go, and how to go, and some players after years of traveling are almost as helpless as if they never had been on a train. . . . There was a player with the St. Louis club a few years ago who asked permission of the manager to lay over on Sunday at Cincinnati en route from Boston to Philadelphia.

The trials of a manager with twenty men, the majority of them grown children, under his charge, who is forced to soothe their injured feelings, condole with them in their troubles, cheer them in their blues, and check them in their exuberance, may better be imagined than told.

One evening after Frank Chance had won two World Championships, he sat gloomily silent for a long time. The big, hearty, joyous boy who had come from California a dozen years before was battered, grizzled, . . . and weary. Still young, his fine face showed lines of care and worry and a few gray hairs streaked his head. He was thirty-two and looked old. For a long time he sat musing. Then he looked up and smiled grimly.

"This business is making a crab out of me," he remarked.[1]

Al Kaline

It's awful hard to manage a team where players are making five, six, seven times as much as you are and are very independent and can go from one club to another as free agents. It's tough to have discipline and tough to plan and tough to build.

Rube Marquard in 1912

I don't guess any man in the big leagues today had a harder time making good than I did. I came up to the Giants with a record price tag attached to me, and the newspapers and fans expected a lot. I did poorly at first and received as artistic a roasting as one could desire. If it hadn't been for Mr. John McGraw, and our pitching coach, Wilbert Robinson, I doubt I'd have had the nerve to stand up under the abuse. I got my confidence from Robbie, who worked with me constantly, and from McGraw, who kept plugging at me even when I was getting worse instead of better.

Those two men deserve all the credit for my success.[2]

And in 1966

I'll never forget one day we were playing Pittsburgh, and it was Red Murray's turn to bat, with the score tied in the ninth inning. There was a man on second with none out. Murray came over to McGraw—I was sitting next to McGraw on the bench—and he said, "What do you want me to do, Mac?"

"What do I want you to do?" McGraw said. "What are you doing in the National League? There's the winning run on second base and no one out. What would you do if you were the manager?"

"I'd sacrifice the man to third," Murray said.

"Well," McGraw said, "that's exactly what I want you to do."

So Murray went up to the plate to bunt. After he got to the batter's box, though, he backed out and looked over at McGraw again.

McGraw poked his elbow in my ribs. "Look at that so-and-so," he said. "He told me what he should do, and I told him what he should do, and now he's undecided. I bet he forgot from the bench to the plate."

Now, in those days—and I guess it's the same now—when a man was up there to bunt, the pitcher would try to keep the ball high and tight. Well, it so happened that Red was a high-ball hitter. Howie Camnitz was pitching for Pittsburgh. He wound up and in came the ball, shoulder high. Murray took a terrific cut at it, and the ball went over the left-field fence. It was a home run and the game was over.

Back in the clubhouse Murray was happy as a lark. He was first into the showers and out boomed his wonderful Irish tenor, singing "My Wild Irish Rose." When he came out of the shower, still singing, McGraw walked over and tapped him on the shoulder. All of us were watching out of the corner of our eyes, because we knew The Little Round Man—that's what we used to call McGraw—wouldn't let this one go by without saying *something*.

"Murray, what did I tell you to do?" McGraw asked him.

"You told me to bunt," Murray said, not looking quite so happy anymore. "But you know what happened, Mac. Camnitz put one right in my gut, so I cow-tailed it."

"Where did you say he put it?"

"Right in my gut," Murray says again.

"Well," McGraw said, "I'm fining you one hundred dollars, and you can try putting that right in your gut, too!" And off he went.

Oh, God, I never laughed so much in my life! Murray never did live that down. Years later something would happen and we'd yell to Murray, "Hey, Red, is that right in your gut?"[3]

John McGraw in 1925

Napoleon, I believe, said that one poor general was worth more than two good ones. He was right. Nine mediocre players pulling together under one competent head will do better work than nine individuals of greater ability without unified control.[4]

Burleigh Grimes

I always respected John McGraw the most of any of my managers. I was a veteran when I was traded over to his club in 1927, and I figured it was about time. I'd always wanted to play for McGraw for the simple reason that he was the smartest manager in the league and his teams played the best ball. Baseball was his business. In fact, it was his life.

"He was the smartest manager in the league and his teams played the best ball." John McGraw managed the New York Giants to ten pennants between 1902 and 1932.

Unfortunately, I was only with him that one year. But I'd say that in that one season I learned more baseball than I had in all the years up to that point. Just for an example—I learned a whole new and better theory of curveball pitching in about five minutes. He taught me how to make those right-handed hitters *pull* that curve with men on base—which meant more double plays, fewer runners advancing from first to third on a single, and, naturally, more success for me. It was a *simple* adjustment—took five minutes. Only problem was I'd never thought of it before and neither had any of my managers. I won nineteen games that year and twenty-five the next.

Yeah, McGraw and I got along fine. He had a reputation for fining fellows and being rough on them, but if you did your job, he didn't bother you. He just did what he had to do to keep his kind of team playing his kind of ball. And remember, this was New York. One time he said to me, "You know, Burleigh, I pay the top prices in baseball for good young players. They're green kids, from way out in the country most of them; and they come to New York with all these bright lights, and pretty girls, and start getting all this publicity and attention. Then before you know it they run away with themselves. If I can keep a young kid from himself for three years, I got me a good ballplayer." He was strict for his players' own good; and the ones had any sense respected him for it.

On the field he played an aggressive, slashing kind of game. You'd think he was gonna bunt and lay one in there, and boy, he'd *rip* it. Frank Frisch was the same way—as a player under McGraw and later as a manager. A perfect McGraw-type player—he'd cut it *wide* open. Those kind of guys weren't afraid to gamble.

Now I also had a manager up in Boston, and a pretty successful manager, who was just the opposite—Bill McKechnie. He was a staid, careful, sacrifice-bunt-type manager. He wasn't gonna hit and run and try to shake things up. He was gonna bunt you to death. I thought he was always too conscious of what the newspapers would write. There wasn't gonna be any second-guessing on Bill. If the situation called for a bunt, you could bet all the tea in China he was gonna bunt. But he had success—won four pennants. He was the kind that can always get a job with somebody 'cause he's so dependable.

But for my all-time manager—give me John McGraw.

Fred Lindstrom

Bill Terry and I broke in together with the Giants in 1924. He took over first base from George Kelly, and I took over third from Heinie Groh. We'd been together before that on the Toledo Mudhens.

We joined a great team and a tough team under the leadership of a great and tough manager—John McGraw. Back in those days you had tough, rough customers in baseball, and a man like McGraw had to rule them with an iron hand—the [Hugh] McQuillan, [Mule] Watson, Bugs Raymond type of characters. If someone made a mistake in a game, McGraw would tear him apart right in front of the team. He got away with it; in fact, it was probably necessary.

But with the advent of fellows like Terry and [Mel] Ott, and [Carl] Hubbell and [Travis] Jackson and me, we were a different breed. We didn't need someone hitting us over the head to keep us in shape. In fact, we wouldn't take it—at least Terry and I wouldn't. I don't think McGraw was able to adapt his methods of handling his men. On the field, yes, he adapted to the lively ball; but he wasn't able to cope with the more modern-style players. And after 1924 he never won another pennant.

Al Lopez

I was lucky. I played for six managers, and they all made the Hall of Fame. They were good in different ways, and I learned something from all of them. I thought Bill McKechnie was great at handling pitchers. He was a "pitcher's manager," which I also tried to be. So I learned a lot from him.

Max Carey was a guy who loved to steal as a player, and when he became a manager, he wanted his club to run. I remembered some of his lessons when we were putting together the "Go Go White Sox" of 1959.

Frankie Frisch was an offensive manager and a great one. Used his pinch hitters perfectly and usually stayed a step or two ahead of the other team's defense.

Lou Boudreau was an inspiring leader who led by example. He also knew how to delegate authority very well. I guess Lou and I have won the only two pennants for Cleveland since 1920.

Wilbert Robinson liked pitchers who were big and strong and could throw hard. He'd rather have guys with a real good fastball that moved than guys who nibbled too much. Guys like Dazzy Vance. Vance was his pet. I always agreed with Robbie about that: Good stuff is the foundation of good pitching.

John McGraw was a great manager. Real fiery guy. You can tell how smart he was by looking at all the smart managers who played for him. Casey Stengel for instance, who's the last guy I was gonna mention. You could see how much Casey was influenced by McGraw.

Casey was a smart baseball man. I think his greatest asset was that he was willing to gamble on young players. When he first took over the Yankees in 1949, they were ready to start skidding, but Casey put Mantle, Ford, Martin, McDougald in there. Took chances with a *bunch* of young kids. And won ten pennants in twelve years.

McGraw'd do that too—stick with a young guy and kind of nurse him along. For example, he had Mel Ott on the bench one full season

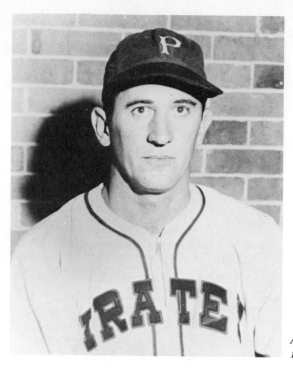

Al Lopez with the Pirates in the 1940s

and kept bringing him along until finally Ott became a superstar. Fred Lindstrom was just a kid when McGraw brought him up, and McGraw stuck with him until Freddie turned out to be another great player for him.

So I'd say both McGraw and Stengel were very good with young kids. Especially Casey'd sit and talk to them by the hour. He never had any kids of his own, so he had a lot to give to these young guys, and I guess some of them like Mantle and Billy Martin felt like he was a father to them. As I think of it McGraw had no children of his own either. Just thirty years worth of baseball teams.

Charlie Gehringer

Of all my managers I liked Bucky Harris the best and [Mickey] Cochrane probably next. Cochrane was a super leader when he was playing, but after he got beaned and had to manage from the bench, he didn't call them quite so well because he wasn't close enough to the scene. I think if he can handle it, a playing manager is great, especially if he's a catcher because the catcher is the quarterback. When Mickey was managing the Tigers from behind the plate I can't remember him ever fouling up anything. Seemed like he made snap judgments that always worked out well, especially in '34 and '35 when we were win-

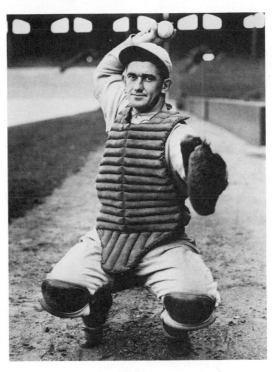

"Seemed like he made snap judgments that always worked out well. . . ." Mickey Cochrane in the 1930s.

ning our two pennants. After he became a bench manager it seemed like he weighed everything a little more, and you can't do that in baseball—in politics maybe, but not in baseball—you've got to jump into things or you miss your chance. And after Mickey got hit in the head, it seems like we missed more chances.

So I'll choose Harris for my best manager. He was most fair, and I don't think I ever heard him second-guess a player, no matter how lousy they'd done. He seemed to enjoy managing, and he didn't take it out on the players when things were going bad.

Now, Cobb was a little different. Golly, he could be rough. He had a path worn from center field to the pitcher's mound. He'd grab that ball away from the pitcher, show him up in front of the crowd. They *hated* that, and I remember guys jerking away from him. That was bad news. He was great with the hitters, a very astute batting instructor, but he didn't have much luck with pitchers. We'd have great hitting, but we'd get beat 10–9. So he was a tough man to play for, very demanding and very thin-skinned. I'll take Harris.

Ted Williams

Nobody in the world was nicer and easier to play for than Joe Cronin. He was a big, good-looking Irishman, and everybody liked Joe

Cronin. God, he was a hitter's manager if there ever was one. You know, I copied the way he was with young guys when I managed in Washington and Texas, and I still do in teaching hitting. He was always optimistic and enthusiastic and always trying to stir up good conversation with the youngsters about baseball, and especially hitting. We'd sit around for hours in the clubhouses, in the hotels, on the trains talking pitchers and the psychology of the game. He was a real heads-up guy, and he kept us thinking.

But Cronin had the greatest obstacle to beat in the fact that he was playing shortstop, trying to be manager, and planning day by day and long range. I mean that's pretty near impossible. I know Lou Boudreau was able to do it over in Cleveland. He managed superbly, worked his pitching staff, played great shortstop, and had great years. But remember, nobody in baseball had better coaches surrounding him than Lou Boudreau. Cronin didn't have that group around him.

Now when he quit playing he was the greatest manager I ever played for.

But the guy who was a manager who was *really* a manager was Joe McCarthy. He hadn't been a great player like Cronin, but he knew how to run the team and handle his personnel. He had so much psychology about him that he was just terrific. Strict curfew, strict rules, no joking around with the players. He *always* had complete control of the players. Really, he probably had fewer discipline problems than anybody. When his hiring was first announced some of the writers thought there was sure to be trouble between McCarthy and Williams, and I'll admit I was just a little nervous about it myself. But we got along just fine.

We had some good ballplayers on our club who were scared to death of Joe McCarthy, and maybe they didn't play as well for him as they had for Cronin because they tightened up or they didn't want to play for him as much. But for every player like that there were ten that McCarthy got the most out of. Overall, Joe McCarthy got more out of his players than any other manager I ever saw, and I loved Joe McCarthy.

Joe Cronin

Looking back, I wish I'd been a player first and a manager later, but not both at once. I think player-managing is the toughest job in the world. You just can't win. There's a lot more to the job than just playing and running the ball game. You've got to plan, and handle the men—and every personality is different. You've got to cooperate with the office and cooperate with the press. And it's all in a goldfish bowl.

From the very first I had doubts about it and almost asked to step down after that first year. But I didn't. And looking back, I regret it.

Al Lopez

I managed for seventeen years after nineteen years as a player, so I know a little bit about both. I loved both and I'm proud of the job I did in both, but I guess I'd say managing can be more discouraging than playing, especially when the team is losing, because when you're a player at least you have individual goals you can shoot at. When you're manager *all* the worries of the team become your worries.

At the same time it's a very lonely life. After the game or after the workout, the coaches go off by themselves, go out and have a few drinks. But the manager has to meet with the press until they have whatever they need from him. After that, the writers go off and finish their work, and then maybe hang out together. But the manager is by himself. He can't mingle with his players. I enjoyed my players, but I couldn't socialize with them. So I spent a lot of time alone in my hotel room. Those four walls kind of close in on you.

Eddie Mathews

I managed Atlanta in 1972, '73, and '74, but it gradually became apparent to me that I wasn't cut out for it. The actual managing of the ball game was no big deal. You make a decision, it works, you're a good manager. You have the tools to make it work, it'll work. But it's after hours that can be rough. You get wives calling you, for God's sake, "Where's my husband? I just called his room. He's not in. Don't you have a curfew? It's after midnight." It's crazy; you're dealing with irate wives and irate mothers and sometimes even irate husbands.

When you've got twenty-five guys and their families, different nationalities, different values, different *everything*, and you're trying to get them to pull together in a pressure situation, it's *tough*. At least it was for me.

As a player I had ups and downs, but they were my *own* problems. As a manager the phone's likely to ring at any hour of the day and it's somebody else's problem, which is now also *your* problem. What you say may determine whether a guy gets divorced or goes to jail or whatever.

It's also very lonely because ultimately you alone have to make the decisions. Not on the baseball field, you've got a lot of help there. It's the other stuff—the disciplinary actions. 'Cause I was always a carouser and a hell-raiser, and now I had to turn around and keep these other guys in line.

You set a curfew for 1:00 A.M. Five minutes after one, you're sitting in the lobby. Here comes one of your players. He's five minutes late, right? Now, what happens? Do you fine him two hundred dollars, or do you accept his claim that he had a tough time getting a cab or some silly thing. Now suppose you let him off for only five minutes late.

Eddie Mathews in 1980. INSET: *manager of the Braves, 1972–1974.*

Next time somebody else is a half hour late. What the hell do you do with him?

Nowadays there's absolutely no control over the ballplayers. Fines don't mean anything to them because money doesn't mean anything to them. Five hundred dollars is nothing to them. Reggie Jackson reports a day late to spring training. They fine him a day's pay. Considering his salary that's a healthy fine. But it doesn't hurt Reggie. He'll tell them it's fair and pay with a smile. He probably made a lot more money on that day than he lost in the fine—making a commercial for jeans or something.

So it's just a constant aggravation. One that I didn't need.

YOGI BERRA in 1947, addressing the crowd on Yogi Berra Night:

"I want to thank all you people for making this night necessary."

9.

Fans

Albert G. Spalding in 1884

Every wholesome American boy knows everything worth knowing about baseball—the famous players, the historic contests, and the notable features of the sport.

And in 1911

Folks marvel at the great throngs which attend important baseball matches. They really need not be wondered at. The spectators have mostly been players, and once the germ of baseball gets in their blood, they never get it out. Here is the evolution of the game up through the boy into the man. The boys of the past generation are the spectators of this. The boys of this one will be the spectators of the next. Like an endless chain . . .[1]

John Montgomery Ward in 1888

The excitement of the spectators at an important match is itself worth going to see. . . . The pent-up enthusiasm breaks forth like a whirlwind; the crowd is on its feet; cheer follows cheer, men standing upon chairs and benches; hats, canes, umbrellas, parasols, and hand-kerchiefs are waved wildly in the air; the crowd is swayed like trees in a tempest, and the sound is like the roar of a cataract. I have often stood and looked and listened, lost to the game, forgetful even of the victory just won, carried away by the influence of the impassioned scene. . . .

The excitement over the games in the old days is said to have been even greater than now. Men's passions were aroused to the highest pitch, and scenes of violence were not infrequent. Not the umpire alone, . . . but the visiting players too, became the objects of the pub-lic's wrath, and it was no unusual thing to see a player escorted from the field, when the game was over, guarded by several policemen. . . .

I am often asked whether the players themselves become as deeply interested in the game as the spectators. In one sense they do, and in another they do not. The difference in position between player and spectator must be taken into consideration. . . . The man whose every wish is directed toward the success of a certain club, and who yet is simply an onlooker, powerless to promote the desired end, is in a most trying position. . . . The strain upon the nerves becomes intense, and in addition to being interested, he grows excited.

With the player, however, it is different. . . . Instead of being help-less he is in a position to do something to promote the cause. . . . It is just as well, . . . if he grew one-half as excited as many of the spectators, he would scarcely be able to see a ball, much less hit or field it.[2]

King Kelly in 1888

I always received the very best treatment at the South End grounds in Boston. This is saying a great deal considering the fact that I was a member of a visiting club and had the reputation of being a tricky man on the field. How a Boston audience would shout and roar, with min-gled feelings of anger and joy, when I would cut the third bag on my way home. It almost reminded me of hundreds of insane people on the loose.[3]

John McGraw in 1923

It was seldom that we went to Pittsburgh without having some kind of run-in with the fans. I suppose we did antagonize them too much, but it certainly was a lot of fun. There were hot doings anytime the Giants arrived. We were roundly hated. . . .

We used to stay at the old Monongahela Hotel and from there drove in open carriages to the ball park. The Pittsburgh park then was in Allegheny City, across the river. To reach the bridge we had to pass by the public marketplace. If we escaped a shower of small stones and trash outside of the park, we were sure to get it as we passed the market.

One afternoon, after a hot game with the Pirates, the fans started after us while we were getting in our carriages. . . . Of course, we were not altogether blameless. If the fans started razzing us we would razz right back at them. To tell the truth, we sort of delighted in tantalizing the overheated rooters.

On this particular day we had dodged handfuls of gravel, loose pieces of brick, and so on, all the way to the bridge. Just as we crossed on the other side, one of the market men started razzing us. We came back at him strong. In another minute we were greeted with a shower of old vegetables—potatoes, onions, tomatoes, and even cantaloupes.

Joe McGinnity, always a quiet sort of fellow, arose in his carriage to try and quiet things down. He was just about to tell the other players to keep quiet when he lurched forward. As if in concert four big tomatoes hit him squarely in the seat of the pants. The stains stayed there until we got back off the trip.

Sammy Strang, in another carriage, was hit on the side of the head with an overripe cantaloupe. When we finally escaped and reached the hotel, anyone to look at our carriage would have thought that we had been hauling garbage. That sort of thing happened frequently.

Instead of curing us, though, it made the players more eager to fight and to win. They loved to lick the Pirates—our main rivals—and then drive by the market.[4]

Johnny Evers in 1925
I have played baseball when literally thousands of people were yelling at me until they were black in the face. I let them rave. I could yell as loud as any of them but not as loud as all of them put together. They had the floor, so I went about my business.[5]

Ty Cobb in 1914
Probably no big league ballplayer has had as much experience with crowds as I have. Once, I went into a grandstand because a fan irritated me beyond endurance by the names he called me, and again I was threatened with being shot if I played in Philadelphia after the time I unfortunately spiked Frank Baker.

The crowd makes the ball game. How much pepper do you suppose a player would show if games were played to empty seats? Probably nearly every spectator who has ever attended a big league contest has noticed that he sees the best baseball when the crowd is biggest. . . . Many big leaguers claim that the crowd and its rooting has no effect on them. This is not generally true. I know it has a big effect on me. Most ballplayers, however, like to give the impression that they are indifferent to the roasts or applause of the crowd.

The two worst towns on the American League circuit for rooters riding visiting ballplayers are St. Louis and Philadelphia.

With their club generally a tail-ender . . . there does not appear to be any occasion for the fans of St. Louis to be so rabid, but it seems as if about half the spectators there attend the game for the fun of panning the visiting players. The names that the occupants of the bleachers call the outfielders could not be printed on asbestos paper. If they ever get a winner in St. Louis, every visiting ballplayer will have to have police protection each time the home club loses a close game.

The sentiment of the Philadelphia fans is easier to understand because they have a winning club to support, but still it is unusual, since, otherwise, Philadelphia is a nice, quiet, well-behaved city where the citizens go to bed early. After I was accused of deliberately trying to spike Baker when the Athletics were fighting for the flag back in 1910, I received numerous letters telling me that I would be badly treated the next time the Tigers played in Philadelphia. The spiking incident occurred in Detroit. One of these communications stated positively that if I played in the next series, I would be shot by a man standing on top of one of those houses outside the right-field fence. . . .

Mrs. Cobb did not want me to play, but I figured that the writer was bluffing . . . and, anyway, I could not afford to remain out of the game. So I worked through the series, but I make no pretense of bravery for my action. It would have required more courage for me to stay out of the game because most of the newspapers had printed stories about the letter at the time, and I would have been called yellow. . . . I would rather take a chance on being shot than have that epithet applied to me. I do not want to pose as a hero in this incident and will freely admit that I spent several uncomfortable minutes during the series in my exposed position in center field.[6]

And in 1961

[Al]though I was wide open to a bullet or knife in the back, nothing happened to me. It was a rough ball game. Eddie Collins and Jack Barry of the A's both were hurt. The A's beat us behind Plank, 2–1. Fans rushed the field, overrunning the safety police after the last out.

I suppose I should have run for the dugout. But here is a true fact. *I never ran off a diamond in my life*. . . . And I didn't take to my heels this time. I walked at my own pace toward our bench.

The crowd, snarling and threatening, was all around me, but especially close were six or seven men who seemed trying to box me in. "Just a minute," I said. "What's the idea here? Just give me a little bit of elbow room."

One of the men leaned close to tell me, "Ty, we know you're a Mason, and we're Masons, too. And that's why we're here around you."[7]

John McGraw in 1923

The rowdyism that prevailed in baseball in the earlier days was not entirely due to the players. Fans were just about as rough as the men on the field. In fact, it was their encouragement of rough tactics that egged the players on. An attack on the umpire often was a genuine treat for them. . . .

To win at any cost was just as much of a slogan of the fans as of the players. They would resort to all kinds of tricks to handicap the opposition. A favorite practice, for instance, was for some enthusiast to sit in the stand with a small mirror and throw a reflection of sunlight into the batter's eye. That was considered good sport and perfectly proper. . . .

All over the country the sportsmanship of the spectator is improving. . . . Thirty years ago the applauding of an opposing team was looked upon as little less than treason. It is very common now for the stands to give the opposing team, even an individual player, an ovation.[8]

Paul Waner

I remember soon after I came up, Pie Traynor said to me, "Paul, you're going to be a very popular ballplayer. The people like to pull for a little fellow."

And that's the way it turned out. In all the fifteen years I played with Pittsburgh, I was never booed at home. Not even once. The same with Lloyd. No matter how bad we were, no booing. . . .

Now on the road I *liked* to be booed. I really did. Because if they boo you on the road, it's either 'cause you're a sorehead or 'cause you're hurting them, one or the other. In my first year in the big leagues, the players all told me to watch out for the right-field fans in St. Louis. "That right-field stand is tough," they said. "They ride everybody." And, of course, the fellows didn't know whether I could take a riding in the majors or not.

So the first time we went into St. Louis, I figured if they jumped on me I'd have a little fun. And sure enough, as soon as I showed up in right field they started in and gave me a terrible roasting. I turned around and yelled, "They told me for years about all you fans in St. Louis, that all the drunken bums in the city come here. And now that I'm here, I see it's true." I said it real serious and madlike, you know, never cracked a smile.

Oh, did they scream! Well, such as that went on back and forth between us for two or three months. Then one day in the middle of the summer we were giving them an awful licking. I bounced a triple out to right center and drove in two or three runs, and after the inning was over and I came running out to my position, they stood up and gave me the very devil. And then, for the first time, I laughed and waved to them.

It so happened that on the very last out of that game a fly ball was hit out to me. I caught it and then ran over to the stands and handed it to some old fellow that I'd noticed out there every time we played in St. Louis. Well, by golly, they started to clap, and soon all of them were cheering, and do you know that from then on all of them were for me.[9]

Ted Williams
Before the war, if a guy was heckling me I'd try to foul one into the stands and hit him. No way I could do it, but I'd try to pop them in there. Until I had two strikes. Then I'd try to get a hit. That's silly I know, but that's what I did.

Then later there were other incidents I regretted, although I do think I grew up somewhat. Maybe not enough though.

But you know the funny thing—I had those people in Boston in the palm of my hand all those years and I never even realized it.

Al Kaline
Fans? All you have to do is smile at 'em and say hi and shake their hands. They're satisfied.

Duke Snider
I had one run-in with the fans that I'll never forget. One game in 1956, a night game at Ebbets Field, I went zero for five and left almost a

Autograph mania. The Hall of Fame game, Cooperstown, New York, 1980.

dozen runners on base. I couldn't buy a hit all night, and the last time up I was booed.

When I came into the clubhouse after the game, I was really upset, and I gave the fans a little blast. Really I was upset with myself, but my frustration came out against the fans. This was around the time when Mr. O'Malley was talking about moving the club to Los Angeles and I said Brooklyn didn't *deserve* the Dodgers. Pee Wee was looking at me and shaking his head, but I said, "Go ahead and print it."

President Eisenhower had had a heart attack three or four days before, but the next morning you had to go to page 4 to find out his condition. *I* was on page 1 in bold headlines.

I was sorry for what I said, and I retracted by saying that I'd spoken in a fit of anger.

Well, that night, my first time up there were about 75 percent boos. I got a single. My second time up I got another hit, and it was about 50–50 boos. The third time up there were still some boos, and I got another hit. Then they gave me a standing ovation.

That was Ebbets Field.

Sandy Koufax

Walking to the dugout for the start of the game in Ebbets Field was an experience in itself. To get from the clubhouse to the bench, you had to walk down a long dirt runway, which was separated from the main concourse by a high picket fence. Every day, as you left the clubhouse, there would be a mass of fans lined up from one end of that

LEFT: *Yogi Berra.* RIGHT: *Duke Snider.*

fence to the other. . . . They'd be reaching through the picket fence to shake you by the hand or pat you on the back. They'd be yelling, "Newk, you're the greatest pitcher in the whole world. . . . Get 'em today, Pee Wee baby. . . . Today's the day, Gil."

When you went back they'd be there to shower you with affection. If you had won.

You'd lose the game, though, and, as Leo Durocher puts it, "You gotta go back the same way you came." They'd be waiting there, the same loyal rooters, and they'd be screaming, "You bums! You bums couldn't beat anybody, you couldn't beat my grandmother! What's the matter with you?" They'd throw sand through the fence, and sometimes a dislodged rock or two. . . . You really needed a shower by the time you got to the clubhouse. . . .

That was the Dodger fan of blessed memory. They came to root, and they rooted for their own. Brooklyn against the world.[10]

Roberto Clemente

I send out twenty thousand autographed pictures a year to the kids. I feel proud when a kid asks me for my autograph.

I do it because baseball has given me a good life. I am a human being. . . . I have achieved something. Some players complain. I tell them we do not have to stand in the street with a heavy drill going rat-tat-tat-tat. We come to the park in a clean shirt. We smell from perfume all the time.

I believe we owe something to the people who watch us. They work hard for their money. When we do not try 100 percent, we steal from them.[11]

Mickey Mantle

They'll boo the ass off anybody sometimes. I used to get it . . . and in Yankee Stadium besides. They'd get on me for not going in the army or not being able to run so fast if my legs were bad. . . .

Sometimes you even get it from the family, and that's when it really hurts. Once I struck out three times in a game, and when I got back to the clubhouse, I just sat down on my stool and held my head in my hands, like I was going to start crying. I heard somebody come up to me, and it was little Timmy Berra, Yogi's boy, standing there next to me. He tapped me on the knee, nice and soft, and I figured he was going to say something nice to me, you know, like "You keep hanging in there," or something like that.

But all he did was look at me and then he said in his little kid's voice, "You stink."[12]

Many fans look upon an umpire as
a sort of necessary evil to the
luxury of baseball, like the odor
that follows an automobile.
                    —CHRISTY
                    MATHEWSON in
                    1914, *Pitching in
                    a Pinch*

10.

Umps

Connie Mack

In the early days of baseball, when umpires wore high silk hats and
dressed as if they were going to a wedding or funeral, they would turn
to the spectators when close plays were made and ask their opinion.
The crowd was usually as divided in opinion as the United Nations,
but they felt complimented by the umpire's consideration of them.
The umpire would then make his decision. This was a practical
method of stopping wars at their point of inception.

It was in the eighties and nineties that the game passed through its
turbulent era. Umpire-baiting became a popular pastime. As the
crowds became tougher the umpires became tougher.[1]

Ty Cobb in 1914

The best recommendation for an umpire in the old days was: "He
licked somebody in the Three I League. He ought to do."[2]

109

Christy Mathewson in 1914

Tim Hurst, the old American League umpire, was one of the most picturesque men who ever spun an indicator. He was telling a story just the other day in McGraw's billiard room in New York which gets better every time I hear it. Tim tells of umpiring in Baltimore in the old days when there was a runner on first base.

"The man started to steal," said Tim, "and as he left the bag he spiked the first baseman, who tried to trip him. The second baseman blocked the runner, and in sliding into the bag, the latter tried to spike Hugh Jennings, who was playing shortstop and covering, while Jennings sat on him to knock the wind out. The batter hit [Wilbert] Robinson, who was catching, on the hands with his bat so that he couldn't throw, and Robbie trod on my toes with his spikes and shoved his glove into my face so that I couldn't see to give the decision. It was one of the hardest that I have ever been called upon to make."

"What did you do?" I asked him.

"I punched Robbie in the ribs, called it a foul, and sent the runner back," replied Tim.[3]

Ty Cobb in 1914

When the subway was first put into New York, many out-of-town folks were confused by the Broadway and Bronx trains. Frequently passengers would get on a Bronx express and forget to change at Ninety-sixth Street, so that instead of arriving at the old American League Park they found themselves in the Bronx Zoo. . . . This would make a difference of about an hour in the time of arrival at the ball park. I would not call this a plain bonehead play because I made the same mistake myself, once.

Tim Hurst was scheduled to work a game out at American League Park when the Detroit club was playing there one day, and he got carried up into the Bronx instead of going on the right route. Hurst has told me since that he was reading some promising prizefighter's history at the time and paid no attention to the stations. Nobody was scheduled to help Hurst umpire this game, so that when the time for the contest arrived and Tim had not showed up, we were up against it for an umpire. [Clark] Griffith, then managing the Yankees, sent for [Hughie] Jennings, and they held a confab at the plate while the players of both clubs gathered around.

"I'll tell you what I'll do," said Foxy Griffith. "One of my extra players will work behind the bat, and you can put one of your men on the bases." The rule book provides for substitute players to umpire in the event of an emergency.

"All right," replied Jennings, and selected an extra player from the bench. . . .

Germany Schaefer was playing second base on the Detroit club in those days, and he smashed the ball to right field in the first inning. It was really a single, but Germany, figuring that he wasn't going to get any the worst of it from a player of his own club umpiring, decided to take two. . . . The play at second base was close, Schaefer being forced to slide for it, but our volunteer umpire was properly on the job and shouted: "Safe!"

Germany was up and brushing himself off, being rather tickled with the fact that he had made a two-base hit, when he heard a deep, contradictory voice break out behind him: "Yer out!"

Germany looked and saw Hurst right behind him. He had come hustling across the field when he saw the hit and had got close enough to second base to take the play there. . . . Schaefer put up an awful kick . . . but Tim . . . stuck to his decision.

"You were late, and you are incompetent," declared Schaefer. "If you would keep away from the racetracks, you might be on the job. How do you expect to call them from the clubhouse?"

"You don't make the plays close enough for me to need to be any nearer to see them," replied Hurst, who was always there with the comeback. "Now get to the bench before I put you out of the game."[4]

Christy Mathewson in 1914

There are several types of umpires, and ballplayers are always studying the species to find out the best way to treat each man. . . . There are autocrats and stubborn ones and good fellows and weak-kneed ones. . . . The autocrat of the umpire world is Silk O'Loughlin. . . .

"There are no close plays," says Silk. "A man is always out or safe, or it is a ball or a strike, and the umpire, if he is a good man and knows his business, is always right. For instance, I am always right."

He refuses to let the players discuss a decision. . . . If a man makes any talk with him, it is quick to the shower bath. Silk has a voice of which he is proud and declares that he shares the honors with Caruso and that it is only his profession as an umpire that keeps him off the grand-opera circuit. I have heard a lot of American League ballplayers say at various times that they wished he was on the grand-opera circuit . . . but they were mostly prejudiced at those moments by some sentiments which Silk had just voiced in an official capacity.

As is well known in baseball Silk is the inventor of "Strike Tuh!" and the creased trousers for umpires. I have heard American League players declare that they are afraid to slide when Silk is close down over a play for fear they will bump up against his trousers and cut themselves. He is one of the kind of umpires who can go through a game on the hottest summer day, running about the bases, and still keep his collar unwilted. At the end he will look as if he were dressed for an afternoon tea.

Always he wears on his right hand, which is his salary or decision wing, a large diamond that sparkles in the sunlight every time he calls a man out. Many American League players assert that he would rather call a man out than safe, so that he can shimmer his "cracked ice," but again they are usually influenced by circumstances. . . .

Corresponding to him in the National League is Billy Klem. He always wears a Norfolk jacket because he thinks it is more stylish . . . and he refuses to don a wind pad. Ever notice him working behind the bat? But I am going to let you in on a secret. That chest is not all his own. Beneath his jacket he carries his armor, a protector, and under his trousers' legs are shin guards. He insists that all the players call him

Johnny Evers. INSET: *Bill Klem.*

"Mr." He says that he thinks maybe soon his name will be in the social register.

Larry Doyle thought that he had received the raw end of a decision at second base one day. He ran down to first, where Klem had retreated after he passed his judgment.

"Say, Bill," exploded Larry, "that man didn't touch the bag—didn't come within six feet of it."

"Say, Doyle," replied Klem, "when you talk to me call me 'Mr. Klem.' "

"But Mr. Klem—" amended Larry.

Klem hurriedly drew a line with his foot as Doyle approached him.

"But if you come over that line, you're out of the game, Mr. Doyle," he threatened.

"All right," answered Larry, . . . "but, Mr. Klem, I only wanted to ask you if that clock in center field is right by your watch, because I know everything about you is right."

Larry went back, grinning and considering that he had put one over on Klem—Mr. Klem.

For a long time Johnny Evers of the Chicago club declared that Klem owed him five dollars on a bet. . . . He kept pestering Klem about that measly five dollar bet, not in an obtrusive way, you understand, but by such delicate methods as holding up five fingers when Klem glanced down on the coaching lines where he was stationed, or by writing a large "5" in the dirt at home plate with the butt of his bat. . . .

One day John let his temper get away from him and bawled Klem out about the neglected debt.

"Here's your five, Mr. Evers," said Klem, handing him a five dollar bill, "and now you are fined twenty-five dollars."

"And it was worth it," answered Evers, "to have a few words with you, Mr. Klem."[5]

Johnny Evers in 1910

Umpires, in spite of the theory upon which baseball is conducted, . . . are human beings. . . . Umpires . . . are likely to blunder, to be carried away by prejudice, . . . and more than likely to become confused by the fierce heckling of players or spectators, and to blunder worse and worse. Umpires may even be dishonest. . . .

Yet baseball, as an institution, is more dependent upon the honesty, courage, and fairness of umpires than upon any other element in the game. One incompetent or dishonest official . . . can mar an entire season. . . .

In spite of these facts the rulers of baseball have adopted an extraordinary code; first, that the umpire always is right; second, that those who differ with him are "anarchists"; third, that all criticism of umpires should cease "for the good of the game." . . .

The umpire, from being the abused, downtrodden victim of fanatical frenzy, as pictured in the comic supplements, has in the major leagues at least, become the czar, armed with arbitrary power to use or misuse, and certain of the support of his league in any case.[6]

And in 1915

I was fired out of so many games on my ear last summer by these human walruses in umpires' suits that I think my ears must have callouses on them. And instead of sympathizing with me, everybody seemed to sympathize with the umpires. . . . I have made up my mind that my mouth will be hermetically sealed this season. So far I have got along fine. I've been in two games already and haven't bawled anybody out yet. I believe I can keep on being a human Sphinx, though they say that steam under pressure exerts tremendous force and is liable to cause an explosion.[7]

Bill Dickey

I think the maddest I've ever been in my life was in 1929. We were playing the Philadelphia Athletics. I don't remember what inning it was, but the bases were loaded and two outs. The ump was Bill Dinneen, who was a good ump, and a good guy. Cochrane was the hitter. He hit a swinging bunt down the third-base line, and Henry Johnson, our pitcher that day, made a great play and threw the ball to me. I looked around at Dinneen, and he said, "Safe!" I said, "Why was he safe?" He said, "You didn't tag him." I said, "Bill, I didn't have to tag him! The bases were loaded!" Then he said, "You weren't on the base."

I was so mad, I couldn't see! I had the ball in my hand and I threw it, but I didn't mean to let it go. But I was so mad, and I threw it so hard, that it slipped away from me and rolled toward the A's dugout. Well, I took out after it, and the men were running the bases. When I got back another runner had scored, and I was crying. Well, of course, Dinneen put me out of the ball game, and they suspended me for three days.

But here's the funny part. I was so mad that I stayed mad all night. I got up early 'cause I couldn't sleep and went down to eat breakfast. Got me a newspaper and I opened it up. There I was in a cartoon throwing off my mask, my chest protector—everything's up in the air—and there was a little old lady in the front row of the grandstand with her hands over her eyes, pleading, "Please, don't take off any more!"

John McGraw

If a ballplayer is high-strung—and all good players generally are—he cannot entirely control himself when he thinks the umpire has given him the worst of it. . . . I would rather have a ballplayer who fought for every point, even if wrong, than one who meekly submitted to everything without a word.[8]

Al Lopez

In my third or fourth year at Brooklyn, I was made team captain; and I got to arguing too much with the umpires because I thought it was part of my job as captain. But the bad part was that I was getting thrown out of too many ball games.

Finally, I was traded to Boston, and Manager McKechnie made me field leader for that club. And I started arguing with umps for that team and got thrown out of a couple more games. Finally, McKechnie took me aside and said, "Look, Al, you can't help us win games if you're in the clubhouse." That made sense to me, and I stopped pushing the umps so hard. I've never forgotten that lesson. It's good to express your opinion, but don't push it to the point where you're ejected.

As a manager, if one of my players got into a hot dispute, I'd jump in between player and ump to protect my player. Maybe I even agreed with the ump, but I'd jump in there. A lot of managers do that. Let the player cool down. And then talk to him in the dugout. Tell him what Bill McKechnie told me.

Bob Feller

It's show business on TV. The coaches and some of the players want to get out there and put on a big act. The manager might be protecting his players from ejection or showing the club owner that he's in there fighting to win. The player might be covering up for some mistake he made. Or they may just feel that the ump is 100 percent wrong and can't help but let him know how they feel. Anyway, I do think maybe there's a little more of a show made of it now because of TV.

Wahoo Sam Crawford

I was an umpire for a while—in the Pacific Coast League from 1935 to 1938—long after I finished playing. Umpiring is a lonesome life. Thankless job. Thankless. You haven't got a friend in the place. Only your partner, that's all. . . . Everybody else is just waiting for you to make a mistake. There's a bench over here, and a bench over there, and thousands of people in the stands, and every eye in the whole damn place is watching like a hawk trying to get something on you.

I had a good partner, too. I booked in with a fellow named Jack Powell, a wonderful umpire and a wonderful person as well. He'd tell me not to fraternize with the players. I felt that I could kid around with them a little, you know. What the heck, I'd been a ballplayer myself. But he said, "Don't do it, don't fool with the players, don't have anything to do with them. If you do, sooner or later they'll put you on the spot."

And that's the way it turned out. He was right. It's a thankless and a lonely way to live, so I quit it.[9]

Mickey Mantle

When a player makes a bad play, he gets booed and yelled at. An umpire gets booed . . . not only when he makes a bad call but when the crowd *thinks* he has made a bad call. When a ballplayer makes a really fine play, he gets cheered. . . . But when an umpire makes a good play—when he is in the right spot at the right time and makes the right call on a difficult and confusing play—nobody notices. Nobody cheers. Nobody even cares. . . .

How does he keep his morale up?

Self-respect . . .

But it's not easy.[10]

DIZZY DEAN, when asked why he
gave different places of birth to
different interviewers:
"Them ain't lies. Them's scoops."

11.

The Media

Albert G. Spalding in 1911

As showing the importance of taking advantage of opportunities
presented for the gratuitous advertising of the game, I recall an incident
following the sale of King Kelly to Boston. The newspapers of Chicago
did not take kindly to this transaction. One paper—the Chicago
News—was particularly severe in its criticism. The *News* strenuously
urged, among other things, a reduction in the price of admission to
games, claiming that if Chicago was to have cheap players it ought to
have cheap admission.

Frequent caricatures were printed, some of them occupying a half
page, illustrating the slave pen of antebellum days, with the auction
block, upon which, instead of the familiar forms of the unhappy slaves,
abject ballplayers were displayed for sale to the highest bidder. Being at
the time president of the Chicago Club, and having been instrumental
in the sale of Kelly, I came in for much notoriety. While these daily
"roasts" were being served out to me, I noticed that the attendance

kept increasing. Gradually the controversy quieted down. Then one day on the street I met the prominent baseball writer "Harmony" White and asked him, "What's the matter with the *News?* You haven't been giving me the usual amount of space of late."

He replied that he was absolutely *out of ammunition.* I offered to furnish him fresh ammunition if he would only keep up the onslaught. His incredulous look indicated that he was not impressed with my sincerity. I then explained to him that simply as a business proposition I could not afford to be neglected in his paper, for since he had let up in his attacks our attendance was dropping off.

"Well," said he, "if you feel that way about it, and will supply the ammunition, I will open up again. . . .

As a result of this casual conversation it was then and there agreed that he would send a trusted messenger to my office on two days of each week to secure the necessary ammunition. This plan was carried out to the end of that season, and, as a result, the Chicago club made more money that year than it had ever made during its history up to that time.[1]

Connie Mack in 1950

How did baseball develop from the sandlots to the huge stadiums—from a few hundred spectators to the millions in attendance at professional games today?

My answer is: through the gigantic force of publicity.

When I entered the game we first received only a few lines as news. These few lines expanded into columns and pages; in ratio the crowds in our ball parks grew and grew and grew. News, like advertising, is a powerful momentum behind any enterprise.

The professional sporting world was created and is being kept alive by the services extended by the press.[2]

Johnny Evers in 1925

A ballplayer has two reputations, one with the other players and one with the fans. The first is based on ability. The second the newspapers give him.[3]

Honus Wagner in 1925

A player would stand a better chance if no one ever heard of him until he put on his uniform. Then, if he had the goods they would know it instead of beginning to look for it before he started. A fellow with a big reputation must start hitting .300 right away or they think he's a frost.[4]

Rube Marquard

I had an awful time when I first came up to the Giants. The New York papers gave me a great send-off, but they really overdid it. They set a standard I could never live up to, and it began two years of bitter disappointment for me. It still makes me uncomfortable when I think about it.

Joe Cronin

I always got along with the press, but some of the fellows had a rough time—like Ted [Williams]. Oh, he had some run-ins with those Boston writers! I'll never forget one year when he was young—it might have been his rookie year—Ted sprained his ankle just as we were leaving on a road trip. So we left him behind in Boston while we went to Washington, and he was gonna rejoin us in New York.

So while he was home some newspaperman got him to give an interview, and Ted said he didn't like the trees, he didn't like the streets, he didn't like the people, he didn't like *anything* about Boston.

Well, here we are on the road in Washington, and all the newsmen come up to me waving this article and asking, "What're you gonna do about it? How can you play a guy like that?"

So we went to New York and Ted joined us there. And I sat down with him and said, "Now, Ted, goodness gracious. You really put yourself on the spot! Now what're you gonna do?"

He said, "Joe, I'll tell you one thing I'm gonna do. We're going home after this series. *I'll hit .400* during that next home stand. Don't you worry about it."

And he did. He hit .400.

Mickey Mantle in 1967

The newspapers were nearly my undoing. The writers . . . probably felt that they were doing me favors by writing me up as if I were already ticketed to the Hall of Fame. The result was that many of the home fans . . . resented me right from the beginning, or resented my not delivering immediately on my newspaper promise. It may have been, too, that the write-ups had an effect upon me, scaring me with the goals they set for me.

It took me a while to learn to be wary of writers. At first I thought you could talk to them just the way you might talk to any of the guys in the clubhouse—none of whom would think of running out and repeating some dumb thing you said, trying to make it sound dumber. It was a real shock to me to discover that when I said something in front of a writer, I was shouting it from the New York rooftops.[5] . . .

I was only nineteen, and I came out of a little bitty town in Oklahoma and there I was in New York. That'd be tough on anyone. And then they started writing that I was the next DiMaggio; that really put the pressure on.

It really wasn't for about five years that I began to do what they expected of me. I used to wish I could get away from the pressure sometimes.

Well, after they fired Yogi and brought in Johnny Keane—I got my wish. I had a bad year and the team had a bad year, and all of a sudden there weren't those big crowds in the clubhouse. That's when I decided "pressure" wasn't all that bad.

Lou Boudreau

Late in the summer of 1948, as the American League pennant race stayed tied in a three-way knot—Cleveland, Boston, and Philadelphia—baseball was front-page news in Cleveland. The smallest item about our ball club was of major news value. The difficulties presented by such microscopic coverage . . . began to mount. They reached a climax when one paper assigned a columnist to follow us on a road trip and act as a grandstand manager whose sole duty was to second-guess my managerial decisions.

Lou Boudreau, player-manager and MVP of the 1948 World Champion Cleveland Indians

A manager would have to be a full-fledged saint to put up with such journalistic tactics without squawking, and I'm no saint.[6]

[Eventually, on the team's last road trip, Boudreau closed the Indian clubhouse to all newspapermen for the rest of the season.]

Whitey Ford

The 1961 season became a nightmare for Roger Maris after he got into this thing of catching up to Babe Ruth's record of sixty home runs. . . . The writers, TV, radio, fans, everybody began hounding him, and he even began to lose some of his hair. The doctors said it was nerves.[7]

Mickey Mantle

Once, when Roger was taking all that heat, he even got a big list of questions that was sent to New York from some paper in Japan by cable, and he said, "No wonder I'm going nuts." Another time, some writer asked him, "What's a .260 hitter like you doing hitting all those home runs?" And Maris just looked at him and said, "You've got to be a fucking idiot." After a while he came to me and said, "I can't take it any more, Mick." And I had to tell him, "You'll have to take it, you'll just have to."[8]

One little and two big leaguers: Mickey Mantle, Roger Maris, and fan

Eddie Mathews

I was Aaron's manager the year he broke Ruth's lifetime home-run record, and it did have aspects of a nightmare. Very few people could have handled the pressure as well as Hank did. I had problems with it, and I was just the manager. Would you believe two or three hundred writers were traveling with us? And everyone wanted an exclusive interview. We had to change Hank's name, hide him in the hotels, hire special limousines to chauffeur him in and out and around. Of course, that left me taking the brunt of everything, 'cause I was the only one available. It was "You no-good S.O.B., I'm here all the way from Japan, and I've *got* to interview him."

It was an interesting but aggravating experience. There'd be two hundred writers in the clubhouse after a game. You couldn't even move. TV cameras pushing people aside to get in and get their close-ups. Between games of a doubleheader even they'd try and get in, and I had to make a rule to keep them out. They were mad at me the whole goddamn time. Hell, I didn't do anything right. Oh, it was a mess. It started in spring training and ended the day after he hit number 715. They *all* left. Jesus!

Ralph Kiner

I work in television broadcasting and, yes, the media situation has become more and more of a factor in baseball. I think also the trend of reporting has changed considerably, which I think has to do with TV. The reporters today are looking for psychological elements more than they were when I was playing.

The media

Al Kaline at his induction into the Hall of Fame, August, 1980

Back then it was "How did the game go?" Today it's "What happened to your psyche when you were seven years old?"

Casey Stengel

Some ballplayers think the writers are always out to knock them. That's silly. Four-fifths of them will write what's good about you if they can.[9]

Al Kaline

I've learned to like my work in the broadcast booth. When they first asked me to do it, I said I'd try it on a temporary basis. If I liked it and they liked me, I could continue.

I liked it, although I'd had no background at all in broadcasting. My main problem was getting up the nerve to point out something I thought was wrong. I found myself, when something went wrong on the field, purposely keeping my mouth shut. Well, I wasn't doing my job. I was hired because I know baseball, not because I know and like all the players on the Detroit Tigers. It would be the easiest thing in the world to just sit up there and root for the Detroit Tigers. I love the Tigers, and I always will. But I'm not going to sacrifice my reputation as an honest person just to keep some player's wife from getting mad at me.

Two cranks in a family means
domestic bliss—if they are both
baseball cranks.

—ALBERT G.
SPALDING in
1911, *America's
National Game*

12.

Wives and Families

John McGraw in 1923

Very few players are ever as valuable to a team the first year they're married as they are before or after. Wait a minute—I'll explain.

When a young fellow gets it into his head to get married, there's no stopping him. He thinks of nothing else. He is entering a new phase of life and is taking on new responsibilities. Naturally, he and his wife think their marriage the most important thing in the world. In working out their early problems they forget all about baseball. It takes a full year for him to get down to business and concentrate his mind on the game.

I am convinced that nothing helps a young man so much in baseball or in any other profession as a good wife. I think, though, that they ought to get married immediately after the World Series. By the time the next season comes around, they will be able to understand things.

I have known young bridegrooms, on the bench, to forget whether

124

there were men on bases or not. They are thinking about that new apartment, about that new furniture, that fancy gas range, and so on.

It is a beautiful state of bliss, but, take it from me, a young man in that state of mind doesn't win many ball games.

It is quite natural for the wives to want to attend the ball games. Baseball has become a part of their lives. If they are sensible women—which most of them are—they will encourage and criticize their husbands so as to be of help. I've had brides come to me and ask what kind of food they ought to prepare for their husbands.

There are other wives who will not attend a game in which their husbands appear. They get so nervous over his possible success or failure that they fear they'll make themselves conspicuous. I wish all of them thought that way.

The wives and sweethearts who really cause the player trouble and embarrassment are the foolish ones. Many ballplayers, you know, come into the leagues with little knowledge of life, especially big city life. They're carried away with hero worship and marry some girl who really seeks the limelight more than the love of the young fellow. There have been many cases of that kind.

These foolish wives or sweethearts who sit in the stand and yell out endearing encouragement to their husbands are genuine distraction. They not only embarrass the player but often make it very uncomfortable for those about them in the stands.

You can well imagine the feelings of a player when he leaves the bench to go to bat at a critical moment and suddenly hears a soprano voice from the stands: "There goes my dearie!"

It is the real, wholesome woman of good, hard, common sense who helps the ballplayer to success. Often she has been my very helpful ally in getting a player to improve his work or to take care of himself.

As a rule I do not approve a wife's accompanying her husband on the road trips. She seems to distract his attention. Again, a lot of wives, when thrown together in such close association, are bound to talk and gossip over what they've heard. While they mean no harm the husbands are often worried over this. They learn of things about other players that otherwise would not have interested them.[1]

Stan Musial

Wives traveling with the team can present problems, but more often they have a stabilizing effect. Some players can't be controlled by anybody else *but* their wives.

Early in my career the wives weren't allowed to travel with us as much. In fact, they weren't even allowed to come to spring training. That's all changed today. Now players can afford to bring their wives down and rent a cottage on the beach, and they can bring their wives on trips. Which I think is great—as long as it doesn't just become a family vacation or a family trip at club expense.

Joe Cronin

After two years in the National League, the Pirates outrighted me to Kansas City in the spring of 1928. They'd seen enough of me I guess. Things looked bleak, but in July of that year my luck began to change. Joe Engel, a Washington scout, saw me play and recommended me to Clark Griffith and the Washington Senators. My contract was assigned to Washington on July 13—Friday the thirteenth—and I arrived at the club's front office on July 16, which is my wife, Mildred's, birthday. But that's another story. That's the main story.

You see, Mildred was Clark Griffith's niece—that's right, Calvin and Thelma Griffith [owners of the Minnesota Twins] are her brother and sister—and at that time, she was working in the Senator's office, and Joe Engel dropped her a note saying, "I'm bringing you home a 'real sweetie.' " Isn't that a strange coincidence? I walked in the office and there she was—the girl of my dreams, though she didn't pay any attention to me for a number of years there. But I finally won her over. We got married in September of 1934 at St. Matthew's Cathedral in Washington, later made famous by poor Jack Kennedy having his funeral there.

We went through the Panama Canal on our honeymoon and arrived in San Francisco. There I received a phone call from Mr. Griffith telling me he had an opportunity to sell my contract to Boston for an unheard price of two hundred and fifty thousand dollars. Well, he'd never sold a player before, but it was the Depression and he needed the money. He wanted me to think it over and call him back. It was a golden opportunity for me, really. Mr. Yawkey wanted me to play shortstop and manage the Red Sox. He had big plans to build the team into a contender. My wife and I mulled it over, and the next day we called back to say okay. Neither of us ever regretted it. We've lived in Massachusetts ever since. Raised three boys and a girl, and now we have seven grandchildren as well.

My wife could write a book about baseball. She knows more baseball than anyone. I'll put her against anybody in America. She can tell you how many strikeouts some guy in Yakima, Washington, has. And our oldest boy, Tommy, is working for the Twins. So we have a lot to talk about. Things are never dull around the Cronin house.

Jackie Robinson in 1948

When my wife gave birth to a bouncing baby boy, we named him Jackie, Jr., and vowed that we'd give him all the things we missed as kids.

I hope my son will be an athlete, too. I'm sure it will keep him out

The Robinsons

of trouble. A lot of boys get in trouble because they don't have anything to do. When they're playing games, wrestling, or boxing, they don't have time to loaf on street corners or get mixed up with tough gangs. Sports have kept me out of plenty of trouble.[2]

In 1957, having announced his retirement

Now I'll be able to spend more time with my family. My kids and I will get to know each other better. Jackie, Sharon, and David will have a real father they can play with, talk to in the evening and every weekend. They won't have to look for him on TV.

Maybe my sons will want to play ball, as I have, when they grow up. I'd love it. But I'll see to it they get a college education first. . . .

Just now Jackie still feels badly about my quitting. It's tough for a ten-year-old to have his dad suddenly turn from ballplayer to a commuter. I guess it will be quite a change for me too. But someday Jackie will realize that the old man quit baseball just in time.[3]

In 1968, after Jackie, Jr., was arrested for illegal possession of narcotics and a firearm

He quit high school. He joined the army. He fought in Vietnam and he was wounded. We lost him somewhere. I've had more effects on other people's kids than on my own.

I can talk about Jackie. Rachel and I have been able to piece things together. He's a bright boy and a good athlete. If he'd worked I think he could have become a major leaguer. I would have liked that, but he's an independent kid, and look where he was. You know Rachel has a master's degree. She teaches at Yale. So there was the culture stuff. He felt blocked there. And he was Jackie Robinson, Junior, so he felt that he was blocked in sports. He wanted to be something; he wanted to be great at something. So he decided, when he was pretty young, that he was going to be a great crook.[4]

[Jackie Robinson, Jr., successfully arrested his heroin addiction at a drug rehabilitation center in Connecticut, where he was later invited to join the staff. However, his life was tragically cut short by an automobile accident on the night of June 17, 1971.]

Yogi Berra in 1961

Carm won't let me do a lick of work around the house because she's afraid I'll get hurt. If she sees me get up on a ladder she hollers, "You'll fall off." So when we have to put up curtains or something like that, Carm gets up on the ladder and I hand them up to her.

Of course, Carm knows I won't be playing ball forever, so she's saving up a few chores for me. I figure she'll get even. For now, she puts up with the life of a ballplayer's wife without complaining. It's only when I'm gone nights that I could be home that she complains. "I don't mind you not being here in the daytime," she says. "I'm busy then, anyway. But at night, when the kids are in bed and all the housework is done, I want you around."

That's all right with me. I like to be around then.

I also like to be around at mealtimes. Carm is a real good cook. I like things like pork chops and lamb chops as much as steak and roast beef, and I still love ravioli and lasagna and spaghetti. Carm always makes spaghetti at least once a week, sometimes with meatballs, sometimes with sausage, and sometimes with meat sauce. I like it any way she cooks it. Actually, my only eating trouble is that I like to eat too much. I can eat a three- or four-pound steak with no strain, and Carm says her food bills are cut in half when I go on a road trip. Gil McDougald's wife, Babe, loves to watch me eat. She's Russian and she likes to cook, and she says the best part of cooking is seeing somebody eat it and enjoy it. She makes me a dish she calls "galumpe," which is cabbage rolls filled with meat and rice, and they're pretty big, but I can eat six or seven of them. Carm always give me a lecture when we're going out. "Don't make a pig out of yourself," she says. "Lay off after you have seconds." But I love to eat.[5] . . .

Carmen and Yogi Berra

"Sometimes with meatballs, sometimes with sausage, and sometimes with meat sauce."

Casey Stengel

We never had any children, but Edna had so many in her family—nieces and nephews and their children that came along—that we became very active with the family. We'd have big Sundays in which our home in Glendale became a playground for the kids.

Edna also got very much interested in the Yankee players and their wives and took an interest in the way those families grew. There were very few divorces. It got to where there were about fifty young children, and then probably seventy-five. And this is the way it goes in most ball clubs. . . .

All in all, I would have to say that her end of things has been handled in a first-class manner, with me being a man that's been up and down.[6]

Whitey Ford

I'll tell you one thing, if you think it was fun traveling around with Casey, you should've seen him when his wife was along. Edna was a tall, good-looking woman, who dressed magnificently; you know, they had a fair amount of money anyway because her family owned a bank

"You should've seen him when his wife was along." Edna and Casey Stengel.

in Glendale where they lived in California; and they owned apartment houses, and Casey put money in oil wells in the thirties with Al Lopez and some other old ballplayers, and no kidding, they struck oil. They really struck oil. But Edna was a beauty. She kept their accounts because once she had been a bookkeeper, and she had even acted in the silent movies. Casey'd end up a speech sometimes by turning to her and saying, "And tell them about the time you played with Hoot Gibson."

She took a lot of trips with us because they always lived in the same big house in Glendale ever since they got married, and she'd have to keep crisscrossing the country just to join him in New York every summer. And back home she kept their house filled with things they bought all over the world. They had a Chinese room upstairs and Japanese beds, and stuff like that.

One thing she didn't like was when people would say Casey was a funny old guy—you know, just a clown. She hated it the same way that Carmen Berra hated for people to make fun of Yogi's looks. Edna would always say, "He's not a clown. He's one of the smartest men in baseball, in business, in anything he'd try." And she'd remember that Casey used to ask her to find a job in the family's businesses for one of his old ballplayers. She'd say that on trips he might yell and holler and even insult her in front of the whole ball club, but she said he always quieted down and got all sweet and courtly to her—and she was right.

Once she kept a team plane waiting, and the Old Man got all embarrassed because if it was a player that kept us waiting, Casey would've hit the ceiling. But this time it was his own wife, so he was embarrassed, and he started getting on her for it. On the airplane he bitched and yelled at her, and then he sat there without saying anything for a few hours—you know, letting it sink in and all. He was pretty rough, and she just sat there all red in the face and took it.

When we finally landed they had this chartered bus to take us to the hotel. But by then Casey was beginning to feel a little sorry that he'd been so rough on her. They got on the bus and sat in the two front seats where the manager always sat, then he said, "I'll check and see that your bags are okay," so he hopped down from the bus and went around to where the guy was loading the bags in the hatch on the side of the bus.

Then he came back after a long while—I guess he was trying to show her that he was going to a lot of trouble—and he said, "Yeah, they're all right. They got all three of them packed in."

I guess that's what Edna had been waiting for—sitting there taking all that guff from him. Now she finally gets a shot at him. She didn't change her expression or anything, or even look at him. She just waited a minute and then said, all nice and even and cool, as if he had just screwed up for real, "I had four."[7]

Ralph Kiner

My children were pretty athletic—baseball and tennis. My oldest boy, Mike, went to UCLA on a four-year baseball scholarship and played a couple of years in the minors. My other son, Scott, is a tennis pro. And then I have a daughter, Casey, who plays *very* good tennis.

I guess it's logical. Their mother is Nancy Chaffee, who was ranked in the top four in the world in tennis. When we got married I naturally had to take the game up. I told her, "There's no way a girl can beat me at anything." But she forced me to eat those words. For three years I tried but I could not beat her. Finally, I beat her. That was when she was pregnant. . . .

Al Kaline

I got married in 1954 after my second season. I'd had enough of living alone in that hotel room in Detroit. My wife and I had gone through school together in Baltimore, and marriage to her really made my life better—more stable and less lonely.

And then after we had kids, her role became even more important. All the weeks that I was on the road and all the nights I was at the ball park, she had to fill the shoes of both parents.

Most important though, we shared everything, good and bad. Really, all the fame and glory in the world isn't worth a thing without someone to share it with.

Stan Musial

My son played baseball when he was young, but I didn't get to see him much. People think we can teach our kids to play. But by the time you're done traveling and playing night games and doubleheaders, you don't really have as much time to give to your kids as you'd like. So my son ran track and played high school football and didn't participate in much baseball. Another reason—everybody used to always say, "Can you hit like your dad?" or worse, "Why can't you hit like your dad?" And I think that kind of cooled him off to the idea of baseball.

Reminds me of Dick Sisler. My wife and I used to pal around with Dick, and he'd be introduced to people; and they'd say, "Oh yes, George Sisler's son. How come you can't hit like your dad? Ha. Ha." You could see what kind of position that put him in.

So it's kind of tough for a young guy to follow a famous dad's footsteps.

Al Kaline

I have two boys, Mike and Mark, and I know that it isn't always easy being a ballplayer's child. Did you ever stop to think what it must be like going to school while the old man is fighting a batting slump that may hurt the pennant chances of the home team?

Roberto Clemente

Roberto Clemente

I want my children to suffer some. I want them to have what they're supposed to have, but I don't want them to be rich. I want them to be like normal people.[8]

John McGraw and Hal Chase in 1912, managers of the Giants and Yankees

Baseball is a rough and forceful sport, but there's a lot of heart in the old game.

—JOHN MCGRAW

OF HEARTS AND

THE DIAMOND

Ty Cobb in action

When I began playing the game
baseball was as gentlemanly as a
kick in the crotch.
                    —TY COBB, *My Life*
                         in Baseball

13.

Headhunting and
Other Atavisms

Ty Cobb in 1914
   If basemen find a man afraid to slide in hard, they're going to block
him off sure.[1]

In 1948
   I was their enemy. If any player learned I could be scared, I would
have lasted two years in the league, not twenty-four.
   Don't let anyone ever tell you I was a dirty ballplayer though. When
you're out on those paths you got to protect yourself. The base paths
belong to the runner. . . . I had sharp spikes on my shoes. If the baseman stood where he had no business to be and got hurt, it was his
fault.[2]

Only twice did I deliberately try to spike a man.

One was a Cleveland catcher, Harry Bemis, who roughed me up when I slid into home. I missed Bemis, as it happened, but by so little that it cured him of the habit. The other fellow played for the Boston Red Sox in the days when throwing at a batter's head was everyday procedure. . . .

Hub Leonard would aim bullets at your head, left-handed to boot. . . .

Leonard did it once too often. So I dragged a bunt down the chalk line, which the first baseman was forced to field. Leonard sprinted for first to take the throw and saw that I was after him. He didn't stop at the bag, kept right on going, into the coaching box, which looked like safe territory to him. He wouldn't have been safe that day if he'd scrambled into the top bleachers. I ignored the bag—since I was already out—and drove feetfirst right through the coaching box. He managed to duck, but he knew he was a marked man with me. The escape was close enough medicine for him. He never threw another beanball at me.[3]

Walter Johnson in 1925

The beanball is one of the meanest things on earth, and no decent fellow would use it. The beanball pitcher is a potential murderer. If I were a batter and thought the pitcher really tried to bean me, I'd be inclined to wait for him outside the park with a baseball bat.[4]

Ty Cobb

Walter Johnson was the greatest pitcher who ever lived, and for many years he had me completely buffaloed. I'd never admit it to anyone at the time, but I was really afraid of that fastball of his. How he could *buzz* them in there, and it was impossible to avoid picturing what would happen if he hit you in the head. Not a pretty picture.

But I was determined to conquer Walter's fastball, and finally I hit upon a way to beat him. Walter had only one weakness—he was kindhearted to a fault, and he was always afraid he'd bean a batter and kill him. So—I crowded the plate, forcing Walter to go for the outside corners. Any other pitcher would've backed me up, but not Walter. He had to pitch right where I wanted it or walk me. I knew he wouldn't risk hitting me, and he never let me down.[5]

Babe Ruth

In the 1918 World Series we [the Boston Red Sox] were playing the Chicago Cubs, and they had Leslie Mann and Max Flack alternating in the outfield.

I was slated to pitch one game, and the first time up Mann socked me for a base hit. When I went back to the bench, Bill Carrigan, our manager, called me over to give me some advice.

"Mann is a tough hitter against left-handed pitching," Bill said. "The only thing to do is loosen him up a bit. The next time he comes up *dust him off!* Drop him in the dirt! Maybe that'll stop him!"

I promised Bill I would.

Meantime the Cubs had sent Flack in to replace Mann, and when Max came up I promptly turned loose a fast one that flattened him.

When I went back to the bench, I was feeling pretty proud of myself.

"Well," I said, "I guess I showed that guy Mann a thing or two, didn't I?"

I thought Carrigan would explode. He cussed me up one side and down the other. And I don't blame him. Can you imagine a pitcher not even knowing the difference between hitters and hitting Max Flack in the ribs thinking all the time that he was making Leslie Mann a victim?[6]

Lefty Grove

Never bothered me who was up there with the bat. I'd hit 'em in the middle of the back or hit 'em in the foot, it didn't make any difference to me. But I'd never throw at a man's head. Never believed in it.

Lefty Grove in the late 1930s

I used to pitch batting practice. You know, take my turn at it in Philadelphia. Those guys, Doc Cramer and them, used to hit one back through the box, and they knew damn well when they did, they'd better get out of there, 'cause I'd be throwing at their pockets. They'd try to hit one through the box their last swing, those guys, just to rile me up. Yessir, boy, I was just as mean against them as I was against the others. You can count on two fingers the guys who wouldn't throw at anybody in those days. Walter Johnson was one, and Herb Pennock was the other.[7]

Joe Cronin

I remember one year in the late thirties when I was managing the Red Sox. We had a game scheduled with the A's in Philadelphia; and prior to our game they held an exhibition game between the 1914 pennant-winning A's and the 1929 pennant-winning A's. Eddie Collins was our general manager at the time, and Lefty Grove was on our pitching staff; and of course, both participated in the exhibition, playing for their old teams—Collins with the 1914 team and Grove with the '29 team. And do you know that when Collins came up the first time, Grove threw one right at his chin? That's right, ducked him right out of there.

Collins was mad—he always did have a temper, one of those *determined* guys—and he was cussing Grove. But Grove just stood out there and laughed. That was his fun.

Billy Herman

Pitchers rarely throw at batters like they used to. Once in a while it happens. But not like it used to. See, back in the old days, the umpires couldn't control it . . . which was bad. Once it started it'd get out of hand. And it'd carry over from year to year. You'd have hard feelings between clubs, and the next year, the first series they'd play—boom!—there you go, it'd start again. It was bad for the game of baseball; there was a lot of real sloppy games. It'd get to be just a throwing contest, everybody trying to step on each other and slide into each other. And the pitchers headhunting. Oh, it was terrible. It's amazing more people didn't get hurt bad.

But now the umpire stops it right quick. As soon as he thinks it might be intentional—boom!—that's the end of that. The manager and the player get fined and suspended. But I'll tell you what it *did* do back years ago is separated the men from the boys. 'Cause they tried you out. They tried you *out*. And I see players today, *outstanding* players, who if they had to go up to the plate and get knocked down every time, they'd hit one hundred points less. They'd get a lunch pail and go to work in a hurry. 'Cause it's no fun going up there and knowing you're gonna get knocked down. And sometimes they *get* you.

My first time at bat in the big leagues I got a base hit. The next time up I got hit right in the head. Si Johnson stuck one right in my ear.

See, I wasn't anticipating it. After you play awhile, you know which pitchers to watch out for, Burleigh Grimes and them. You start hitting them a little bit, you better not dig in up there.

It tore up my ear. The funny thing . . . I went to the ball park the next day and I still had this blood all over my uniform. I put it back on, dried blood all over it. They didn't wash the uniforms every day like they do now. You couldn't stand the sight of blood, you couldn't play.

You know, though, I have to admit, my team, the Cubs, was the worst of all. Charlie Root. Pat Malone. Lon Warneke. Guy Bush. Oh, we had a mean pitching staff over there in the thirties. And the Cardinals were bad. Dizzy Dean. He'd come into the visiting clubhouse and threaten us. "So and so, you been hitting me pretty good. You're gonna go on your *ass* today." And then he'd go out and do it. And he'd throw *hard*.

And the Giants had *their* headhunters—Schumacher and Fitzsimmons. Fitzsimmons knocked me down in the on-deck circle one time in Chicago. I hollered at him. He was stomping and storming, getting ready to pitch to the lead-off man, wasting time—he hadn't even thrown a pitch yet—and I hollered at him, "Get in there and pitch, you fat bastard!" And he looked over at me and *wham!* He threw the ball at me in the on-deck circle.

I'll tell you another story about the Giants. We were playing them in Chicago one day, and Schumacher was pitching. And in the tenth inning Chuck Klein doubles off him with a man on base and beats him the ball game.

Well, the next day, Hubbell's pitching against us. Charlie Root's pitching for us. Root gets the Giants out one, two, three in the first. Bill Terry, who's their third hitter, makes the third out.

In our half of the first Hubbell gets the first two men out and up comes Klein, our third hitter. Hubbell drills him right in the middle of the back. Now Hubbell never come *close* to anybody. He could close his eyes and throw strikes; his control was that perfect. So we knew that had to be deliberate. And we knew Hubbell didn't do it on his own. It had to come from Terry, the player-manager, because Klein had beaten Schumacher the day before. So we're all hollering at Root in the dugout, "Goddammit, knock somebody down out there." But he just set there like a wooden Indian. Never said a word.

He went back out there on the mound and pitched on through the Giant lineup—never even come close to anybody—until Terry came up the second time. Root's first pitch hit him right in the neck. They started for each other, but we broke it up before it got anywhere.

That's the way it was back in those days.

Ted Williams

When I first came up, the old-timers all told me, "When they knock you down, get right up, and show no fear. Because if you do, they'll just knock you down again." I don't think there's any question about it—they were right. The pitchers put you through a period of testing, and when it happened, you had to be more determined than at any other time in your career.

Now they have rules against all that jazz, which is *just fine* with me. It's a wonder more guys didn't get killed.

Stan Musial

The only time I ever really lost my head on the field was—well a couple of times. One time in the early forties we were playing the Dodgers, and we always had knockdown drag-out battles with them. Durocher'd have his pitchers knock us down and we'd knock them down. It was automatic. So this game we were playing a doubleheader, and it was early in the first game, like my first time up, and they had a big guy pitching by the name of Les Webber, a right-hander who never did much in the big leagues. So the first pitch went over my head. I said, "Oh, boy, this is early." There was no reason. The game had just started. Second pitch went the same place. I was starting to get a little tight. Then he threw *another* one over my head—*three* straight. So I started out after him. Course, they broke it up.

Mort Cooper was pitching for us, and he told me when I came in the dugout, "I'll get this guy for you. Don't you worry about it." Sure enough, Les Webber came up the next inning, and Cooper hit him right in the neck.

The only other time that I really got mad was another game against Durocher, only he was managing the Giants that time, not the Dodgers. This was in the fifties. I could hear Durocher yelling to the pitcher, "Hit him! Hit him right on that big red number 6!" And by golly the pitcher—I think it was Windy McColl or was it Marv Grissom—anyway, he hit me right in the back. So that got me mad.

Back on the bench I told our pitcher, "First guy that comes up, *hit* him." And the first guy up was Willie Mays. Well, our pitcher threw one way over his head, wasn't even close. So I went over to him from first base and said, "You've got to hit him. We can't let them get away with what they're doing to us." So he threw another one *way* high over Mays's head. Then sure enough, Mays hit a home run that beat us. That was the only time I ever really got on a pitcher on my own team.

Durocher tried to intimidate the other team with this kind of rough stuff, but I think it backfired on him more often than not. He was just stirring up a nest of hornets. When Durocher came to town I was so charged up before the game, man, I could go out there and climb six fences. And I wasn't the only one. Our whole team was up.

Duke Snider

All those years in Brooklyn we hated the Giants above all others. The games usually lasted an hour or two longer than average because of all the knockdown pitches, managerial maneuvering, arguments, and sometimes even fights.

Like the time at the Polo Grounds when Durocher was yelling at his pitcher to stick it in Carl Furillo's ear. The pitcher tried to follow orders, but he ended up walking Carl. So Carl was on first, and he saw Durocher motioning to him to come on into the dugout. Well, Carl charged him like a bull. He knocked down Monte Irvin and Jim Hearn, and he had Durocher down and was choking him, and everybody piled on. I was on the outside of the pile next to Babe Pinelli, the umpire, and I could hear Babe yelling, "Kill him, Carl. Kill him!"

Eddie Mathews

The scary thing is when you know the guy's gonna unload on you, and yet you gotta be man enough to stand up there and show *no fear*. I've watched guys who aren't afraid, but it will affect them to the degree that if they get flipped, the next pitch could be a foot over their head and they'll swing at it. They get that much more aggressive. I tried to be as passive as I could. I didn't want to show any emotions at all at the plate. If I got hit I tried not to even rub it. Now, I might try to step on somebody's foot running the bases, but as far as yelling or fighting over a knockdown—no way. When you're in pro sports—any sport—you're gonna have a certain amount of physical intimidation. I was hit and cut and jumped on, and the whole enchilada; but after I established that I couldn't be intimidated, it dropped way off.

Now, I said I tried to be stoical about getting hit by pitches, which is true; but playing third base it was different. I wouldn't put up with dirty baserunning.

Frank Robinson was a very hard slider. He *hurt* a couple of our guys with his slides. I warned him at third base. I said, "Frank, don't come in here like that." This was where he'd be out by a mile and was embarrassed and was trying to make up for it, trying to kick the ball out of my glove. We ended up finally in a pretty good fight.

I remember Daryl Spencer came sliding into me one time. He was out a long ways, but he ended up sticking his heel spike in my knee. Eighteen stitches. I turned around to slug him, but he was rolling around on the ground. He'd broken his knee. So there wasn't any fight.

I usually had a flash temper that quickly cooled off, but with Spencer I did maintain that mad. You see, Robinson I didn't consider dirty, he was just a damn aggressive hard slider. But Spencer was dirty. He'd do roll slides, and he hurt a number of people. In fact, he ended Mel Roach's career on our club with one of his football slides.

So I went home and pulled a Ty Cobb. Actually sharpened my

spikes for Spencer, because you know he was an infielder. But he never played the infield against us again. Played the outfield a little bit, and then ended up over in Japan. So I was never able to get him, which is probably just as well.

I guess I'd say I didn't enjoy fighting, but I can't say I minded it either.

Ted Williams
I hated that—to see a dirty base runner, like a former football player coming in and knocking a little second baseman nine hundred feet into left field. I could name you several guys that did it, and it's not right. It's not baseball. And it's not baseball when the pitcher throws at a batter's noggin.

Roy Campanella
I had this run-in with Lew Burdette. It was in Milwaukee, and he threw at me twice in one turn at bat. After the second one I hollered, "Now dammit, throw the ball over the plate." Burdette said, "Nigger, get up and hit." I got so damned mad I missed the next pitch. He called me "nigger," then he struck me out. And I was going out there. But you know after I was paralyzed and retired from baseball Burdette seen fit to come and ask how I was feeling. I didn't want to be called "nigger" by no one. I was gonna fight him. But now I can't swing a bat, or nothing, he comes by. I tell you, hate don't get you nowhere. Don't keep hate stirring down inside. The onliest thing I want to remember about Lew Burdette is that whatever he called me, and he shouldn't have, later on he come all the way to Harlem to say hello.[8]

Somebody wanted to know once how many times Mickey Mantle, Billy Martin, and I got fined. All I could think of to answer was, more times than Babe Ruth.

—WHITEY FORD,
Whitey and Mickey

14.

After-hours Hijinks and Other Mischief

Casey Stengel

I played in professional baseball for twenty years . . . but a lot of people seem to remember some of the stunts I pulled better than they do the ball games I helped to win.

The one that's remembered the most was the time I came back to Ebbets Field in 1918 after being traded from Brooklyn to Pittsburgh over the winter. Those Brooklyn fans were riding me. They cheered you as long as you were playing for them, but when you went away you weren't any good, see.

One of my old Brooklyn buddies, Leon Cadore, was out in the bull pen. He was a cutup—loved to do card tricks, loved to do coin tricks. He was very agile with his hands, and he'd caught this young sparrow in the bull pen that day. Just before my first time at bat I got it from him and put it under my cap. I could feel it moving, you know, inside there on my scalp.

So I walked up to the plate swinging three bats very hard. And the crowd yells, everybody gets excited, and they're booing me to death. Then I threw the bats down and grabbed my eye as if something was in it, and said, "Time." Cy Rigler was umpiring behind the plate, and he called time. Then I turned around to face the crowd and lifted my hat off and made a big bow. And when the bird flew out, the crowd just went, "Oh-h-h-h-h-h-h-h-h."[1]

Billy Herman

One guy who was always up to some mischief was my old buddy Dizzy Dean. I wasn't there for this one—Augie [Galan] told me about it, but it was pure Diz. We were headquartered in L.A. one spring, and we had an exhibition up in San Bernardino—that's about two hours drive. Anyway, Larry French lived in L.A., so he got permission to drive up to the game and back while the rest of us rode on the team bus. Well, after the game, for some reason, which I forget, they let Diz and Augie ride back with him. So anyway, late in the afternoon they stopped in Ontario or some little town up there to have a beer. So they went in this little bar—nobody in there—just a girl tending the bar—and they were sitting there washing away the dust from the ball game. Finally Diz looks up at the shelves behind the bar and sees some kind of rare whiskey up there. So he asks the girl how much it costs. She says twelve dollars or fifteen dollars or something like that, and he says, "I'll match you for that bottle."

She said, "Okay." So he played a trick on her using two coins, and by sleight of hand he switched them, so it was impossible for her to win. So he wins the bottle, and then they do it again and he wins another bottle. And he won another three or four after that. Finally, in walks the owner of the joint, and he sees these bottles of rare whiskey on the bar, and she tells him what happened. Diz says, "I won 'em fair and square. You got another one?"

The guy says, "Yeah, I got another one."

Diz says, "Bring it over. I'll match *you*."

So he did the trick again, cheated again, and won that bottle. Then they walked out and got in the car and drove off.

The guy probably had a gun behind the bar, and if he caught Diz cheating he'd probably have shot him. But that's the way Diz was. He kept one bottle and gave the rest away. He never even wanted them. He just wanted to win. That was Diz. Cheat you on the golf course, tee them up in the rough, he'd do anything in the world—just to win. He'd cheat you out of fifty cents in a card game and then take you out and spend one hundred dollars on you. Didn't care about money—he just wanted to win.

Casey Stengel: outfielder with the Giants in the early 1920s . . .

. . . manager of the Yankees in the 1950s.

"Cheat you on the golf course, tee them up in the rough, he'd do anything in the world—just to win." Dizzy Dean in the 1930s.

Dizzy Dean

I'll tell you a day in Boston I got a helluva kick. Remember seeing a big fat guy around with me a lot? Well, he was Johnny Perkins, and he worked in a nightclub around St. Louis, and he made this trip with us. He made us a bet I wouldn't strike out Vince DiMaggio the first time he came up. I did, and when I went back to the bench I made motions to Perk I'd double the bet the next time. I struck him out again, and I put everything back on a third bet, and I fanned him three straight times. Then Perkins wanted to make it all or nothing so I took him, and when DiMag came up again he lifted a pop foul back of the plate. I thought Ogrodowski was gonna catch it, and I ran and hollered: "Let it go, let it go." He couldn't get the ball anyway, as it turned out, 'cause it hit the screen, but I'd bumped him sure as hell if he'd got under it. I wanted to win that bet. I struck DiMaggio out next pitch . . . four straight times.[2]

Lefty Gomez

We were playing at Cleveland, and Bob Feller had just come up to their club, and he was still pretty wild. It was getting close to twilight. I didn't feel too great about hitting against a guy who threw that hard and fast but wasn't completely sure where the ball would go. So I took a book of matches up to the plate and lit one as I stepped into the batter's box.

Bill Summers was the umpire, and he blew his top. "What's the matter with you, Gomez?" he yelled. "You know you can see Feller perfectly well."

"Yeah," I said, holding up the match. "I just want to be sure he sees me."[3]

Burleigh Grimes

You know, Gomez was kind of a clown. When I came over to the Yankees at the end of my career, I'd played all my years in the National League, and Ruffing and Gomez, who were pretty good buddies, called it a "semipro" league. So they called me "the semipro." It came time for the All-Star Game, and Joe McCarthy came to me with those two and said, "These two guys are gonna pitch in the All-Star Game, and I want you to give them some dope about some of the National League hitters."

Well, one of the guys on the National League squad that year was Ducky Medwick. So I told them the truth about Medwick. "This guy can hit a high fastball out of town."

Well, those two were both high fastball pitchers, and I guess they decided to challenge him in spite of my advice because in the All-Star Game Medwick tommy-hawked two home runs off high hard ones— one off Ruffing and one off Gomez.

"Kind of a clown." Lefty Gomez in the 1930s.

After-hours hijinks. The notorious Yankee trio—Mickey Mantle, Billy Martin (shaking hands with Del Webb), and Whitey Ford.

The next time I saw them I just said, "Well, what about it, semi-pros?"

You know, they never called me "semipro" again after that day.

Whitey Ford
[Whitey Ford began his professional career in Class C pitching for Edenton, North Carolina, under manager Lefty Gomez.]

Gomez had a rule that we all had to be in our rooms by ten o'clock every night, and you don't have to be a genius to see trouble right there. We tried, though. But one night about nine-thirty one of my room-mates and I decided to go to a carnival in town; we wanted to take a ride on the Ferris wheel. You know, we figured about five minutes of that and we'd be back in our room on time. So we got on and rode for about ten minutes, but then we couldn't get off. Every time it came our turn to get off, the guy running the ride would pass us, and he kept doing this till ten o'clock. I didn't know why, then.

We finally got off and ran back to our hotel, which was only about two blocks away. We got there about five minutes after ten, and there was Gomez in the lobby. I said, "Skip, you'll never guess what happened, you'll never believe it. We got on the Ferris wheel and the guy wouldn't let us off."

And Gomez said, "You're fined five bucks each."

Years later Dizzy Dean had Gomez as a guest on his after-the-game television show from Yankee Stadium. And Lefty tells this story how he'd given this guy a couple of bucks to keep us on the Ferris wheel. Now I'm in the clubhouse watching the show, and when it's over Lefty comes into the clubhouse and I say: "You son of a bitch. All these years you never told us."

So I say, "Give me my ten dollars back." Now he's laughing his head off but gives me ten dollars. Then I say, scoring big, "Good, you son of a bitch, you only fined me five."[4]

Casey Stengel in the 1950s

Now that I'm a manager I see the error of my youthful ways. If any player pulled that stuff on me now, I would probably fine his ears off.

Mickey Mantle

You couldn't fool Casey because he'd pulled every stunt that was ever thought up, and he did it fifty years before we even got there. He didn't mind it too much, either, so long as you didn't start to lose it on the ball field. That's where it all came out, on the field. You could run around like some of the guys, or you could travel with the club looking like DiMaggio in those beautiful blue suits. But, either way you did it, if you played like DiMaggio, you'd keep Casey off your back.

Casey was smart . . . he always pretended like he was mad at us, even if he wasn't. When the club was going bad he'd have a meeting and tear into the guys, and he'd always point out Whitey and Billy and me in the meetings. I think he did it to show the older players on the club that we new guys weren't getting away with anything just because we maybe were having a big year on the field. He really liked us, but he'd lay into us at the meetings, and then on the way out he'd throw us that big wink of his.[5]

Casey Stengel

There are men that don't have bad habits, but have bad spirit. I'd rather have men with some ability and some fight and some spunk, and who like their teammates. Some of the players who got bad publicity were men I could never have won without.

These are pretty well-known ballplayers. You get big money when you play baseball if you are a Mantle. Mantle should get money. Mantle excites the public. Mantle has been booed in New York. I don't know why it is. It's silly for them to boo him. He still fights to win and wants to stay in New York City.

Billy Martin was a good, winning ballplayer for me in Oakland and when I had him in New York. I couldn't have done without Martin on some of the plays he made. Somebody else couldn't have made them.

Maybe there's better pitchers than Whitey Ford. I couldn't have gone without Ford. What would I have done in the 1960 World Series if I hadn't had Mr. Ford around?

Players violated the nights on Mr. Stengel once in a while. But the four that did, or five, they had the spirit of that ball club, and were trying to win, trying to get to home plate.

We don't advocate drinking. But to say that a ballplayer doesn't ever take a drink—regardless of advertisements, some do. Now no ballplayer should ever get into the habit where he drinks before a ball game. . . . When I had one of those boys, I said, "Well, this man is limited . . . if he doesn't want to change—why, disappear him."

But if you're in a pennant race you can put up with any kind of character except a man that is lazy. A lazy man is a terrible thing on a ball club. And he may be a man that never breaks a rule. He says, "I go to bed at eleven o'clock every night." But he's not awake when he's on the ball field.[6]

Whitey Ford

One day Marvin Miller was over at the clubhouse talking about the players' pension plan, how you could start collecting when you got to be fifty. And Mickey kept saying, "Get it cut down to forty."

He always had it in his mind that he wasn't going to make it to forty because of his uncles and his father. [Mantle's father died at age thirty-nine of Hodgkin's disease, and two of his father's brothers also died in their thirties.]

He really used to worry about it. We'd sit in the room and he used to talk more about that probably than anything else. I'd say, "Goddamm it, your father and your uncles never went to the Mayo Clinic every year for a checkup, and they worked in the mines and were probably getting that stuff in their lungs all the time. You'll probably outlive us all."

I really think that's why Mickey acted a little crazy at times. It wasn't what Toots Shor said when we got voted into the Hall of Fame: "It shows what you can accomplish if you stay up all night drinking whiskey all the time."

It wasn't that. I think Mickey acted a little crazy at times because he just figured he was only going to be around a little while and he might as well enjoy it.[7]

Mickey Mantle in 1981

I'm forty-nine years old, that's nine years over what I ever thought I'd be. So I don't worry about it anymore. . . .

I never slept when I lost. I'd see the sun come up without ever having closed my eyes. I'd see those base hits over and over and they'd drive me crazy.

—ROBIN ROBERTS in *Baseball Between the Lines*, by Donald Honig

15.

Boners, Losses, and Slumps

John Montgomery Ward in 1888

Younger players are not infrequently attacked by what in baseball vernacular is known as "the rattles," a complaint much akin to what sportsmen call the "buck fever" and actors "stage fright." There are times, too, when even the most seasoned seem to lose their heads, though long experience usually deadens the sensibilities.[1]

Ty Cobb in 1914

I could name countless men in baseball with great natural ability and no brains. These players will always be mediocre performers because what's above the collar is worth more in the big league than what's below it, provided a player's not paralyzed.

I'm not going to name any of these men who lack brains because it might cause some hard feelings. They're, however, absolutely dependent on the heads of their managers, and when they have to make a decision they generally pull a "bone."

"If that guy's brains were made of nitroglycerin and they exploded, the bust wouldn't muss his hair," I heard Jennings remark of a player one day. "Give me a man who can think and with arms and legs, and I'll make a ballplayer of him." . . .

Many coaches get panned for the "bones" of a base runner when the latter refuses to pay attention, which is often. On almost every ball club there are some men known as "hog wild" runners, and it is almost impossible to stop them once they get going. To men of this type, third base is a point at which they hate to pause, and many coaches in the National League will tackle a runner of this kind and throw him back on the bag. I have seen McGraw do this in a World Series with Red Murray, but they are stricter about this sort of football coaching in the American League.[2]

Billy Herman

We're playing the Orioles one night in Boston in the sixties, and the game goes into extra innings. I'm coaching third base. Baltimore scores a run in the top of the tenth. It's one of those foggy nights, raining and drizzling. So we're just gonna get that inning in and that's it. We get the first man on, nobody out, and Gary Geiger's the hitter. So Mike Higgins, the manager, lets him hit. No bunt to tie. We're going for all or nothing. And sure enough, Geiger hits one of those towering shots high off the left-field fence. The guy in front of him scores, and the game is tied, and here comes Geiger into third base, stand-up triple. I signal him to hold up. Then I turn around and look into the dugout at Higgins to see if he wants a squeeze or what he wants to do. And I hear a big gasping roar from the crowd. I look up and there's Geiger jogging toward the dugout. The shortstop had taken the relay and was standing there with the ball in his hand. So he throws the ball to the catcher and Geiger's tagged out.

After the game I ask, "What in the hell happened?" He says, "I forgot Baltimore scored a run in the top of the tenth. I thought I'd driven in the winning run." He says, "I wondered why you didn't come over and shake my hand."

Guess who got the blame for it?

Paul Waner

After the 1927 pennant we never won another one, not one single one, all the years Lloyd and I played in Pittsburgh. Gee, that was tough to take. We ended second about four times, but never could get back on top again. We had good teams. But we never quite made it.

It'd just tear you apart. We'd make a good start, but before the season was over they'd always catch up with us. And when you're not in the race anymore, it gets to be a long season, really long.

The closest we came was in 1938. God, that was awful! That's the year Gabby Hartnett hit that home run. We thought we had that pennant sewed up. A good lead in the middle of September, it looked like it was ours for sure. Then the Cubs crept up and finally went ahead of us on that home run, and that was it.

It was on September 28, 1938. I remember it like it just happened. We were playing in Chicago, at Wrigley Field, and the score was tied, 5–5, in the bottom of the ninth. There were two out, and it was getting dark. If Mace Brown had been able to get Hartnett out, the umpires would have had to call the game on account of darkness, it would have ended in a tie, and we would have kept our one-half-game lead in first place. In fact, Brown had two strikes on Hartnett. All he needed was one more strike.

But he didn't get it. Hartnett swung, and the damn ball landed in the left-field seats. I could hardly believe my eyes. The game was over, and I should have run into the clubhouse. But I didn't. I just stood out there in right field and watched Hartnett circle the bases, and take the lousy pennant with him. . . .

When I finally did turn and go into the clubhouse, it was just like a funeral. It was terrible. Mace Brown was sitting in front of his locker, crying like a baby. I stayed with him all that night, I was so afraid he was going to commit suicide. . . .

I still see Mace every once in a while. He's a scout for the Boston Red Sox. Heck of a nice guy, too. He can laugh about it now, practically thirty years later. Well, he can almost laugh about it, anyway. When he stops laughing, he kind of shudders a bit, you know, like it's a bad dream that he can't quite get out of his mind.[3]

Duke Snider

You know, we learned early on the Dodgers that the game in April means just as much as the game in September because *every year* it was a close race in the National League and every year we were in the thick of it. I think it's indicative that Pee Wee and I are the only players in history to have played in three different postseason play-offs. He was in 1946 against the Cardinals, 1951 against the Giants, and he was a Dodger coach in 1959 against the Braves. I was in 1951, 1959, and 1962 against the Giants. So the Dodgers were in four straight National League play-offs—and lost three of them. And that was almost all the play-offs that have ever been played in big league baseball. It's awfully tough to have it all come down to one game and then lose it, believe me.

Another year we lost it on the last day was 1950, and that went into extra innings. I played a big role in that game. Let me set the scene. We'd been playing great ball to catch up to them, and we'd beaten them on Friday and Saturday. All we needed was a tie on Sunday to force a play-off.

We were playing at Ebbets against Robin Roberts and the Phils, and we went into the last of the ninth tied 1–1. Newk was going great guns for us, and Roberts was still strong for them. So anyway, Cal Abrams led off the inning with a walk. Then Pee Wee singled him to second. So it's first and second with no outs. I went over to Burt Shotton, our manager, and asked, "You want me to bunt them over?"

He said, "No, I want you to get a base hit, and drive that run in."

Well, I wish he had told me that more often because I walked up there and lined a single on one hop right to Richie Ashburn in center field. He might've been shortening up a little—he says he wasn't. But the ball was hit so hard . . . Abrams broke back toward second for some reason. So when he reached third, I was almost to first.

I guess our third-base coach, Mel Stock, lost his job because of what happened next. He sent Abrams on in, and he was out by yards on Ashburn's throw. Pee Wee advanced to third and I went on to second.

Then they walked Jackie deliberately to fill the bases.

Next up was Furillo, and he popped it up. Then Hodges hit a *long* fly to the base of the scoreboard in right-center for the third out.

The next inning Dick Sisler broke our backs with his home run, and that was it. Another year of might-have-been.

Al Lopez

Sometimes I'd go to bed after losing a tough ball game where we blew several opportunities to win it, and I'd lie there second-guessing every move I'd made. Now if you get beat 9–1, all you worry about is "So and so's in a slump" or "Our pitching was bad." Those are problems you just have to go out and work on.

But when you get beat 2–1 and your pitching was good and your fielding was good . . . I remember one game in Chicago we got beat 4–3 by the Red Sox. Ted Williams knocked in all four runs.

My instruction to the pitcher before the game was "Pitch Williams low, and if he don't want to swing at it, let him go to first base." At that time Ted was almost through—he'd been to the war a couple of times—and he wasn't running that good anymore. So we were just gonna let him go over to first base. But we aren't gonna let him beat us.

Ted's first time up, the pitcher threw him two low ones. The third one was up in the strike zone, and he hit it up into the right-field stands.

Well, to make a long story short, Williams hit three home runs, knocked in four runs; and the fourth and last time up, I walked him on purpose with two men on. That's right, I filled the bases. I wasn't gonna let him beat me. Even though we ended up losing.

I held a workout after the game because I was dissatisfied with our offensive performance. We just hadn't moved the guys around the bases when we needed to, and we blew several chances to win. And besides I was burned up about this guy Williams hitting those three home runs against us when I had told the pitcher not to give him one good fastball. All three were off the same pitcher, and he pitched a good ball game—except for Williams. In fact, they only got four hits total, including Williams's three.

So anyway, I'm keeping the club for some extra hitting practice after the game. And here comes this little newspaperman from Boston who comes all the way down from the press box way up on the roof, and he says, "Hey, Al, that was quite a ball game! How about that Williams!" I'm kind of looking at him out of the corner of my eye. He says, "Why didn't you pitch to Williams that last time?"

I say, "What the hell's the *matter* with you? If I'd've been a good manager, I'd've walked him the other three times too, and we'd've won the ball game."

He says, "I guess I wanted to see him hit four homers."

I say, "Well, fine—but let him go hit four homers against the damn Yankees!"

Stan Musial

The key to a good season for a team or an individual is consistency. Avoid those slumps. What I did was to listen to advice from only one person—our coach Buzzy Wares, who used to hand the balls to the batting-practice pitcher. If I had two or three bad days in a row, I'd ask Buzzy to watch me carefully. He knew my style better than I did, and he could pick it up if I was overstriding, or standing up too straight, or turning my head. After he left the team Harry Walker took over that job. I'd only listen to Harry then. Otherwise, you just get confused because everybody has a different theory. I'd keep it simple, listen to Buzzy or Harry only, just try to meet the ball, go the other way with it, and try not to get all worried. Maybe *that's* the most important thing. Worry can ruin you. It really can.

Charlie Gehringer

That's the truth—worry can shorten your career. Heck, worry can shorten your life. I remember one time I was in a bad slump, and my anxiety was making it worse. Finally, one night in Washington I said to my roommate Chief Hogsett, "Let's go out and really turn it on tonight. Forget baseball!" So we got a couple of dates and went out and drank countless beers and danced all night.

"I was in a bad slump and my anxiety was making it worse."
Charlie Gehringer in the 1930s.

The next day I was shaky and had such a bad headache that I sat way down in the corner of the dugout as far away from the manager as possible. But I played, and it was uncanny! I hit the fences with four straight line drives. I was so relaxed!

Yogi Berra in 1961

I never blame myself when I'm not hitting, I just blame the bat. If the slump keeps up I just change bats.[4]

And in 1980

I noticed that if the club was winning, they'd overlook a slump. If we were losing, they'd say, "Berra's not hitting." But Casey used to always emphasize the positive. He'd say, "If you're not hitting, try to outdo the other catcher behind the plate."

Eddie Mathews

You can help a team in more ways than one. Hitting has never been the be-all and end-all. I used to play a game just with myself where I'd go into a town and I'd take on the other third baseman. Now he knew nothing about this, but I wanted to beat him in every department—

fielding, hitting, running the bases. I played that game all my life, and it kept me on my toes.

Baseball is a fun game if you're capable of accepting the lows along with the highs, the streaks along with the slumps. You've got to be able to take a defeat and bounce back the next day. You can't worry or brood. I could strike out four times in a game, and hell, the next day it'd be forgotten. It was over when the last out was made.

That's an ability you've just got to have. You can't moan and groan. Nowadays—I see it more all the time—guys get real uptight for some reason. They don't get their hits every day and they start to pout and it hurts the rest of their game—the fielding and everything else. What I try to tell them is "*Forget* today's game! It's over. Tomorrow the slate is clean." That's the way it has to be in a big league baseball season.

I'll tell you when defeat does hurt though is when there's *no* game tomorrow. We lost a couple of pennants back in the late fifties on the last day of the season. And *that* is a *low!* I guess the one that hurt the most of all was the 1958 World Series. I could *not* hit a baseball. In fact, I set a record for striking out. The whole Series was a disaster. We led the Yankees three games to one at one point, and then they came back to beat us. *That* was a long winter.

The flawless home run swing of Eddie Mathews

Mickey Mantle

I think when we lost the 1960 World Series to Pittsburgh was about the worst I ever felt. That was about the only time I ever felt like the best team lost. You *know* Pittsburgh was good and they weren't just a lucky team. You don't get into the World Series on luck. But in that seven-game Series, every break went their way. We won our three games by scores like 10–0 and 15–3, scores like that. All their wins were real close games. And then in that last game when that ball took that bad hop and hit Tony Kubek in the Adam's apple and then [Bill] Mazcroski hit that home run we just sat there in the locker room afterwards. Nobody could believe it. I could barely get out of my uniform. That one hurt all winter. In fact, it still hurts. Twenty years later I still can't believe they beat us in that Series.

Al Kaline

The most heartbreaking loss of my career was 1967, the last day of the season. All my years in the big leagues I'd been dreaming of getting into a World Series, and there it was within our reach. All we had to do to win the pennant was to take a doubleheader from the Angels, who were in dead last place.

We won the first game and lost the second. I don't recall the exact score, but it was close. I'll never forget the last two outs of the game. Dick McAuliffe hit into a double play, and he hadn't hit into a double play all year.

The thing I remember best about that game is the Angels playing hard baseball. They were out of it, way out of it, but they weren't gonna just roll over and play dead. You have to give those guys a lot of credit. They never gave us an inch.

Ultimately, the story has a happy ending. The next spring we all reported to training camp; and it seems like from the very first day, we *knew* we were gonna win. It was the first, last, and only time of any team I ever played on that *everybody* had one goal, and individual statistics did not mean that much to anybody. We were all determined to win the pennant, and we knew we could. And we did. It was the only time I ever experienced where *everybody* had that feeling.

Once an athlete feels the peculiar
thrill that goes with victory and
public praise, he's bewitched. He
can never get away from it.
—TY COBB, *My Life
in Baseball*

16.

Key Victories and
Other Thrills

Goose Goslin

One year I was hitting way out in front of everybody else in the
league by twenty or thirty points all season. That was in 1928. But in
September Heinie Manush kept gaining and gaining and gaining on me,
and by the last day of the season he was only a fraction of a point
behind me. We played the St. Louis Browns on that last day, and Heinie
played left field for the Browns. I was in left field for the Senators. So
Heinie and I were playing against each other, with the batting title on
the line.

Well, do you know that battle went right down to my very last time
at bat. It came to my turn at bat in the ninth inning of the last game of
the season, and if I make an out I lose the batting championship, and if
I get a hit I win it—his average is .378 and mine is .378 and a fraction. If

I get up and don't get a hit, I'll drop below him. I had that information before I went to bat. One of the sportswriters sent it down to me, with a note that said: "If you go to bat and make an out, Manush will win the batting title. Best thing to do is don't get up to bat at all, and then you've got it made."

Gee, I didn't know what to do. Bucky Harris left it up to me. He was the manager.

"What do you want to do, Goose?" he asked me. "It's up to you. I'll send in a pinch hitter if you want me to."

"Well," I said, "I've never won a batting title and I sure would love to, just for once in my life. So I think I'll stay right here on the bench, if it's OK with you."

Of course, everybody gathered around, wanting to be in on what's going on.

"You better watch out," Joe Judge says, "or they'll call you yellow."

"What are you talking about?"

"Well," he says, "there's Manush right out there in left field. What do you think he'll figure if you win the title by sitting on the bench?"

So this starts a big argument in the dugout: Should I go up or shouldn't I? Finally, I got disgusted with the whole thing. "All right, all right," I said, "stop all this noise. I'm going up there."

And doggone if that pitcher didn't get two quick strikes on me before I could even get set in the batter's box. I never took my bat off my shoulder, and already the count was two strikes and no balls. So I turned around and stepped out of the box and sort of had a discussion with myself, while I put some dirt on my hands.

Goose Goslin in the mid-thirties

I didn't know what to do. And then it came to me—get thrown out of the ball game! The umpire was a big-necked guy by the name of Bill Guthrie, so I turned on him.

"Why, those pitches weren't even close," I said.

"Listen, wise guy," he says, "there's no such thing as close or not close. It's either *dis* or *dat*."

Oh, did that ever get me mad (I acted like). I called him every name in the book, I stepped on his toes, I pushed him, I did everything.

"OK," he finally said, "are you ready to bat now? You're not going to get thrown out of this ball game no matter *what* you do, so you might as well get up to that plate. If I wanted to throw you out, I'd throw you clear over to Oshkosh. But you're going to bat, and you better be in there *swinging* too. No bases on balls, you hear me?"

I heard him. And gee, you know—I got a lucky hit. Saved me. I guess that hit was the biggest thrill I ever got.[1]

Connie Mack

I'll never forget the 1929 World Series. Lefty Grove, George Earnshaw, and Rube Walberg, three of the biggest names in baseball, were with me. The problem was in which order I should pitch them.

The Chicago Cubs, the National League pennant winner, feared Grove, Earnshaw, and Walberg, and I knew that if they could lick one of these star pitchers they could break the spell and ride on to victory. A major surprise at the offset would break their spirit. . . .

Some time before the end of the regular season, I was weighing the problem. Entering the clubhouse one day my eyes fell on Howard Ehmke, a grand old-timer. I beckoned him to follow me. In private, I said to him, "Howard, it looks as if I'll have to let you go."

Ehmke was a veteran for whom I had deep regard. This was a hard decision for me to make. It was a sort of professional death sentence.

"Mr. Mack," Ehmke replied, "I've always wanted to be on a pennant winner and in a World Series, and this is as close as I ever got to it."

"Do you believe you could win a game in the World Series, Howard?" I asked.

"Mr. Mack," he replied, "I've got one more good game in me, and I'd like to give it to you in October."

"Howard," I said, "I've changed my mind. You're going to pitch that game in the Series. You stay home and work out here in Philadelphia. When the Cubs come here in their final games with the Phillies, go to every game and study their hitters carefully."

I asked Ehmke to tell no one. The only man I let in on this confidential agreement was Eddie Collins, who had returned to the team as a coach.

When we arrived at the field in Chicago for the opening of the

World Series, not one of the players knew the identity of our first pitcher. Our opponents were eager to get this information. The newspapermen were all speculating on whether it would be Grove or Earnshaw or Walberg. . . .

Not until shortly before game time, when Ehmke took off his jacket and began to warm up, did the secret come out. The huge World Series crowd, the sportswriters, and the players of both teams were all taken by complete surprise.

Al Simmons was sitting next to me on the bench. He jumped up.

"Is he going to work?" he exclaimed.

"Yes," I said, "have you any objections?"

"Nope," Al replied. "If you think he can win it's good enough for me."

Howard Ehmke proved that he was a great sportsman. He not only won the first game by a score of 3–1, but he struck out thirteen and established a World Series record.

That beating shocked the Cubs: "If a has-been can strike out thirteen of our men," they said, "what can we hope to do against Grove, Earnshaw, and Walberg?"

Here's the answer: We won that World Series four games to one.[2]

Bill Dickey

I'll never forget the day Gehrig hit four home runs in a game in Philadelphia—one in left field, one in left-center, one in right-center, and one in right—and in that order. All well-hit balls. Just went around the horn with it. That day made me very happy. We did have a disappointing moment in that game because the fifth ball he hit looked like it was going into the lower left-field seats and Al Simmons boosted himself up on the left-field fence and made the greatest one-handed catch you ever saw on it. Lou very easily could've had five homers in one game.

[John McGraw resigned as manager of the New York Giants on that same day in baseball history. The resignation received the headlines. Recall Gehrig's wry observation: "I guess I'm just not a headline guy."]

Joe Cronin

In 1933 everything went right for us on the Senators. Two big plays happened in New York.

We're behind 1–0 in the ninth inning. Man on first base. Buddy Myer up. Bill McGowan umpiring. Two outs. Myer hit a foul ball back to the screen. Bill Dickey went back and caught the ball. But McGowan also went back and saw where the ball just grazed the screen coming down. So he ruled it out of play. Next ball pitched, Myer hit it out of the ball park to win the game 2–1.

The other unusual play. We're ahead 7–4. Tony Lazzeri's up. Lou Gehrig's on second base and Dixie Walker's on first base. Lazzeri hits the ball to right-center. And in those days they had a grade out there in right field in Yankee Stadium. The ball hit the grade, ricocheted up against the fence, and Goose Goslin, our right fielder, made a good play on the carom. I went out for the relay because I could throw a little better than Myer. So I took Goose's throw, which was perfect, turned around, and relayed it home.

Gehrig on second had gone back to the base to tag up, thinking the ball might be caught, and Dixie Walker, who was much faster than Gehrig, was right on his heels. Fletcher, the third-base coach, couldn't stop one without stopping them both, so they both went home.

I threw the ball on a line, no bounce. Luke Sewell grabbed it, tagged Gehrig, spun around, and tagged Walker. Double play. So instead of no outs, there were two outs, and the next batter, Bill Dickey, grounded out to me, and we won the ball game 7–4.

Those two plays were very, very important to our winning the pennant, especially since the Yankees were our main rivals. Our team just gathered momentum that year, and I guess because of the way we played, it seemed the breaks fell our way.

Ted Williams in the Red Sox clubhouse after the last game of the 1941 season
Ain't I the best hitter you ever saw!

And in 1980
No question about it, that last day of the 1941 season was an exciting day for me. It all came down to a Sunday doubleheader in Shibe Park. I needed a big day to protect my .400 average, and I felt good. I remember Frankie Hayes, the A's catcher, saying to me at the start of the game that Mr. Mack had ordered them to bear down on me. Unless baseball strategy demanded otherwise, though, they *were* going to pitch to me. That seemed fair enough.

Joe Cronin
Connie Mack did everything he could to stop Williams. Started a left-hander from the University of Richmond, some kid named Vaughan, knowing that the one thing Williams always hated was hitting against a new, unfamiliar pitcher. I also remember he instructed his first baseman, Bob Johnson, not to bother holding the runners on first when Ted came up. He played back to fill that hole.

So what did Ted do? He got three hits in the first game. Between games, Jack Mullaney of the Washington *Post* came down to the dugout and said, "Williams is hitting .403 now." So I went down to the bench and said to Ted, "You're hitting over .400. You want to play this last game?"

He said, "Sure, I wanna play it!" Williams always had great confidence, you know. So he went out and played that last game and got three more hits. Wound up at .406.

[Except for Ted Williams in 1941, no major league batter has posted a .400 batting average since Bill Terry batted .401 in 1930, the year the National League as a whole averaged .303.]

Monte Irvin

The high point of my life would have to be the 1951 season culminating in Bobby Thompson's home run and the World Series against the Yankees. For me personally, the World Series is a fine memory because I had eleven hits in six games and stole home in the first game, but we did lose the Series. But nothing can take away that victory over the Dodgers. See, we were 13½ games behind in mid-August when we started to win, and I mean win. We won 16 straight at one point. That's right. And we won 39 of our last 47 games. So even though the Dodgers did *not* collapse, we gained on them day by day. In my opinion, man-for-man, position-by-position, they had the better team, but that's not what counts. It's who plays better ball.

How do I account for the difference? I think Leo [Durocher] deserves an awful lot of credit. He was just fantastic during the stretch, almost inspired I'd say. Every move he made turned to gold, whether it was replacing a pitcher or shifting the outfielders. He just seemed to be almost telepathic.

So we caught them, and there was the three-game play-off. We won the first game behind Jim Hearn 3–1. I got a homer in that one, and so did Bobby Thompson. But that homer wasn't quite as well known as the next one. I'm getting to that. They won the second game behind Clem Labine 10–0. That set the stage.

In that last game at the Polo Grounds, they got off to a 4–1 lead, and Don Newcombe looked unbeatable. That was the score when we went into the last of the ninth. I'll just give you the facts from there on. Alvin Dark led off for us with a single. Then Don Mueller singled too. Two men on and nobody out, and I stepped in. I'm sorry to have to say I popped out to Hodges. That brought Whitey Lockman up, and he doubled down the left-field line knocking in a run. So now it was 4–2 with two runs in scoring position. Charley Dressen, the Dodger manager, got on the phone with his bull pen. They told him Ralph Branca was looking sharp, so he replaced Big Newk with Branca.

So it was Ralph Branca against Bobby Thompson. And what happened next will always be remembered as long as there's big league baseball in this country.

Ralph Kiner

Russ Hodges, the announcer, was screaming, "The Giants win the pennant! The Giants win the pennant! The Giants win the pennant!"

Bob Prince, who broadcast the Pittsburgh Pirates games, was in the same broadcast booth; so when Russ Hodges left the microphone and took off for the Giants' clubhouse to join the celebration, Bob Prince took over the microphone and said quietly, "And Ralph Kiner won the home-run title."

You know, the best comment on that fateful pitch was made by Carl Erskine, who said that the luckiest pitch he ever threw was the one he bounced in the dirt while warming up just prior to the call on the bull-pen phone. Dressen asked the bull-pen coach, Clyde Sukeforth, who was ready to come in in relief, and Sukeforth said, "Take Ralph Branca. Erskine's wild."

Willie Mays

Now it was a play-off for the 1962 National League pennant—the Giants vs. the Dodgers.

The Giant team of '62 was to win 103 ball games, one of the greatest Giant records of all time, but we hadn't *won* anything. The Dodgers had lost it. They'd lost it because Koufax got hurt. He pitched the first game of the play-off. I hit two homers off him, and everybody else hit too, and we won 8–0.

Then we went down there and built up a 5–0 lead in the second game and couldn't hold it, and the Dodgers came on to win it, so there would be a third game, eleven years to the day from the final game of that 1951 play-off.

But the two situations couldn't have been more different. In '51 we'd closed with that unbelievable rush against a team that was playing winning ball. In '62 the team we were closing on couldn't win for losing.

And it all came down to one game.

The date: October 3, 1962.

It started—that last half of the ninth—with the player I admired most. Only he was no longer a player. Now, Alvin Dark was manager.

That time, eleven years before, Leo Durocher had made a little speech. This time, with us behind 4–2 going into the top of the ninth, our last at-bats, Manager Dark made a little speech, too, except you couldn't rightly call it a speech.

All he said was, "Matty, get your bat."

Durocher? He was there. As a Dodger coach, though, sitting over there in the other dugout, staring at us, snarling, using those words.

And Matty Alou went up to pinch-hit for our pitcher.

He hit the first pitch to right field for a single.

Kuenn forced him, but now McCovey got a pinch walk, and Felipe Alou walked too, to load the bases.

It was my turn, with bases loaded.

Eleven years ago, I'd prayed it wouldn't have to be me to come up with bases loaded in that ninth inning of that last play-off game.

Now, I prayed it *would* be me.

And it was.

That was the measure of how far I'd come as a ballplayer.

I wanted to hit!

Wanted to, and did—slashed one up the middle, off the pitcher's leg, for a run-scoring single that left the bases loaded, and now Cepeda got us the fly ball to right field that scored the tying run. A wild pitch, and big Alou and I both moved up, dictating an intentional walk to Ed Bailey to load the bases.

Now Davenport drew a walk from Stan Williams, forcing in the go-ahead run, and a Dodger error gave us another run.

Once again, we'd scored four times in the ninth to go ahead, just as we had eleven years before. Now we still had to hold them off in their half, but no sweat. Billy Pierce came in, and it was three up, three down.

The last out of the game was a half-liner to right-center that held up for me. I caught the ball and threw it into the stands.

In that crazy clubhouse afterward, I remember them offering me champagne and me just turning it down this time. Who needed it?[3]

Whitey Ford

They played the All-Star Game in San Francisco in 1961. They played the game on Tuesday and we got there on Monday, so Mickey and I headed right for the golf course. It was a place where the owner of the Giants, Horace Stoneham, was a member, and we played with his son, Peter. But we didn't have any equipment with us. . . . So Pete Stoneham said, "Just sign my father's name," and that was the best offer we'd had in a long time.

We didn't go so far as to buy golf clubs, but we did get new shoes, a pack of sweaters, balls and shirts, and the whole bill came to something like two hundred dollars. But Pete Stoneham insisted, "Just sign my father's name to it," and so we signed.

During the match Joe DiMaggio and Lefty O'Doul were playing behind us in a twosome, a real San Francisco twosome, and the ninth hole was on an elevated green where I guess they couldn't see us from the fairway. Anyway, Mickey was getting ready to putt, and this ball came flying down and hit him right on the head, sort of glanced off his head while he was lining up his putt. Mickey thought for a minute that he'd been hit by a bullet, he dropped so fast to the ground. Then he realized it was a golf ball that just glanced off his head, either O'Doul's or DiMaggio's, I'm not sure—and neither one of them would admit who hit it, anyway.

Well, Toots Shor had a suite over in one of the big hotels, and he invited me and Mickey over for a little cocktail party he was having that night. . . .

So we were there telling everybody about our golf game, and how Mickey got hit on the head by a ball. And while they were all talking I went over to Horace Stoneham to pay back the two-hundred dollar tab that we ran up at his club.

Horace is a nice generous man, and he didn't seem to want to take the dough back. So he said, "Look, I'll make a deal with you. If you happen to get in the game tomorrow and you get to pitch to Willie Mays, if you get him out we'll call it even. But if he gets a hit off you, then we'll double it—you owe me four hundred, okay?"

So I went over to Mickey and told him what Horace said, but Mickey wouldn't go for it. No way. He knew that Mays was like nine for twelve off me lifetime, and he didn't have any reason to think I was going to start getting Willie out, not especially in his own ball park. But I talked him into it. Now all I had to do was get Willie out.

Sure enough, the next afternoon in Candlestick, there I am starting the All-Star Game for the American League. Willie's batting cleanup, and in the first inning I got the first two guys out, but then Roberto Clemente clipped me for a double—and there comes Willie.

Well, I got two strikes on him somehow, and now the money's on the line because I might not get to throw to him again.

So I did the only smart thing possible under the circumstances: I loaded the ball up real good. You know, I never threw the spitter—well, maybe once or twice when I needed to get a guy out really bad. But this time I gave it the old saliva treatment, and then I threw Willie the biggest spitball you ever saw.

It started out almost at his chest and then it just broke down to the left, like dying when it got to the plate and dropping straight down without any spin. Willie just leaned into it a little and then stared at the ball while it snapped the hell out of sight, and the umpire shot up his right hand for strike three.

Okay, so I struck out Willie Mays. But to this day people are probably still wondering why Mickey came running in from center field now that the inning was over, clapping his hands over his head and jumping up in the air like we'd just won the World Series—and here it was only the end of the first inning in the All-Star Game. It was a money pitch, that's why, and we'd just saved ourselves four hundred dollars.[4]

Stan Musial

The 1962 All-Star Game at Washington's beautiful new stadium drew a capacity crowd including President John F. Kennedy, for whom I had campaigned. Before the game, the president informed me through an aide that he would like to see me.

When I was escorted over to the presidential box just before the game, Mr. Kennedy and I shook hands. We had met only once before, a couple of years earlier. I had been standing in front of the Schroeder Hotel in Milwaukee, waiting for the team bus that would take us to County Stadium. A man came up to me and said: "You're Stan Musial, aren't you? My name is Jack Kennedy. I'm glad to meet you."

Of course, I recognized the senator from Massachusetts, then campaigning in the Wisconsin primary for the Democratic presidential nomination.

"They tell me," he said, "you're too old to play ball and I'm too young to be president, but maybe we'll fool them."

When I reminded him of that remark, the president chuckled. He remembered.

"I guess we fooled them, all right, Mr. President," I said.

In the sixth inning of the game, I was summoned by Fred Hutchinson, my old St. Louis boss who was managing the National League team, to pinch-hit. The game was scoreless when I faced Camilo Pascual, the Minnesota Twins right-hander with a good old-fashioned overhand curve.

Mr. Kennedy leaned over to one of his staff and said, "I hope the old man gets a hit."

I lined a two-strike curve into right field for a single and trotted off to a warm reception, replaced by Maury Wills, whose baserunning and daring led directly to the game's first run and then another in a 3–1 National League victory.

My good friend Senator Stuart Symington of Missouri had arranged a tour of the capital for us the next day, and my daughter Janet's eyes bugged when we reached the White House and were taken into Mr. Kennedy's office for a pleasant visit. Then we were escorted all through the building, including the first family's living quarters.

If only Lukasz Musial could have seen his boy then.[5] . . .

If a team is winning all the players
start thinking, How can we win? If
a team is losing then everyone
starts to feel more individual. To
me, that's the main difference
between playing on a winner or a
loser.

—AL KALINE

17.

Champs and
Cellar Dwellers

Johnny Evers in 1910

Creating a championship baseball team is a question of luck, patience, brains, and money, with patience and luck the principal elements. Critics of weak teams complain always, "Why don't they buy some ballplayers?" Nothing more suggestive of ignorance of the game and conditions prevailing was ever voiced than that wail.

Baseball players are not for sale. . . . If a good man is placed in the market something is wrong. Either the player is dissatisfied, has had troubles with other players, has taken to drink, or has developed some ailment or weakness. Investigation of every case of sales by major league clubs will reveal some such cause.

Often clubs will trade one good player for another; but money will not, alone, make a team. A manager may best strengthen his team when by knowledge of the inside conditions existing on the other clubs he may make advantageous purchases or trades. Players worthless to one club often prove valuable to another.

In spite of the optimistic announcements early each season few managers believe their teams will win pennants. Most of them are content to improve a few positions and continue to improve each year up to a stage of development which justifies straining every nerve to win highest honors. Seldom do more than three clubs have any real hope of winning.

Usually ten years, frequently more, are required to create a pennant-winning team, and it is of pennant-winning caliber not more than three years before it begins to retrograde. Occasionally after reaching its highest form a team collapses entirely in one season and the work must be begun all over again.

Teams are built on various theories. [Charles] Comiskey works on the theory that pitchers and conditioning will win. Detroit and Pittsburgh both are teams built with the idea of hitting power first. The Chicago Cubs are built on the theory of teamwork, inside play, and baserunning. The Boston American team is built with the idea that speed of foot will capture pennants. Generally speaking, harmony, united effort, brains, and conditioning will win over speed, individual brilliancy, and heavy hitting.

The first problem of the owner of a franchise is to get a leader. The next is to get the team, then teamwork, and having all these there remains nothing to do but to pray for luck and good umpiring.[1]

Babe Ruth in 1928

Take the time to go over the records and you'll find the great teams of history excelled in one department or the other. They can be classified either as defensive teams or offensive teams.

The greatest defensive team of all time, I guess, was the Chicago White Sox of 1906. Those boys hit so little that whenever a player got a two-bagger he wrote home about it. But just the same they won a pennant and a World Series.

They had great pitching. And along with their pitching they had wonderful fielding strength plus baseball brains. And brains is one of the biggest assets in defensive play. A fellow can stand up there at the plate and take his cut without any deep thinking, but to play the field properly he has to have something besides curly hair above his shoulders.

The old Athletics were another great defensive team. I've played against them and I know. But coming as they did—at the time when baseball was changing—they had real offensive strength too. Just the same it was the fine pitching of fellows like Combs and Bender and Plank, plus the high-class work of that million-dollar infield, that made them one of the greatest teams of all time. Despite the swatting power of Baker, McInnis, Collins, and the rest, I still figure that they class as a defensive rather than an offensive team. Among modern teams the Washington Senators of 1924 rate as one of the best defensive teams, combining fine pitching with some corking work in the infield and outfield. You'll go far and look plenty before you'll find a better infield combination than Bucky Harris and Roger Peckinpaugh.

When it comes to great offensive teams I'm just cocky enough to believe that the Yankees of 1927 were the best ever. Believe me, that outfit of ours could hit and score runs.

Incidentally, there's another place where I've had to argue with John McGraw. John maintains that the old Baltimore Orioles were one of the great offensive clubs. And he has me there. John saw both the Orioles and the 1927 Yankees while I wasn't taking much interest in baseball at the time the Orioles were good. Under the circumstances I'll have to take his word for it—but I'll never admit that the Orioles packed a greater wallop than the Yankees last year. I don't think it's possible.

The Detroit Tigers, winners of the American League pennant in 1907, 1908, and 1909, were a great offensive club. They had Cobb and Crawford and McIntyre and Jones and big Schmidt—all hitters. And as an offensive club they stood out in an age when defensive play was considered the thing. Real hitters those fellows, and they have proved it during the years that have followed, with the now-bald Tyrus still able to stand up there at the plate and hit with the best of them, despite the weight of more than twenty-two years of baseball activity.

Discussion of great offensive teams would not be complete without some mention of the 1912–1913 Giants—the team that was responsible for the gradual swing from defensive to offensive play. There was a team that was great offensively, not so much on account of its hitting power but because of its baserunning. Old-timers still maintain that the Giants team of that era literally "stole" the pennant. They were masters at baserunning in an age when baserunning was a real art.[2]

John McGraw in 1923

That was the greatest baserunning club I ever saw. The players got the notion that they could steal on anybody, and that belief was so strong that they went out and did it. On one trip west we arrived in Chicago with a club in rags and tatters—had to telegraph for new uniforms—nearly every man on the club had slid the seat out of his uniform pants. We had patched and patched until the principal feature of our pants was safety pins. This telegram of ours created a lot of amusement at the time.

Our club was pretty well worn-out and shot to pieces when we faced the Athletics in the World Series in 1911. I don't give that as a reason for our defeat, but it was a contributing cause. The main cause of our losing that Series was the wonderful hitting and pitching of the Athletics, one of the greatest clubs of all time.[3]

Connie Mack

We enjoyed two magnificent eras when our Philadelphia A's were on top of the world. At the end of both of these eras I have broken up the great teams. Why? To meet urgent emergencies! The pressure of uncontrollable conditions created a crisis.

I will try to give you a full accounting. The first of these breaks occurred in 1914, at the outbreak of World War I.

A third major league known as the Federals invaded the baseball field in 1914. With the bankroll of Harry F. Sinclair, the oil magnate, and money from Ball, the ice king, the Wards of the baking fortune, and the Gilmore greenbacks, our players were being lured with big salary checks.

Our pennant winners were the targets of these financiers. They waved the "long green" in front of our players' eyes. Our team was divided into two factions: one for jumping to the rich Federal League, and the other for remaining loyal to the American League. Even with this split we had won our sixth pennant. But during the World Series our team fell apart. The Boston Braves slaughtered us.

I felt this keenly, as I knew we could walk away with the Series if only we had been united. I was especially hurt, as we were paying our players the highest salaries in our circuit.

Baseball fans throughout the country did not realize what was behind our collapse against Boston; neither did many of the sportswriters. They said that the wonder team was taking it lying down. I knew that the "wonder team" was engaged in a civil war, fighting one another.

After giving the crisis much careful thought, I decided that the war had gone too far to stop it by trying to outbid the Federal moneybags. Nothing could be more disastrous at this time than a salary war.

There was but one thing to do: to refuse to be drawn into this bitter conflict, and to let go those who wanted to risk their fate with the Federals.

The first to go were Bender and Plank. I didn't get a nickel for them. This was like being struck by a hurricane. Others followed. There was only one way to get out from under the catastrophe. I decided to sell out and start over again. When it became known that my players were for sale, the offers rolled in.

If the players were going to cash in and leave me to hold the bag, there was nothing for me to do but to cash in too. So I sold the great Eddie Collins to the White Sox for fifty thousand dollars cash. I sold

Cornelius Alexander McGillicuddy (Connie Mack), manager of the Philadelphia Athletics from 1901 to 1950

Home Run Baker to the Yankees. My shortstop, Jack Barry, told me he wanted to go to Boston, so I sold him to the Bostons for a song.

"Why didn't you hang on to the half of your team that was loyal and start to build up again?" This question has often been asked me.

My answer is that when a team starts to disintegrate it is like trying to plug up the hole in the dam to stop the flood. The boys who are left have lost their high spirits, and they want to go where they think the future looks brighter. It is only human.

World War I was raising havoc with gate receipts. It took star players away from the game to send them to battlefronts. I struggled along through seven lean years, establishing a record for remaining in the baseball cellar.

When the war was over I formulated plans for recovery. I kept my eyes on prospective players. Aspiring youngsters flocked to Shibe Park. One year I tried out more than three hundred of them.

The rumor got around that Connie Mack was going to build another great team. Farsighted owners, such as Ruppert and Huston, put their capital and brains behind a revival of baseball. I watched them cautiously before I began to plunge again. Baseball came back faster than I had expected, and I had to put on speed to keep up.

While I was hard at work on my plans, I saw the Giants and the Yankees forge to the front. New York teams fought in the World Series for three years in succession.

The time had finally come to rebuild. This means, as it does in every line of business, heavy investments. I bought players for big prices.

My new team was finally molded into winning shape, and we finished second in 1925. We were coming along fast in 1926 and for the next two years. We won the pennant finally in 1929 and also the World Series, our seventh pennant and fourth World Series. In 1930 we won the eighth pennant and fifth World Series. We did it again in 1931 when we won our ninth pennant, but we lost the World Series. In 1932 we finished in second place; in 1933 in third place.

Our pennant teams of 1929, '30, '31 were world-beaters. What a magnificent pitching staff we had, what an aggregation of power hitters! Jimmie Foxx, our first baseman, was dynamite, second only to the great Ruth as home-run king. . . .

Here is a fact that may surprise you: Our Philadelphia Athletics in 1932 was the highest-priced ball team in the history of the game, not even barring the New York Yankees.

On the other hand the gate receipts were rapidly diminishing. During four years (1924–28) while we were only contenders, more people passed through the turnstiles each year than when we were World Champions. Figure that out in terms of human nature.

Another great era had come and gone. The big Depression was on. Attendances at ball games were dropping down. Another crisis loomed ahead.[4] . . .

[Baseball history repeated itself. Faced with a situation of diminishing returns, Mack began to sell his high-priced stars to other, more prosperous owners. In 1934 his team dropped into the second division, where it remained for thirteen years while Mack endeavored to lay the groundwork for a third Philadelphia dynasty. In 1950 age finally overtook him and he retired from baseball, his final great dream unfulfilled.]

Harry Hooper

From 1912 to 1918 we had a great, great ball club in Boston. We won the American League pennant in 1912, '15, '16, and '18, and in between we finished second twice. From 1912 to 1918 we won four pennants *and* four World Series.

We played four different National League teams in four different World Series, and only one of them even came close. That was the

Waite Hoyt with the Pittsburgh Pirates in the 1930s

Giants, in 1912. We beat them four games to three. We beat Grover Cleveland Alexander and the Phillies four games to one in 1915, the Dodgers four games to one in 1916, and the Cubs four to two in 1918. The best team in all of baseball for close to a decade!

Harry Frazee became the owner of the Red Sox in 1917, and before long he sold off all our best players and ruined the team. Sold them all to the Yankees—Ernie Shore, Duffy Lewis, Dutch Leonard, Carl Mays, Babe Ruth. Then Wally Schang and Herb Pennock and Joe Dugan and Sam Jones. I was disgusted. The Yankee dynasty of the twenties was three-quarters the Red Sox of a few years before. All Frazee wanted was the money. He was short of cash, and he sold the whole team down the river to keep his dirty nose above water. What a way to end a wonderful ball club!

I got sick to my stomach at the whole business. After the 1920 season I held out for fifteen thousand dollars, and Frazee did me a favor by selling me to the Chicago White Sox. I was glad to get away from that graveyard. [5]

Waite Hoyt

I'll never forget 1925. We'd had four great seasons without a replacement, and in that fifth season—1925—we were tired. [The New York Yankees won pennants in 1921, 1922, and 1923, and finished second in 1924. In 1925 they slumped to seventh.] A team can get tired just as an individual gets tired. We were tired of the pressure of being on top; tired of the pressure of having everyone try so hard against us.

It was still a good ball club, but we seemed to lose our desire. We had bickering and fights. We thought we should have won our fourth straight pennant in 1924 and thought it was an accident that we didn't. Nobody bothered to make any changes; nobody realized the team was falling apart.

Our shortstop and second baseman were through and so was our catcher. Our first baseman was slowing up, and Babe Ruth hit only .290 after hitting .378 the year before. I won only eleven games, and we finished almost thirty games back of Washington, the pennant winner.

But in 1926 Lou Gehrig started at first base, then came Earl Combs and Mark Koenig and Tony Lazzeri. We won pennants again in 1926, 1927, and 1928. It sure was great to be young and to be a Yankee. [6]

Billy Herman

I believe the greatest team I ever saw was the 1932 Yankees. Course, I may have been overly impressed because that was my first full year in the big leagues and they destroyed us in the World Series, but I remember them as being just awesome. An all-star at every position. Joe Sewell on third. You couldn't strike that little son of a gun out. Crosetti and Lazzeri at short and second, one of the all-time key-

"An all-star at every position." The *1932* World Champion Yankees.

stone combinations. Gehrig on first. Dickey catching. Combs, Ruth, and Chapman in the outfield. Gee whiz, half of those guys are in the Hall of Fame. The pitching was probably the weakest part of the club, but it was still *good*. And they had *great* defense. Most of your great ball clubs are strong defensively, and these guys were no exception. Their offense goes without saying.

Best team I ever saw.

Joe Sewell

I'll never forget I was watching the World Series in 1978 and comparing the modern Yankees to the champs of 1932. Do you know how many boys of that '78 team would've made our team in '32? I might be a little prejudiced now, but I say *two*. That's right, two. Guidry and Munson. Both of them in the bull pen!

I might be a little prejudiced now, but go back and check the records. I believe our team batting average was around .300, and our pitching was *strong*. Gomez. Ruffing. Johnny Allen, Pennock, Pipgras—those boys knew what they were out there for. Look at the records and decide for yourself, but for me, I've seen every good team in the last sixty years, and I never saw a better one than the '32 Yanks.

Waite Hoyt

I've always maintained that a Yankee pitcher should never hold out because he might be traded and then he'd have to pitch against them.

Pepper Martin and Dizzy Dean in the mid-thirties

Stan Musial

I came up to the Cardinals after the era of the Gashouse Gang, but I did play with Pepper Martin and Ducky Medwick, and I knew Durocher and Frisch and they had a lot of good stories. I used to love to hang around those guys. I always thought I would've enjoyed playing in that Gashouse era, although I didn't have the same color as a guy like Pepper Martin. I spent a year with Pepper during the war. A fantastic guy, high-strung, excitable, and nice to be around. He loved life, everything from baseball to playing music and tinkering with old cars. He took life so casually and enjoyed it so much. Martin and Dizzy Dean and Frisch and Frenchy Bordagaray. These kind of characters come along once in a lifetime. And they were a great, great Cardinal team.

However, I think the greatest Cardinal teams of all were in the forties. We just missed the pennant in '41, won it in '42, '43, and '44, missed by a game or two in 1945, and won it in '46. Then we finished second in '47 and '48 and '49. So we very easily could've won six or seven times in a row, maybe even more. And we should've won more than we did. I'll tell you why. A couple of things happened. First, they traded John Mize away, and he was our left-handed power. Then a couple of years later, I think it was 1945, they traded Walker Cooper away, and he was our right-handed power. They acquired a couple of pitchers and a bunch of money, but they didn't come close to replacing the players lost. After we lost Cooper, and [Whitey] Kurowski hurt his arm, the opposition was able to throw a lot more left-handers against us and that gave our lefties a lot of trouble. In baseball, you've got to have balance, and with Cooper gone, we lost our balance.

I say that with John Mize and Walker Cooper in our lineup all those years, we would've been *unbeatable*. Really! So that's one of the reasons we didn't win more pennants.

The second reason was this: Up to 1947, there weren't any colored players in the big leagues. In '47 Jackie Robinson came along and then Campanella and Newcombe—three great ballplayers from the colored leagues. The Dodgers started winning immediately with those three guys. They'd been just average, but they become a dynasty. And most of those years they were winning, we were finishing second. So we might've won eight or nine pennants in a row if it weren't for those trades and the Dodgers getting the jump in signing black players. No question about it.

Eddie Mathews

The worst team I ever played on was my first one—the '52 Boston Braves—the last year the team was in Boston. We were terrible. I couldn't catch a ball at third base. I remember in tight spots I used to think, Hit the ball somewhere else—I don't want to blow the ball game. It took me two or three years to gain confidence in my fielding. At the plate too. I hit twenty-five home runs that year, but it wasn't until my second year out in Milwaukee that I felt like a major league hitter. And the rest of the team was just as bad. *No* pitching, except [Warren] Spahn of course, but even *he* lost nineteen games that year. They wouldn't pitch him the last two weeks because they didn't want him to be a twenty-game loser.

We *lost*—that's all I can say. We were all trying, but it became a *very* long season. It got so bad the last week, guys were asking to go home, and Charlie Grimm, our manager, was saying, "Go on, beat it. As long as I can put nine guys out there."

The last series, we went into Ebbets Field with only about fifteen guys on the squad. It was crazy. Now the Dodgers had cinched the pennant, and we were way down at the bottom. And I ended up hitting three homers the next-to-last game. The fourth time up, Campanella says to me, "You're gonna get a fastball right down the middle." I didn't believe him, so I took the son of a bitch, right down the middle. Next pitch, I grounded out to shortstop. So I didn't hit my fourth. But the following day, last game of the year, about the sixth inning—the trainers have got all the bags packed, the clubhouse guys've got everything loaded, and we're getting beat about three runs—I hit a three-run homer and tie the game back up. I came back to the dugout, and everybody in there was hissing and throwing things at me. At the end of nine innings it was still tied and—it was about four-thirty in the afternoon, sun still high in the sky—the umpires called the game because of darkness. End of a long year.

See, here's the way it all came about. The ball club had had a bad year in '51, and they decided to clean house and bring up all young players. Which they did. I actually wasn't quite ready for the big leagues, but they brought me up anyway. Same thing with George Crowe, Bob Buhl, Del Crandall—*none* of us was ready. All kids. But that one year's experience did wonders. We were ready the next year and did well out in Milwaukee, finished second. So it turned out to be real good planning on management's part. They just sacrificed that one year for the experience.

That bunch was the nucleus of the champion Braves of '57 and '58. There were Del Crandall, George Crowe, Billy Bruton, Logan, and me. They made a couple of trades, too—picked up Joe Adcock, Red Schoendienst, and Bobby Thompson. And of course Hank [Aaron] came up from the farm system in 1954.

For many years that club was in contention. Later on of course, in the sixties, the same thing happened to us that happened to the team we all replaced in 1952. We got old and they started cleaning house again.

But in our heyday we had a real good club. We probably could've won more pennants than we did. Let's see . . . we ended up one game out in '56, won it in '57 and '58, and tied for it in '59 when we lost to the Dodgers in the play-off game. It was nothing to be embarrassed about when we *didn't* win. There was stiff competition, and we always gave it a good run. But we could've very easily won four or five in a row instead of just the two.

We had a real well-balanced club. Good consistent pitching with Spahn, Burdette, and Buhl starting and McMahon in the bull pen. Good hitting and power. Good defense. Good catching with Del Crandall. We had some speed—Billy Bruton could fly! We were a very close-knit team, got along great. We really didn't need much leadership; if somebody got a little out of line, started dogging it, three or four of us would take him out to dinner and have a talk with him. We helped each other keep on an even keel. It was a good situation.

Mickey Mantle

The year that Roger hit the 61 home runs, I think that was the best team I ever played on. Me and Roger hit 115 home runs together that year. Our three catchers hit 60 homers between them—Ellie [Howard] and [Johnny] Blanchard and Yogi. And Ellie hit about .348 that year, hitting sixth I think. Whitey won twenty-five games. And we had a great infield. Cletis Boyer was the third baseman. Tony Kubek, shortstop. Bobby Richardson, second base. And Moose Skowron on first base. And that was the best *infield* I ever saw. And also, a lot of people didn't realize this, but Roger Maris was a hell of a right fielder. And I played center field, and I think Tommy Tresh and some other guys traded off in left. It was just an unbelievable team. Johnny Blanchard was probably the best pinch hitter in baseball at that time. He hit 21 homers, and it seemed like most of them were pinch-hitting. And Luis Arroyo. He was probably the best relief pitcher in baseball that year. That was in '61 I think. Just a hell of a team.

Now, the best team I ever played *against* was the Dodger team that beat us four in a row in the World Series a couple of years after that [1963]. Their pitching was their strongest point—Koufax and [Don] Drysdale and [Johnny] Podres.

Another great team with a great pitching staff was the '54 Indians. We won 104 games that year, and they still beat us. Great pitching! Early Wynn, Mike Garcia, Bob Feller, Bob Lemon for starters, and [Don] Mossi and [Ray] Narleski and [Hal] Newhowser in the bull pen. When they lost that '54 Series to the Giants in four games, that was the biggest surprise of my life. I thought they'd *beat* the Giants four in a row.

As far as cellar dwellers go, I guess probably the *worst* team I ever played against was when I first joined the Yankees, the old St. Louis Browns. They were weak everywhere almost, especially their pitching.

The 1961 Yankees—Maris, Berra, Mantle, and Moose Skowron

I think Ned Garver was their best pitcher. If you knocked him out, or maybe [Duane] Pillette, the second starter, they didn't have any long relievers out in their bull pen, and you could run the score up on them, like 19–2, scores like that.

They did have one good short reliever too—Satchel Paige. He could still pitch all right. I couldn't hit him. Only way I could get on was to bunt him, 'cause he couldn't hardly get off the mound. But he'd throw *hard*. He could still throw hard, believe me. All kinds of different pitches and moves. Kind of like Luis [Tiant]. Change-ups, curveballs . . . he just knew how to pitch. And I was only nineteen at the time too, you know. I could be fooled. . . .

One year I remember we had won nineteen straight games, which might be a record, and those old Browns came to New York for a series. So we figured there's at least four more. Well, they beat *us* four in a row.

And that was probably the worst team I ever saw.

Billy Herman

Go back twenty-five years to the mid-fifties. Everybody was predicting that the Yankees were headed for a fall because they were trading their top minor league talent away each year for pennant insurance—the John Mizes, Enos Slaughters, John Sains. Well, finally in the mid-sixties, it did catch up with them. The old stars they brought in were gone after a year or two, and their farm teams had been stripped and they had no replacements for them. So they had some bad years there during the late sixties.

Now their minor league system is strong, and they're also spending freely in the free-agent draft, so they've built themselves a pretty good ball club. But it's an old ball club and could be on the verge of going down again. [Lou] Piniella, [Graig] Nettles, [Reggie] Jackson—how many more years do these guys have left?

You know you can top off a team with free agents, but you can't build a team with them. 'Cause you're getting *older* players normally . . . a lot of their free-agent investments are already long gone. Tom Yawkey proved the limitations of trying to build a ball club with high-priced old stars, golly, over forty years ago. He was in love with those big names—the Pinky Higginses and Jimmie Foxxes. Lefty Grove. Several of them. So he went out and got these guys, and they were all over the hill. They just could not jell.

Can the Yankees jell? I just don't know. Their organization has some good people, but it has more than its share of controversy between [George] Steinbrenner and his general managers and field managers. I use the plural because there's been so much turnover. Steinbrenner demands results and doesn't have much patience. So if things blow up there, they may *really* blow.

Casey Stengel in 1962, after his New York Mets lost the first nine games of their maiden season

The trouble is, we are in a losing streak at the wrong time. If we were losing like this in the middle of the season, nobody would notice. But we are losing at the beginning of the season, and this sets up the possibility of losing all 162 games.[7]

[The maiden Mets, perhaps the most celebrated cellar dwellers ever, went on that year to post an atrocious won-lost record of 40 and 120. Looking back in later years Stengel mused, "When I go back in my mind to our play in 1962, I just wonder how we ever got to win 40 games."]

Duke Snider

[In 1963, after sixteen years with the Dodgers, Snider returned to New York to play for the lowly Mets.]

Without Casey on the Mets, I would've gone nuts. He used to call me kid, which at my age [thirty-seven] was nice of him. I learned Stengel-ese that summer, and we did manage to have some fun. He used to call me over to sit next to him in the dugout, and he'd say, "We're gonna talk about the '49, '52, and '53 Series" [all Yanks over Dodgers]. One day I said to him, "Why do we always talk about those years, Case? When are we gonna talk about the '55 Series?" 'Cause that was the year we finally won it all. And he'd say, "One of these days we will, kid, one of these days."

Every player is nervous before
every World Series. You find me
one who says he ain't and I'll tell
you he's a damn liar.

> —ROY CAMPANELLA
> in *The World
> Series*, by Joseph
> Reichler

18.

October Fever

OCTOBER 1919

Edd Roush

Yes, I knew at the time that some finagling was going on. At least
that's what I'd heard. Rumors were flying all over the place that
gamblers had got to the Chicago White Sox. . . .

We beat them in the first two games, 9–1 and 4–2, and it was after
the second game that I first got wind of it. We played those first two
games in Cincinnati, and the next day we were to play in Chicago. So
the evening after the second game we were all gathered at the hotel in
Cincinnati, standing around waiting for cabs to take us to the train
station, when this fellow came over to me. I didn't know who he was,
but I'd seen him around before.

"Roush," he says, "I want to tell you something. Did you hear
about the squabble the White Sox got into after the game this afternoon?" And he told me some story about Ray Schalk accusing Lefty

187

Williams of throwing the game, and something about some of the White Sox beating up a gambler for not giving them the money he'd promised them.

"They didn't get the payoff," he said, "so from here on they're going to try to win."

I didn't know whether this guy made it all up or not. But it did start me thinking. Later on in the Series the same guy came over to me again.

"Roush," he says, "you remember what I told you about gamblers getting to the White Sox? Well, now they've also got to some of the players on your own ball club."

That's all he said. Wouldn't tell me any more. I didn't say anything to anybody until we were getting dressed in the clubhouse the next day. Then I got hold of the manager, Pat Moran, just before the pregame meeting.

"Before you start this meeting, Pat," I said, "there's something I want to talk to you about."

"OK," he says, "what is it?"

"I've been told that gamblers have got to some of the players on this club," I said. "Maybe it's true and maybe it isn't. I don't know. But you sure better do some finding out. I'll be damned if I'm going to knock myself out trying to win this Series if somebody else is trying to throw the game."

Pat got all excited and called Jake Daubert over, who was the team captain. It was all news to both of them. So at the meeting, after we'd gone over the White Sox lineup, Moran looked at Hod Eller, who was going to pitch for us that day.

"Hod," he said, "I've been hearing rumors about sellouts. Not about you, not about anybody in particular, just rumors. I want to ask you a straight question and I want a straight answer."

"Shoot," says Hod.

"Has anybody offered you anything to throw this game?"

"Yep," Hod said. Lord, you could have heard a pin drop.

"After breakfast this morning a guy got on the elevator with me and got off at the same floor I did. He showed me five thousand-dollar bills, and said they were mine if I'd lose the game today."

"What did you say?" Moran asked him.

"I said if he didn't get damn far away from me real quick he wouldn't know what hit him. And the same went if I ever saw him again."

Moran looked at Eller a long time. Finally, he said, "OK, you're pitching. But one wrong move and you're out of the game."

Evidently there weren't any wrong moves. Because old Hod went out there and pitched a swell game. He won two of the games in that Series.

I don't know whether the whole truth of what went on there among

"Yes, I knew at the time that some finagling was going on."
Edd Roush in the 1920s.

the White Sox will ever come out. Even today nobody really knows exactly what took place. Whatever it was, though, it was a dirty rotten shame. One thing that's always overlooked in the whole mess is that we could have beat them no matter what the circumstances!

I don't care how good Chicago's Joe Jackson and Buck Weaver and Eddie Cicotte were. *We* had Heinie Groh, Jake Daubert, Greasy Neale, Rube Bressler, Larry Kopf, myself, and the best pitching staff in both leagues. We were a very underrated ball club. Sure, the 1919 White Sox were good. But the 1919 Cincinnati Reds were *better*. I'll believe that till my dying day.[1]

OCTOBER 1920

Burleigh Grimes

Yeah, I pitched three games in the 1920 Series. Pitched the last one with one day's rest. Started out great with a shutout in game two, but it was downhill from there. I found out later what the problem was: This fellow Jack McCallister, who became my friend later, was a scout for the Indians at the time; and after we were friends he told me that Pete Kilduff, our second baseman, had been giving my pitches away. See, Kilduff would pick up a little handful of dust and put it in his glove every time the catcher called for a spitball. This was so the ball wouldn't be so slippery if it came to him and he had to throw it. Well, that wasn't too bright. None of the other fielders felt it was necessary. But Kilduff was doing it, and by the time we caught him doing it, the damage had been done. They knew when my spitter was coming and mostly they laid off it 'cause it was my best pitch.

The other thing that was hard to take was that I got some bad dope from Jack Coombs, who'd been coaching for Detroit that summer. See, in those days we never sent scouts ahead to look at a ball club. Now they have guys on them all summer, but in those days they couldn't afford such things. So I had to rely on Coombs, who said to pitch Elmer Smith high fastballs. That's the guy who hit the grand slam home run off me in game five. I pitched him high and hard, and he lowered the boom. Bad dope, and I don't know how it could have been an accident cause Coombs'd been in the American League all his life.

Joe Sewell

That home run by Elmer was the first grand slam in World Series history. That came in the fifth game, and it's only *one* of the reasons that that was one of the most famous historical games ever played in the World Series. The other reasons are that Jim Bagby, our pitcher that day, hit the first home run ever by a pitcher in a World Series, and Bill Wambsganss, our second baseman, made the only unassisted triple play *ever* in the World Series. That's the thing most remembered—that play. And I was standing right there at shortstop just a few feet away. It all happened in a flash, a beautiful sequence. It was the fifth inning. No outs, of course. Pete Kilduff was on second base and who was that big catcher on the Dodgers?—Otto Miller. He was on first. Clarence Mitchell was the batter.

He hit a line shot up the middle, and I thought the ball was gone for a sure hit. But Bill was off with the crack of the bat running toward the bag and leaped unbelievably high and backhanded the ball. It took everyone in the ball park a few seconds to realize that the ball was not a hit, including the runners. Bill's motion carried him right to second base, which he tagged for the second out—Kilduff was still running full speed. Then he turned around to throw the ball to first to double Miller—I should say *triple* Miller off; but I noticed Miller was just a few steps away from him, so I hollered, "Tag him! Tag him!" Which Bill did.

If he'd thrown to first it would've been a triple play, but not an *unassisted* triple play. It's that "unassisted" that made it a play that people still talk about.

Joe Sewell, Burleigh Grimes, and Earl Averill, Cooperstown, New York, 1980

Like I said, it took everyone in the park a few seconds to adjust to what'd actually happened. There was a long breathless silence. Then the place went wild. You know those old straw hats that men used to wear? Well, some fellows started scaling their hats down onto the field, and then everyone was doing it. Hats all over the field. We had to call time for the grounds crew to come up and pick them all up.

It was a moment I'll never forget.

OCTOBER 1926

Babe Ruth in 1928

In the 1926 World Series when Grover Alexander struck out Tony Lazzeri in that crucial inning and won a championship, a lot of fellows raved about Alex's great curves. Let me tell you a little secret. Alex threw Tony just one curveball in all those pitches. And the ball that Tony fanned on wasn't a curve at all. It wasn't even a fast one. It was a half-speed ball that cut the corner of the plate within a half inch of the spot Bob O'Farrell called for.

No, sir, the thing that fanned Tony Lazzeri that day and the thing that cost the Yankees a World Championship was Alexander's uncanny control. He was putting that ball right where he wanted it, on

Grover Cleveland Alexander in the late 1920s

every pitch. And the fellow who was up there at the plate with a bat on his shoulder felt like a sucker. For he knew that the balls were so bad he couldn't hit them squarely, yet they were good enough that they were sure to be called strikes if he let them go.

I know. I stood up there. And I felt like a sucker along with the rest of the boys.[2]

Grover Cleveland Alexander in 1945

There must be a hundred versions of what happened in the Yankee Stadium that dark, chilly afternoon. It used to be that everywhere I went, I'd hear a new one, and some were pretty farfetched. So much so that two or three years ago I ran across Lazzeri in San Francisco and said: "Tony, I'm getting tired of fanning you." And Tony answered: "Maybe you think I'm not."[3]

Rogers Hornsby

Everybody figured the Series was going about as expected when we left St. Louis trailing three games to two with the last two games scheduled on Yankee home ground. About the only surprise was that we'd carried them that far.

Alex pitched for us in that sixth game, and we finally got around to giving him some support with our bats. We won by 10–2, and the Series was squared again.

After that game, the second for Alex and his second victory, I told him to take it easy that night.

"I'll be ready if you need me, Rog," was all he said, and I didn't worry about him. I knew if he could walk from the bull pen to the mound, he'd be all right if we got into a jam.

We got into a jam all right. . . . Trailing 3–2 in the seventh inning of the last game, the Yankees filled the bases with two out.

I figured Alex was our best bet. I left my position at second base and walked out to meet him. Naturally, I wanted to get a close look at him, to see what shape he was in. And I also wanted to tell him what the situation was, in case he'd been dozing. He was a great guy to relax and probably had got himself a little shut-eye in the bull pen. But he was wide awake when I met him. And his eyes were clear. . . .

Alex didn't say much.

"Bases filled, eh?" he said. "Well, don't worry about me. I'm all right. And I guess there's nothing much to do except give Tony a lot of hell."

Alexander took care of Lazzeri, all right, striking him out. On the second strike Tony hit a tremendous line drive that crashed into the left-field seats, foul. Then Alex fooled Tony with a low curve outside, and we were out of the jam. Two innings remained, but Alex protected that 3–2 lead and emerged as the popular hero of that Series, one of the most exciting, people have told me down through the years, that ever has been played.

That was a great celebration on the way home. Alexander drank enough black coffee to float a battleship as we tried to have him in condition for the reception we knew was ahead of us when we got back to St. Louis. But the old boy stayed in character.

"They're calling me a hero, eh?" he said quietly, as they served him more coffee. "Well, do you know what? If that line drive Lazzeri hit had been fair, Tony would be the hero and I'd be just an old bum."[4]

OCTOBER 1929

Mickey Cochrane

The most amusing "jockeying" experience I ever had was provided by, of all people, Judge Kenesaw Mountain Landis. It was during the Cubs-Philadelphia Series of 1929. We had started the Series with a fine appreciation for invective and were hurling it from bench to bench across the infield until the air around home plate was blue.

Lots of these sounds, none too refined, carried over the dugout aprons and into the ears of spectators in the immediate vicinity of the players' benches. After one of the games, Judge Landis issued an order putting a stop to the language and threatening a sizable fine.

The next game was at Wrigley Field, and just before the game I walked over in front of the Cubs' bench and yelled: "Hello, sweethearts, we're going to serve tea this afternoon, come on out and get your share."

Judge Landis had ensconced himself in a box adjacent to the home dugout. He never by the slightest movement betrayed that he heard my wisecrack. He did not even lift his chin off the rail.

After the Series, when we had won, the Judge came into the locker room and congratulated us. He singled out many players individually and paid tribute to them in flattering terms. He never gave me a tumble, sitting over in a corner. . . . I thought he was sore and was going to pass right over me.

Finally, just as he was leaving, he stopped in front of me.

"Hello, sweetheart," he said; "I came in after my tea; will you pour?"[5]

Joe Sewell

The fifth game of the 1920 Series was one of the *two* historical games I was in. The other one was in the 1932 Series, the third game. That was the day that Ruth pointed to the fence. He sure did. Ask Burleigh Grimes. Ruth was fussing at Burleigh at the time, and he sure did point, 'cause I saw it myself. I've told the story one hundred times.

Take it back a little farther. There were some hard feelings in that Series right from the start all on account of Mark Koenig. See, late in the season, they'd lost their regular shortstop to an injury, and they brought [ex-Yankee shortstop] Koenig in to replace him. Well, Koenig was more than just a fill-in. He played great baseball, and a lot of people felt like they couldn't have won without him. But the Cubs only voted him a half share of the Series money. Well, a lot of the fellows on the Yankee ball club were great friends of Koenig—like Ruth, Gehrig, Dickey, Combs, Lazzeri, Pennock—and they took offense.

The day that the World Series opened we were taking hitting practice, and the Cubs had to come out along a runway right by our bench to get to their dugout. So Ruth and them boys, they'd take a turn hitting, and then they'd go back and sit on that bench by the runway. So Ruth happened to be sitting there when they came out. First thing he said was "Here comes the Squeeze-the-Eagle Club!" Well, that started it. You never heard such foul language in your life. I didn't know such words existed in the English language. Now I'm gonna tell you the truth, didn't a one of them say a word back except Gabby Hartnett. The rest of them were quiet, but you could tell they were steaming.

We rubbed it in on the field. Won the first two games in the Yankee Stadium.

The third game was in Chicago. By now the Cubs were yelling back, and the language was getting brutal. Mrs. Sewell told me they could hear it in the stands, and it was embarrassing.

The big inning was the fifth. I led off with a fly ball to Hack Wilson in center field and came back to the bench to get me a drink of water just like I always did. Ruth batted after me and the ball park was jumping. Everybody in the place was screaming at the Babe. Burleigh Grimes was sitting there on the Cub bench with a towel on his head, and he and Ruth were cussing each other—I'm talking about *cussing* each other. The Babe took a strike and the yelling got louder. He took another strike and the yelling got even louder than before. He backed out of the box, and he had his bat in his left hand, and with two fingers on his right hand, he pointed to center field. Didn't say a word to the pitcher, Charlie Root. Next pitch—crack! I've still got a clear mental picture of that ball going out of that ball park. You ever seen a golf ball hit? That's exactly how it went. There was a tree full of boys beyond the fence in center field, and they all dropped out of it and chased that ball.

Someone on our bench said, "Look at old Burleigh." He was waving that white towel, asking for a truce.

Ruth came around third with boos rolling down and a lot of rotten fruit, cabbages, and oranges pelting around him. The fans must've brought whole loads of that stuff out to the ball park. Finally, they got it cleaned up, and things quieted down.

The next batter up was Lou Gehrig, and he hit another home run. Things were really quiet then. I don't guess there were too many people betting on the Cubs by that time. We won the game 7–5.

That night Joe McCarthy got a letter from Judge Landis. The judge said that from then on, any player using profanity would be fined five hundred dollars. The next day McCarthy read us the letter in the clubhouse before the game. And do you know you could've heard a pin drop?

We sat there on the bench like mummies. But our bats made a lot of noise. We won it 13–6 for a four-game sweep.

Burleigh Grimes

I never said nothing to Ruth. Guy Bush and Bob Smith were the guys who were riding him, calling him a "big ape" and a lot worse, and

The Babe

he was hollering back at them. I was always supposed to be the bad guy, so they were always faulting me, but Bush was the ringleader.

Ruth held up his finger to say that he had one strike left, and the next thing you know everybody's saying he called his shot. Sure, Ruth played along with it. Why not?

Babe Ruth in 1945

Right now I want to settle all arguments: I didn't exactly point to any spot, like the flagpole. Anyway, I didn't mean to. I just sort of waved at the whole fence. All I wanted to go was give that ball a ride . . . anywhere.[6]

Billy Herman

He didn't point, don't kid yourself. If he'd pointed do you think Root would've thrown him a strike to hit? I'll tell you what he would've done. Remember he was ahead on the count. Right, you guessed it—Ruth would've been sitting in the dirt, maybe rubbing himself where it hurt.

Waite Hoyt in 1933

Gabby Hartnett

Babe waved his hand toward our bench on the third-base side. One finger was up, and he said quietly—and I think only the umpire and I heard him—"It only takes one to hit it." Root came in with a fast one, Babe swung, and it landed in the center-field seats. Babe didn't say a word when he passed me after the home run. If he'd pointed out at the bleachers, I'd be the first to say so.[7]

Bill Dickey

I know the true story—I was in the on-deck circle with Gehrig at the time—but I'm gonna hold my tongue.

I used to get in arguments with Gabby Hartnett. He'd say, "Ruth did *not* point." And I'd say, "Oh, yes he did, Gabby. Oh, yes he did." And he'd get so mad at me he couldn't see.

Let's leave it just like that.

Waite Hoyt in 1933, to a dugout of bench-jockeying Cubs:

If you guys don't shut up, I'll put on my old Yankee uniform and scare you to death.

Satchel Paige

[Satchel Paige was the pitching star of the 1942 Negro World Series.]

The night before that fourth game I drove back over to Pittsburgh.

I'd been staying there each night and driving to our games in Philadelphia. As much as I was thinking about the Series, there was a mighty nice gal over there I just had to see.

Going back and forth like that really wasn't much of a drive for a man who likes cars the way I do and who got a nice, powerful piece of machinery to zip around in.

But I always had to make good time.

The morning of the fourth game I started early. I was scheduled to start again and was all set on doing me a little winning.

I really stepped on the gas and was clipping right along when I heard this siren while I was busting through Lancaster. It was a cop. I pulled over. . . .

"You're under arrest for speeding," he said to me.

"But I got to pitch a ball game over in Philadelphia—the World Series."

"All you got to do is see a justice of the peace," he said, and took me to town. We stopped in front of a barbershop.

We went inside, and the justice was cutting somebody's hair.

"You'll have to wait," he said.

Well, I could tell there wasn't any use arguing so I just sat and waited.

Then he came over, wiping his hands on his apron.

"What is it?" he asked the officer.

"Speeding."

He turned and looked at me. "Guilty or not guilty?" he asked.

All I could think about was getting out of there.

"Guilty," I said.

"That'll be three dollars."

I threw the money at him and got out of there quick. It's just a good thing that cop didn't follow me anymore. If he had he'd of found out that speeding I was doing before was just snail-walking when you looked at what I did the rest of the way to Philadelphia.

Even as fast as I was going I didn't get to the ball park until the fourth inning, and we were behind, 5–4, then. I jumped into a uniform and ran out there. My manager sent me in there real quick. I didn't even have time to warm up.

There was two [Homestead] Grays on base and two outs. I knew I wasn't warmed up enough to pitch yet, so I tried picking off that runner on first about ten times until I'd gotten loosed up. Then I looked in at my catcher, got my signal, and started firing. I struck out the batter for the third out.

Going into the seventh inning we still was behind by that 5–4 score. Then the roof fell in on the Grays. We scored two runs in the seventh to go ahead and three more in the eighth for icing. While all that was going on, I kept pitching no-hit, no-run ball, I didn't give up a hit or a run for the 5⅓ innings I pitched.

We had us the World Championship in four straight games.[8]

DODGERS VS. YANKEES
1949   1952   1953   1955   1956

Roy Campanella
You know, I played in five World Series in the ten years I was on the Dodgers. I consider myself pretty lucky. The only disappointment was that we did not win more of them. We lost in '49 and '52 and '53 and '56, and won our only World Championship in '55. One of our problems I believe is that we were trying too hard. You know there is such a thing as trying too hard. You get all knotted up. Some people said we were afraid of the Yankees. We weren't afraid of the Yankees. We just wanted to beat them so badly that we maybe became a little overanxious.

Duke Snider
The most disappointing event in my personal career was the World Series of 1949 when I struck out eight times in five games and tied

The 1956 World Series—Campanella catching, Mantle batting.

Rogers Hornsby's record. When Reggie [Jackson] hit the five homers in '78, breaking my home-run record, I told my friends I'd rather have had him break my other record. But no, Rogers and I still share the strike-out record. And of course we lost the Series. I was down in the dumps, and when my home-town folks gave me a dinner that winter, I promised them things would be different if we got in the Series again. But inside, I had my doubts, and I carried them for years.

Finally, in 1952 we got back into the Series and again our opponent was the Yankees. Their starter in the first game was Allie Reynolds, who'd struck me out five of the eight times in '49. Well, I straightened my inner doubts out in a hurry. My first time up against Reynolds I hit a home run. As I rounded the bases I thought, This is it. I can handle the pressures of World Series competition. And I went on to hit four homers in that Series. That *made* my confidence—erased all doubts from my mind.

The pinnacle of my World Series career though had to be 1955. I'll never forget that last game.

Johnny [Podres] threw Elston Howard a change-up and got him out on the front of his foot, and he hit a grounder to short. I can see it like it was yesterday. And if the ground ball should have gone to anyone it was Pee Wee because he'd had a few more years of frustration than we had. He was there in 1941 when Hugh Casey wild-pitched and all that. I can still see him picking up the ball taking dead aim at [Gil] Hodges and Hodges stretching out. Then the place went wild. . . .

I remember the ride back to Brooklyn. See, we took two buses over to Yankee Stadium from Ebbets Field. We parked our cars there at a service station on Bedford Avenue and rode over on the buses. I remember Johnny Podres getting on the bus, and he'd beaten the Yankees earlier in the Series. He said, "Just get me one run, that's all I need fellows." He said that all the way over there. . . . We got him two and that was it.

The bus ride going back now, it was like the end of World War II. Ticker-tape parade. I don't know how everybody in New York found out what route we were taking back to Brooklyn, but whatever street we went down there were people hanging from the light standards and everywhere. . . . People were just going crazy.[9]

Yogi Berra

Yeah, they beat us in '55, and then they won the first two games in '56. But then we won three straight. The last one was Don Larsen's perfect game, and catching that was my greatest thrill. Best-pitched game I ever saw. I'll never forget that game. He used that no-windup delivery and worked very fast and made it look very easy. He said he got the no-windup idea from a comic book. It worked, didn't it?

The 1956 World Series: Yogi congratulates Don Larsen on his perfect game.

Twenty-seven up and twenty-seven down. That was a very happy moment for me, and it felt good to win the Series again.

[In defeating the Dodgers in the 1956 Series, the Yankees regained the World Championship that some observers had begun to think of as rightfully theirs. It was their sixth championship in eight years.]

OCTOBER 1958

Mickey Mantle

I played in twelve World Series, and a lot of great things happened in them, but one moment I remember particularly had to do with something—and someone—who wasn't even on the ball field.

It was in 1958. We had lost the first two games of the Series to the Braves in Milwaukee, and now we were back in Yankee Stadium for the third game. I was in center field in the top of the second inning when, apparently for no reason, a cheer started in the stands and grew and got bigger and louder until it seemed that everyone in the stadium was standing and applauding. It took a minute or so to figure out what was happening. Then it became obvious.

Roy Campanella had come into the ball park.[10]

Roy Campanella in 1980

Roy Campanella

[After the January 28, 1958, automobile accident that ended his playing career and very nearly ended his life, Roy Campanella spent over nine months in hospitals. Shortly before his scheduled release from Rush Institute, he was offered an assignment to write a syndicated column on the 1958 World Series. He accepted.]

We left the house around noon and arrived at the stadium just a few minutes after the game had started. I admit I was a little nervous as it was the first time I was out in a big crowd since the accident. The nervousness almost turned into panic when it came time to put my wheelchair in the aisle and they found the aisle wasn't wide enough for the chair. Before I knew what was happening, a couple of husky firemen lifted me out of the chair and carried me down the aisle. For just that first minute I felt like some sad freak. It was awful. If I could have run I'd have been out of there in two seconds flat. But there I was, being carried in somebody's arms, like a helpless child. As the firemen, with the help of my attendant, were getting me to my seat, I could hear the buzzing of the crowd. Then came a tremendous roar, and following that a great deal of cheering and clapping and whistling. At first I thought the people were cheering some play on the field. But when I was finally seated—there between my wife, Ruthe, and my boy Roy, Jr.—and looked around, I saw that everybody around me had their eyes in my direction. . . . It's hard to explain the feeling that came over me. At first I thought, I don't want this! But what could I do? I couldn't get up and leave. And then I accepted the cheers, in my heart. Just like they were meant. I knew that they came from the heart.

As I sat there tears rolled down my cheeks. I remember Roy, Jr., looking up at me kinda funny. "Daddy, are you crying?" he asked. He had never seen his daddy cry before. Then I looked hard at Ruthe. She also had tears in her eyes. I could see the players looking my way leaning out of the dugouts and all. And I remember several of the Braves players waving at me. Yogi Berra, who had been squatting behind the plate, stood and waved to me and smiled. I could see he wanted to come back to the screen and talk to me, but I think he was too embarrassed or maybe he didn't want to embarrass me.

That box seat was in the first row in back of the screen behind home plate. It was the first time I had sat in anything but my wheelchair. I was worried whether I could sit in the seat without a belt or some other means of support. When you're paralyzed you worry about everything that's new. You don't know how you're going to cope with it. But with Ruthe on one side and with Roy on the other, I made out all right.

And I took those Series games in stride.[11]

Aerial view of Yankee Stadium in the 1950s. Note Polo Grounds beyond the Harlem River. The far river is the Hudson.

There's no question about it. To star in baseball you have to have some sort of drive that'll motivate you to make the necessary sacrifices. It doesn't come easy, even to the most talented ones. You've got to be able to drive yourself all the time. It's a long season with ups and downs, and you've just got to keep grinding it out.

—RALPH KINER

THE LONG

AFTERNOON

Buck Leonard in 1980. INSET: *with Durango in the 1950s.*

I declined the honor. I wasn't sure which year those gentlemen had in mind.

—SATCHEL PAIGE commenting on his nomination for American League Rookie of the Year in 1948

19.

Jim Crow

Buck Leonard

It was tough playing in the Negro leagues, but we loved baseball and we just made ourselves content playing in our own league. I played with the Homestead Grays for seventeen years out of the twenty-three I played. I also played every winter in Latin America—Cuba, Venezuela, Puerto Rico, and Mexico. My last five years I was down in Mexico for the summers too, playing for Durango. We had to play year-round to make enough to live.

If you had a family you couldn't support them. They never used to pay us a nickel during spring training, for example, only board and room and laundry. And sometimes maybe four dollars or five dollars to spend. I remember one fellow—a *good* pitcher—came to our spring training camp in Orlando, Florida. But he had three kids. We couldn't pay him enough, so he had to quit us.

From February to May our living expenses were covered by the gate from our exhibition games, no payday until May 1 when our official season opened in Pittsburgh.

When I first started with the Homestead Grays in 19 and 34, they were giving us sixty cents a day for meals. We'd only eat two meals a day, a big cheap breakfast and a meal at four in the afternoon. No steak. If you had a night game, you'd eat after the game.

And we stayed in rooming houses. We couldn't afford hotels. We'd double up, two men on one bed. No air conditioning. Sometimes a fan maybe. If we traveled overnight it was two men would sleep in the upper berth and two in the lower berth of a Pullman. If you wanted to get up in the night to go to the bathroom, you had to climb over everybody. Mostly though, we traveled by bus. We'd go thirty thousand miles and play 200 games in a season. In 1938, we played 210. About half of them were league games. Mondays, Wednesdays, and Fridays were for exhibitions.

It was tough, but we did it 'cause we loved the game. Naturally we'd have preferred playing under major league conditions. We used Wilson balls, bats off the shelf. The lights were bad, and a lot of the fields were in rough condition. I think this hurt our playing.

Another thing, we weren't organized like the major leagues were. If it started to rain we couldn't give the people a rain check. We didn't have the established ball park and the established schedule that a team needs.

And we never kept proper statistics, so there's no permanent record, and you're liable to get a different story from each one of us. It's just what we can remember—and pass along. Like this conversation. . . .

Cool Papa Bell

I remember one game I got five hits and stole five bases, but none of it was written down because they didn't bring the scorebook to the game that day.

Satchel Paige in 1934

I sure get laughs when I see in the papers where some major league pitcher says he gets a sore arm because he overworked, and he pitches every four days. Man, that'd be just a vacation to me.

And in 1971, at his Hall of Fame induction

We traveled around and played; and if I didn't pitch every day, they didn't want the ball club. And that's how I started to pitching every day. I pitched in 165 ball games in a row. . . . So I began to learn to pitch by the hour. . . .

Buck Leonard

Anything would go in the black leagues, spitball pitching, cut-ball pitching, all kinds of tricky baseball. We'd use the tricks against each other and we'd use them against the white boys. I played quite a bit against major leaguers. Generally every Sunday in October until it got too cold to play, I'd travel from my home in Rocky Mount, North Carolina, all the way up to Baltimore to play a doubleheader against a major league all-star team. *We'd* win sometimes; *they'd* win sometimes. Sometimes we'd make two hundred dollars each for the day's work. Then I'd drive back to North Carolina that same night.

Then I went with Satchel Paige's all-stars to California in 1943. We played against the major league All-Stars in Wrigley Field in Los Angeles every Sunday. They had Lou Novikoff, Peanuts Lowrey, Roy Partee, Buck Newsom, Johnny Lindell, Junior Stephens, Wally Moses, George Case—twelve or fifteen of them. The promoter tried to bring in different big names every week. We kept pretty much the same group for every game—Josh Gibson, Vic Harris, Sammy T. Hughes, Cool Papa Bell, Double Duty Radcliffe. Satchel Paige was our pitcher, and he got five hundred dollars a game. The rest of us averaged about two hundred dollars. They'd have a top player at every position. We had to fill in some. But we won our share of the games. We played hard all the time 'cause we wanted to *win*. It was a matter of pride. I wouldn't say they *always* put forth their best efforts, but we did have some very good games.

We were drawing twelve to fifteen thousand in that little ball park. But then they got a telegram from Judge Landis telling them not to play us anymore. They had everything to lose and nothing to gain. Andy Pafko kept playing, and Landis fined him four hundred dollars.

After that, we began scheduling games with the Pacific Coast League All-Stars, but attendance fell way off because the fans had been seeing *them* play all year. Finally, when the income tax man started coming around, we decided to give it up and head on home.

Lou Gehrig in the 1930s
Baseball is our national pastime, and there's no place in it for racial discrimination. I've seen many Negro players who should be in the major leagues today.

Dizzy Dean in the 1950s
I have played against a Negro all-star team that was so good we didn't think we had a chance against them.

Bob Feller
I barnstormed with Satchel Paige annually, starting back in 1937 when both of us could really hum that ball. . . . I had an all-star major league club behind me. They all bore down to see what they could do against such a fabled figure as Satchel Paige. They didn't do much.

By the time he came to the majors, of course, Paige was getting by mostly on savvy. Still, nobody ever stopped Joe DiMaggio as cold as he did. I've seen Satch walk a man deliberately to get at DiMaggio.[1]

Ted Williams

I used to play pinochle with my friend Chuck Moran's father. His father was from back east, and we'd sit on the porch and play, and he'd tell stories about seeing Joe Wood and Walter Johnson and some of the great players of the day. He told about seeing Walter Johnson pitch an exhibition against an all-Negro all-star team at a little park in New Haven where you were so close you could hear the players talking. He said in the first inning one of the Negro players got up and called out to Johnson, "Mr. Johnson, I sure heard plenty about that fastball. You throw it, Mr. Johnson, and I'm gonna hit it right out of this park." And he did, and the game ended 1–0.

Hearing that story, I thought to myself, What's this he's feeding me? I knew Mr. Moran used to cheat at pinochle, so any kind of story like that was suspect as far as I was concerned. Six or seven years later I finally met Walter Johnson in Washington. What an impressive man. Big, lean, strong-looking, soft-spoken. A very gentle man. I remembered Mr. Moran's story, and I couldn't help asking: "I've got a friend in San Diego who says he saw you pitch against this Negro team in New Haven, and he said in the first inning one of the players . . ." and Johnson began nodding his head. "That's right," he said. "That sure is right. He hit that ball a mile."[2]

Cool Papa Bell

They used to say, "If we find a *good* black player, we'll sign him." They was lying.

Roy Campanella

The Phillies invited down a few high school players to work out at Shibe Park. I was one of them. I guess from my name, Campanella, which is Italian, they didn't realize I was black.

But after I got there they said, "Gee, you can't work out here." I knew why, but I asked them, "Why?" They were a bad team and needed help. They said, "Well, you're black; no black boy plays in the big leagues." I couldn't quite understand it 'cause I went to an integrated high school. So at the age of fifteen this really started me thinking. My father was white, an Italian, and my mother was black, and in our home we had an interracial family. And it never even phased me one bit. But I was learning fast. When I started traveling with the Baltimore Elite Giants, I started learning that there was segregation everywhere. I won't say so much that it made me *mad* as that it made me *aware*. I always felt that getting mad I didn't accomplish anything. But to be *aware*, I thought I could accomplish more.

Buck Leonard

We expected that baseball was going to be integrated someday; but when it happened it took a lot of us by surprise. It happened faster than we thought it would.

The Dodgers signed Jackie Robinson. We didn't think he was the best. He ran well and he was a fighter, but he wasn't one of the Negro "stars." It just shows you that you can't always tell about a ballplayer. Branch Rickey saw something there and he was right. Robinson was the man for the job, college-educated, a winner, a man with good self-control.

I guess they thought about bringing me up at that time, but I was too old. They wanted someone they could bring up gradually who could give them four or five years at least on the major league level. That meant guys like Jackie Robinson and Monte Irvin. Cool Papa Bell, Satchel, and me—it was too late for us.

Cool Papa Bell

Most of the black ballplayers thought Monte Irvin should have been the first black in the major leagues. Monte was our best young ballplayer at the time. . . . He could hit that long ball, he had a great arm, he could field, he could run. Yes, he could do everything.[3]

James "Cool Papa" Bell, fleet flyhawk of the Negro Leagues

Monte Irvin

Satchel Paige says it very well. He says, "You know if I had been pitching to Ruth and Gehrig, you could knock a few points off those big fat lifetime batting averages." He's right too. Maybe they should put asterisks on all the records made before the Jim Crow barrier was broken. And you know, there were plenty of other great pitchers in the Negro leagues. I'm talking about guys like Raymond Brown and Leon Day and Bill Byrd. And Barney Brown. Slim Jones. These guys were legends. Now had they been pitching in the major leagues, things would've been just a little more competitive.

It's very difficult for me to try to tell you how good these men were. Cool Papa Bell? He might've been the fastest baseball player who ever lived. Just like they'd talk about Josh's [Gibson] slugging, they used to tell stories about Bell's running. He was known to score from second base on a *bunt*. That's right. Now, suppose he'd played under good conditions—you know, get a massage after every game, not have to drive five hundred miles to play a doubleheader, this kind of thing. There's no telling how many bases he would've stolen. It's just a shame that more people didn't get to see him.

The only comparison I can give is—suppose Willie Mays had never had a chance to play big league. Then I were to come to you and try to tell you about Willie Mays. Now this is the way it is with Cool Papa Bell. This is the way it is with Buck Leonard. Just a fantastic hitter. With Oscar Charleston, who they say was just as good as Willie—or *better*. But very few people ever saw him play.

There were others. I'm thinking about John Beckwith. Ray Dandridge, third baseman. Willie Wells, shortstop. Sammy T. Hughes, second baseman. Leon Day, who was a pitcher just like Bob Gibson. And

Tips from a pro: Monte Irvin coaches kids in the Bronx, June, 1980.

on and on. I'm thinking about Smokey Joe Williams and Mule Suttles and Biz Mackey, and right on down the line.

If they could have removed the Jim Crow barrier even just ten years earlier, there would've been twenty to twenty-five men they could've taken right onto major league clubs as regulars and they'd have been potential Hall of Famers. There were *that* many.

So Jackie Robinson was *not* the best. He was just the first. And a very fine choice as it turned out. What made Jackie so outstanding was his personal color and his competitive fire. He wasn't a good hitter at the beginning, but he *made* himself into one. He had great natural speed and quickness and used it to full advantage. He *made* himself into an all-star second baseman, and he developed the knack of stealing bases and particularly stealing home. He'd drive pitchers *crazy*, and he was very thrilling to watch. So he drew fans to the park and sparked his team to victory and, as I said, turned out to be an excellent choice for the pioneering role. Not many people could've controlled themselves so well in the face of all that pressure and abuse.

Later, after he didn't have to be a pioneer anymore and could let himself fight back, we all saw what kind of fires Jackie really had burning inside.

Eddie Mathews

When I was playing against him in the fifties, Jackie [Robinson] had changed. A lot of race crap. He'd pioneered and taken an awful lot of abuse, and in the process he'd become pretty ornery. Not dirty, just ornery. If he got brushed back it was because he was black, not just because he was Jackie Robinson, a helluva hitter. But I only played against him his last few years after he was past his prime.

Actually, he probably had every right to be paranoid; because when I broke in, black players couldn't stay at the same hotels with the rest of the team, couldn't eat in the same restaurants, couldn't even drink out of the same water fountains in some places. So they had a right to be ornery I guess.

On the Braves we had no race problems whatsoever. In fact, Hank Aaron's one of my *good* friends. I can't speak for Hank. He never showed any bitterness. I'm hearing *now* a little bit that he was disappointed by some things. . . .

I don't know how to explain it. That's just the way it was. We were all young kids and that was the American society. But it did change from the fifties on—change for the better.

But . . . with Aaron, there were times when he wasn't even allowed in the dining car of the train. We'd have to bring his meal back to him. Now, at my age, today, if something like that happened, I'd make an issue of it. But at that time I was twenty-one, twenty-two years old, and I hardly gave it a second thought.

Monte Irvin

Most of the white players were fair in their treatment of us when we first came up—I'd say over 50 percent of them. You have to realize that there's a certain amount of fairness among athletes, a certain amount of respect for ability. The attitude is play hard, but play fair; and may the best man win.

You have to remember though, the attitude in the country at large back then—much more conservative. Some of the players who might've wanted to be friendly had to be careful or they'd be criticized as "nigger-lovers" by the folks back home. So they were kind of stand-offish. Now, as the tone of the country became more liberal, they became more liberal themselves. For instance, I remember when Jackie was signed, Pee Wee Reese asked Branch Rickey to be traded. Branch told him, "We have great plans for you. But think about it for a couple of weeks. I won't go against your wishes." In the meantime though, playing around second base with Robinson, Pee Wee got to know him and began to respect him. So he went to Rickey and told him he had changed his mind. He realized that Jackie was gonna help the team win. So you have to admire him for that. On the other hand, Dixie Walker and Bobby Bragan and a couple of others *did* get themselves traded. Some of those same fellows today are *sorry* that they acted that way. They thought that was the way they were supposed to act. Bragan says that when he was a manager in later years, he always tried to give extra help to young Negro players to try to make up for the silly way he reacted back thirty years ago. And he's still doing the same thing today, down there in Texas.

Willie Mays

Did you ever notice that the teams that signed more black players faster tended to win more games? [4]

Monte Irvin

I honestly believe the black and Latin players have been the salvation of baseball, particularly the National League, because they were first. Look over the last thirty years, a *very* high percentage of the stars have been Negro-American, or Latins—black, brown, and white—from Puerto Rico, Venezuela, the Dominican Republic. Baseball is a land of opportunity for these fellows.

Bob Gibson

It's nice to get attention and favors, but I can never forget the fact that if I were an ordinary black person I'd be in the doghouse, like millions of others. [5]

Jackie Robinson

Jackie Robinson in 1964

Integration in baseball has already proved that all Americans can live together in peaceful competition. Negroes and whites co-exist today on diamonds south, north, east, and west without friction, fist fights, or feuds. They wear the same uniforms, sit side by side on the same benches, use the same water fountains, toilets, showers; the same bats, balls, and gloves. They travel from city to city on the same buses, trains, or planes. They live in the same hotels, eat in the same dining rooms, kid each other in the same baseball jargon. Negro and white ballplayers play cards and golf together, go to movies together, swap inside information about opponents, defend each other in rhubarbs, pound each other's backs after a winning game. They attend postseason banquets together, go on club picnics, visit each other's homes. Fans no longer notice the color of a ballplayer's skin. Willie Mays is San Francisco's hero. Now that Stan Musial has retired, Bill White is the most popular Cardinal, as Ernie Banks is the most respected Cub. From Boston, where fans mobbed Earl Wilson after his 1962 no-hitter, to Los Angeles, where Tommy Davis is the toast of the town, baseball is an all-American game.

Now, let's broaden the focus.[6]

That space between the white
lines—that's my office. That's
where I conduct my business.
—EARLY WYNN

20.

The Business End

John Montgomery Ward in 1889, from The Brotherhood of
   Professional Baseball Players' "Manifesto"
   There was a time when the National League stood for integrity and
fair dealing; today it stands for dollars and cents. . . . Players have been
bought, sold, or exchanged as though they were sheep, instead of American citizens. . . . By a combination among themselves, stronger than
the strongest trusts, owners were able to enforce the most arbitrary
measures, and the player had either to submit or get out of the profession in which he had spent years attaining proficiency.

Connie Mack in 1950
   In 1888–89 I joined some friends in the organization of the Baseball
Players Brotherhood.
   We had in the Brotherhood such men as John M. Ward, John K.
Tener, later governor of Pennsylvania, and Charles Comiskey, who
was soon to become the millionaire owner of the Chicago team in the

American League. The purpose of our Brotherhood was to protect the players.

The Brotherhood and the National League broke into open warfare in 1889. It threw a bombshell at the big fellows by stating that the new Players' League, with teams in every major city, would be operated in the interest of the players. Players from National League teams lost no time in rushing to us for protection.

The National League appealed to the courts. Litigation followed, but the National League contracts were held inequitable.

The baseball war of 1890 threatened to throw both the National League and the Brotherhood League into bankruptcy. The magnates dropped about four million dollars in their desperate attempt to break the Brotherhood; finally, at great cost, they succeeded.

Players scrambled back to their old magnates. They had been suspended for life, but they were received with open arms when they came back as prodigal sons. . . .

But the Brotherhood had started a new era in baseball. Club owners had awakened to the realization that ballplayers are human and must be given a fair deal or they will rebel.[1]

"Today it stands for dollars and cents . . ." John Montgomery Ward, captain of the New York Giants in the 1880s and 1890s, founder of the Brotherhood of Professional Baseball Players.

Albert G. Spalding in 1911

It was announced at the beginning that it was to be a fight to the death, and it was carried to a finish along these lines. In place of powder and shell, printers' ink and bluff formed the ammunition used by both sides.

If either party to this controversy ever furnished to the press one solitary truthful statement as to the progress of the war, if anyone at any time made true representation of conditions in his own ranks, a monument should be erected to his memory. No one cared for the score of yesterday's game; all eyes were centered on the question of attendance. Both sides engaged in faking attendance reports. The Chicago papers, for instance, would appear every morning with figures—furnished by club officials—and reading something like this:

"Brotherhood attendance—8,000."

"League attendance—2,000."

Round figures are always suspicious, and the constant reiteration of these attracted my attention.

Securing the services of a bright young Chicago reporter, I placed in his hands the statistical information which had been procured as to faked attendance at Brotherhood games. He published, side by side, the figures as given out by the Brotherhood managers and the *true* figures as sworn to by my agents.

The publication produced a profound sensation and . . . discounted the claims made by the Brotherhood. When explanations reflecting in a like manner upon the league's attendance were attempted, no one paid any attention to them. The Brotherhood had been put on the defensive.

I recall being present at a league game one day at Chicago when the attendance was particularly light. At the close of the contest I was talking to Secretary Brown, when a reporter came up, asking:

"What's the attendance?"

Without a moment's hesitation the official replied: "Twenty-four eighteen."

As the scribe passed out of hearing, I inquired: "Brown, how do you reconcile your conscience to such a statement?"

"Why," he answered, "don't you see? There were twenty-four on one side of the grounds and eighteen on the other. If he reports twenty-four *hundred* and eighteen, that's a matter for *his* conscience, not mine."

Meanwhile, the public had become utterly disgusted with both sides, and all clubs were losing money right and left.

With these conditions present the National League managers believed that an assault should be made to break through the ranks of the Brotherhood in hopes of capturing some of their players. No scruples were entertained. . . .

Michael J. "King" Kelly around 1890

To me was delegated the task of making a capture. I was given a carte blanche in the matter. I didn't fancy the job, but it was urged with force that I'd been a player, knew all the boys, and could gain a hearing where no one else could.

So I reluctantly consented and determined to go after big game. I sent a note to Mike Kelly, "The King,"—then at the zenith of his popular career—whose defection from the ranks of the enemy would cause greater consternation than that of any other, I thought. I invited Kelly to meet me at my hotel. He came. I opened with the question.

"How are things going with the game, Mike?"

"Oh, the game's gone to ———."

"What? You don't mean to say that the managers are getting discouraged?"

"Aw, ——— the managers!"

"Why, What's the matter?" incredulously.

"Everything's the matter; everybody's disgusted; clubs all losing money; we made a ——— foolish blunder when we went into it."

I thought the time was ripe. Placing a check for ten thousand dollars on the table, I asked, "Mike, how would you like that check for ten thousand dollars?"

"Would Mike Kelly like ten thousand dollars? I should smile."

"But that's not all, Mike. Here's a three-years' contract, and I'm authorized to let you fill in the amount of salary yourself."

His face blanched. "What does this mean? Does it mean that I'm to join the league? Quit the Brotherhood? Go back on the boys?"

"That's just what it means. It means that you go to Boston to-night."

"Well," said he, "I must have time to think about this."

"There is mighty little time, Mike. If you don't want the money, somebody else will get it. When can you let me know?"

"In an hour and a half," he answered.

At the appointed time I was waiting—and he came. . . .

"Well, Mike, where have you been?" I asked.

"I've been taking a walk," he answered. "I went way uptown and back."

"What were you doing?"

"I was thinking."

"Have you decided?" I asked.

"Yes," he replied without hesitation; "I've decided not to accept."

"What?" I ejaculated. "You don't want the ten thousand dollars?"

"Aw, I want the ten thousand bad enough; but I've thought the matter all over, and I can't go back on the boys. And," he added, "neither would you."

Involuntarily I reached out my hand in congratulation of the great ballplayer on his loyalty. We talked for a little while, and then he borrowed five hundred dollars of me. I think it was little enough to pay for the anguish of that hour and a half, when he was deciding to give up thousands of dollars on behalf of the Brotherhood.[2]

Casey Stengel in 1918, criticized for not sliding home in a close game for the Pirates

With the salary I get here, I'm so hollow and starving that I'm liable to explode like a light bulb if I hit the ground too hard.

Burleigh Grimes

You know, I used to quarrel with Mr. Ebbets (owner of the Dodgers) about money, but I really liked him and respected him. We dealt straight with one another—player and owner. I didn't enjoy it; but I guess if anyone was qualified to know my worth, it was me. It wasn't like now—you didn't know what every guy in the league was earning—unless some guy spouted it. I guess the top guy in the league was Grover Alexander, who was getting ten thousand dollars. So you tried to work up to that.

I'll tell you one time things got a little tough with Mr. Ebbets. I was pitching in Ebbets Field, and I think the score was 1–1 against Cincinnati. Jake Daubert was up, and Ebbets disliked him. He'd traded him away earlier in the year, in fact—a little disagreement over money. Anyway, I pitched Jake a slow ball, and he hit it off the right-center-field wall for an inside-the-park home run. Ebbets had a direct phone from his box to the bench, and he used it to order them to pull me out of the ball game. I guess that was the only ball that was ever thrown over the top of Ebbets Field.

Mr. Ebbets fined me one thousand dollars. I didn't say anything about it till the next spring.

I started off that next season with eight or ten wins in a row, and then I went on strike. I said, "Gimme back that one thousand dollars or I ain't gonna pitch anymore." I was gonna go home, and Ebbets knew it!

Yeah, I got the thousand back.

Luke Appling

In 1936 Mr. [Harry] Grabiner, our general manager, said he'd give me a twenty-five-hundred-dollar bonus if I had a good year and the team drew so many people. "In fact," he said, "even if we don't draw at all, I'll give it to you if you have a good enough year."

Well, that was the best year the White Sox ever had. We finished third, half a game out of second. And so I went up to check him out. He

Luke Appling in 1980. INSET: *the White Sox shortstop from 1930 to 1950.*

said, "Well, we didn't draw that many people. The newspaper accounts are exaggerated."

I said, "How many people did we draw?" and he told me.

I said, "Heck, I just missed by 185 people." And I figured I'd had a pretty good year. *Hit* .388. But he wouldn't give it to me.

The next spring I held out for twenty-five hundred dollars more than Mr. Comiskey and Mr. Grabiner wanted to pay me. Finally, they called me about ten days after spring training started and said they'd give me what I wanted. So I came on down.

When I got to camp, I said, "Mr. Comiskey, you satisfied?"

He said, "Yeah, I'm satisfied if you're satisfied, but I gave you twenty-five hundred dollars more than I wanted to."

So I said, "Well, then tear this contract up. I'll sign one for twenty-five hundred dollars less." So he tore it up, and I signed another contract for twenty-five hundred dollars less.

When I was signing the second contract, he said, "Tell me, why'd you hold out and raise so much cain for?"

So I told him about Mr. Grabiner not paying me my bonus, and then he said, "Well, I see your point. We'll just tear this one up and give you the first one back again. I wish you'd've come to see *me*."

That's half the fun of it is horse trading with the boss!

Buck Leonard

I got my pay on the Homestead Grays every two weeks May to October for seventeen years. Never missed a payday. See, our owner didn't make his money just out of baseball. He had a fortune also invested in juke boxes—we called them "piccolos"—and he was never short of cash.

My best payday was 1944, over one thousand dollars a month. Josh [Gibson] and I told them we were going down to Mexico to play, so they raised us to keep us. My salary was *doubled* that year from the year before thanks to that offer from Mexico. So I did all right there. But the whole league had to quit playing in 1950. After they started putting blacks on the major league teams, the Negro League was dead. We couldn't draw flies.

Ralph Kiner

Nineteen forty-six was the start of everything. That was the year that the Pascual brothers in Mexico offered huge sums of money to induce players to jump to the Mexican League. After a few did jump the owners decided they'd better change some of their old-fashioned ways. The minimum salary was introduced and meal money and spring-training money. And that was also the start of the pension plan.

And then in 1952, when Allie Reynolds and I were the player-representatives of the National and American Leagues, we decided after tremendous arguments that 60 percent of the World Series TV money and all of the All-Star Game money would be funneled into the players' pension, which was the *basis* of this new financial world in baseball. The owners wanted to have a set fee of a million dollars a year, but we argued very strongly for a percentage. I'd been in the Palm Springs area that winter, and everybody out there was talking cable TV and TV's great future. So that's why we fought for the 60 percent rather than the flat fee. And got it.

You know there's an interesting sidelight to those 1952 negotiations.

The owners would *not* talk to any player's agent back in those days. They really weren't within their rights, but there was an unwritten rule and nobody dared to break it. "Never take legal issues outside the world of baseball." Nothing ever got into the civil courts.

So anyway, in 1952, Allie Reynolds and I were meeting with the executive committee representing the owners, and we were all alone and outnumbered, and in addition, they had their attorneys in the meetings. Well, we figured that was unfair, so we hired an attorney, J. Norman Lewis, but they refused to allow him into the meeting. I've forgotten the details, it was so long ago, but basically we said, "Then we're not gonna meet!"

Finally, they relented and we continued our meetings with legal counsel on hand. And that was *probably* the first time in the history of baseball that any attorney represented players in negotiations with management.

Buck Leonard

A ballplayer goes in the office now with his attorneys with him—attorneys, not one—he's got a *firm* behind him![3]

Sandy Koufax in 1966

Ballplayers do need agents for the same reason that writers, actors, singers, and dancers need them. We need them because *it is difficult to sell yourself when what you're selling is a talent, not a product*. You're put in a position of bragging about yourself, of telling how good you are, a position which most of us find uncomfortable and just a little ridiculous.[4]

Johnny Evers in 1910

Without the reserve clause it is doubtful if any twenty players could be held together long enough to create a strong, coherent team. Without the reserve, and the illegal agreements between owners, some players would receive high salaries for a few years, possibly bankrupt some clubs without much improving their playing strength, destroy the power of owners and managers to discipline players, and for a time at least, weak clubs would be weakened and strong ones strengthened.

The owners claim baseball could not exist without the reserve clause, while the thinking players insist that long-term contracts, safeguarding the interests of both parties, would accomplish just as much.[5]

Ralph Kiner

The end of the reserve clause has revolutionized the business end of baseball. It's probably the biggest change in the history of the game. The original concept was wrong, but that was the way it was, and if you wanted to play baseball you had to accept it. Going back to the Curt Flood case, the Senate committee warned organized baseball that their rules were illegal and needed revision. Well, now of course, we see that that was no idle warning.

Stan Musial

At one time, with the reserve clause, the system worked too much in favor of the owner. Now I think it's gone too far the other way—in favor of the ballplayer. We have to find a happy medium. The player should not be a slave, but the owners need more stability in the ownership of players over a period of years. They spend a lot of money developing a player; it's not fair that they should lose it all without compensation. As far as multiyear contracts go—I believe that the American system always worked on the basis of people being paid *after* they've produced. It's hard to figure down the line five or six years in business *or* in baseball how it's going to turn out. Who's going to keep producing, and who's going to be injured or get fat or lose their ability? It's too hard to analyze.

Eddie Mathews

It's the owner's fault. If you're silly enough to give a back-up catcher seven hundred thousand dollars for two or three years, that's your problem. . . .

Robin Roberts

As soon as someone is declared a free agent, he's someone the owners want to sign, and they can be pretty unrealistic in their judgments, pretty overoptimistic. If they had that someone under contract themselves, would they pay him that kind of money? That to me is the question they seem to be ignoring. So it's out of balance, and I think many of the owners are among the first to admit that they've gone haywire.

The thing is it's not just the profit motive that's operating here. It's the *desire* to be a winner. That's how they've gotten into this mess—rampant competition to *win*. Sometimes I think the profit motive would make more sense.

Some of these people figure if they can sign a couple of high-priced free agents, they'll win it all. It rarely happens that way though. They've made a large expenditure based on a dream rather than on good business sense.

I just hope some of these teams like the Orioles—who do such a marvelous job without throwing money around wildly—can restore some sanity to the situation. Because as is, it's scary. It really is. Crazy and scary.

Duke Snider

My high salary for one season was forty-six thousand dollars and a Cadillac. If I were to get paid a million, I'd feel that I should sweep out the stadium every night after I finished playing the game. But . . . I agree with Bill Lee, the Expos' pitcher. If they're willing to pay the crazy salaries, you're the one who's crazy if you don't take it.

Al Kaline

I never had an agent. Always negotiated one-on-one with the general manager. Always had a pretty easy time of it too. I just made one rule. I said, "Look, you don't go low to settle at a happy medium because I'm not gonna go high. I won't ask for fifteen thousand dollars more than *I* think I'm worth. And I don't expect you to offer me fifteen thousand dollars less than *you* think I'm worth." So we always had that understanding that we'd avoid playing games. There's no question I could have gotten more if I'd been the type to hold out. In fact, I'm sure I could've gotten whatever I wanted. . . .

My highest salary was just over one hundred thousand dollars for each of my final three years. The Tigers offered me one hundred thousand dollars a couple of years before I accepted it, but I'd had a mediocre season, so I turned it down. I felt that the press was pressuring the management to make me the first one-hundred-thousand-dollar player in Tiger history, and I didn't want it under those circumstances. I wanted it as a reward for a real good year.

Billy Herman

If they stopped overpublicizing this salary thing, it might get a little more sane. Some of these players read about themselves in the papers and how much money they're getting, and they *love* it.

Same thing with the free-agent draft. I scouted for seven years, and I saw it firsthand. You draft a kid and then you sign him. Well, maybe he's a pretty good prospect, and you're gonna give him twenty-five thousand dollars. So the next day you pick up the paper and read where you drafted this kid and gave him seventy thousand dollars. The family or maybe the newspaper inflated the figure.

Well, the next kid you go to sign has read about this first kid. Maybe he plays the same position and feels he's just as good or better, which maybe he is. He's gonna demand seventy thousand dollars to sign—maybe eighty. So there you have it—instant inflation.

Mickey Mantle

The way this money thing gets so played up, it usually ends up making everybody look greedy—the players and the owners both.

King Kelly in 1888

There are two classes of people whose wealth is always exaggerated by the great public. They are actors and ballplayers. . . .[6]

Billy Herman

You know, back in the thirties when I was with the Cubs, they figured if they drew between seven hundred fifty thousand and a million fans in a season, then they'd made themselves pretty good profits. That's an average of about ten or twelve thousand a game.

Now I was talking to Bob Fontaine, general manager out in San Diego, a couple of years ago when I was working for them, and I asked him what was the break-even point for the ball club. He said, "We have to draw one million eight hundred thousand to break even." To break *even*.

So you can see a club drawing a million and a half and they're losing money 'cause of the inflated salaries and travel expenses and all.

I'll tell you the truth. I just can't figure out where it's all leading. It's too deep for me.

Stan Musial

Today, most of the clubs, particularly in the National League, have brand-new ball parks that hold fifty thousand or more. When I was playing in the National League, we had eight teams and drew a total of eight million in a season. And the same in the American League. They'd draw eight to ten million so there'd be sixteen to twenty million people coming to a baseball game in an average year. Now there are twenty-six teams instead of sixteen, and almost all of them draw at least a million, and a lot of them draw over two million. So we draw thirty-six to forty million people in a season. That means *money*.

TV has made a difference too. We have much bigger contracts. We televise more games. So from a financial standpoint baseball has really

Ralph Kiner, Cooperstown,
New York, 1980

skyrocketed. It's just a matter of the ballplayers being in the right place and getting their share of the revenues.

I'd say that once pay-TV comes in, everybody's going to be a millionaire.

Ralph Kiner

TV provides a fat revenue, and I can see it only getting fatter. There's a new era coming in TV with cable; and with satellites beaming games around, there's gonna be very interesting developments ahead. That's why I hope to stay in broadcasting as long as I'm capable. It's important to me to be able to understand and adapt to the changes that are coming. You can't live in the past in this world. You've got to come to the future.

DIZZY DEAN after being hit in the head by a thrown ball in the 1934 World Series:

"The doctors X-rayed my head and found nothing."

21.

Injuries, Trades, and Other Disruptions

Edd Roush

John J. McGraw. I just didn't enjoy playing for him, that's all. If you made a bad play he'd cuss you out. That didn't go with me. So I was glad as I could be in the middle of the '16 season when he traded Mathewson, McKechnie, and me to Cincinnati for Wade Killefer and Buck Herzog, who had been the Cincinnati manager. Matty was to replace Herzog as the new manager. I still remember the trip the three of us made as we left the Giants and took the train to join the Reds. McKechnie and I were sitting back on the observation car, talking about how happy we were to be traded. Matty came out and sat down and listened, but he didn't say anything.

Finally I turned to him and said, "Well, Matty, aren't you glad to be getting away from McGraw?"

"I'll tell you something, Roush," he said. "You and Mac have only been on the Giants a couple of months. It's just another ball club to you fellows. But I was with that team for sixteen years. That's a mighty long time. To me, the Giants are home. And leaving them like this, I feel the same as when I leave home in the spring of the year.

"Of course, I realize I'm through as a pitcher. But I appreciate McGraw making a place for me in baseball and getting me this managing job. He's doing me a favor, and I thanked him for it. And by the way, the last thing he said to me was that if I put you in center field I'd have a great ballplayer. So starting tomorrow you're my center fielder."[1]

Casey Stengel in 1923, upon being sold to the lowly Boston Braves a few weeks after starring for McGraw's Giants in the World Series

[Stengel was the hero of the Series with two game-winning home runs.]

Well, maybe I'm lucky. If I'd hit three homers McGraw might've sent me clear out of the country.

Al Lopez

One of my dear friends traded me twice—Casey Stengel. He traded me from Brooklyn to Boston, and then five years later, having come up to Boston to manage, he traded me over to Pittsburgh.

I didn't feel bad. He told me about both trades in advance. I'll never forget the first time. I was up in New York on the off-season, and I was going out with some friends, and we were having a late afternoon drink in my hotel room. The phone rang and it was Casey, so we invited him up. Well, Casey was quite a talker, and he kept us all entertained for I don't know how many hours. Finally, my friends left and Casey stuck around for one last drink. When we were alone at last, he said, "Dammit, Al. I'm gonna have to trade you. We need pitching and you're the guy they want." I said, "Don't feel bad, Casey. If I was managing a club and I felt I could improve the club, I'd trade my own brother." I would too. I *did*, when I managed. Traded some of my favorite players to improve a club.

So Casey traded me and [Tony] Cuccinello and a couple of other players for four or five guys, including a couple of pitchers. The deal turned out to be a bad one for Casey because the two pitchers didn't last long and Cuccinello and I played for *years* up in Boston. Of course, as I said, Casey joined us up there a few years later, and then in 1940 the son of a gun traded me again.

Eddie Mathews

You don't realize how much being traded hurts until it happens to you. I was with the Braves fifteen years, and I saw my best friends, [Warren] Spahn, [Lew] Burdette, and [Bob] Buhl, get traded, and I always felt bad—but not anywhere close to as bad as I felt when *I* got it. "Me? How can they do this to me? I'm their loyal third baseman."

Mine happened in kind of a silly situation. I wasn't notified by the management. I heard it from a sportswriter, and it was Christmas Eve. I got the phone call, and bang! I'm gone.

I didn't resent it. But I was, I'd say, deeply *hurt*. And it hurt for a long time.

Mickey Mantle

The saddest and by far the scariest moment of my career came way back in the beginning, in the 1951 World Series against the Giants—October of my rookie year. My whole baseball career terminated almost on that one play. In the fifth inning of the second game, Willie Mays (also a rookie in 1951) hit a fly ball to right-center, and I chased it. I was playing right field and Joe DiMaggio was playing center, and he called for it. So I put on the brakes and caught my spikes on the rubber cover of a sprinkler head and went down and twisted my knee and tore my ligaments. I just lay there. I thought I'd broken my leg in two and my career was over right there. But they carried me off and took me to the hospital and operated on me. That was the first of four knee operations over the next fifteen years. It was never right again. It still just flops around to this very day. All of my other injuries, and I had them every single year, came from favoring that knee.

So as far as I'm concerned that was the worst thing that could ever have happened to me. It forced me to retire early, and I know I could have set a lot of records that I didn't get a chance to because of my legs. They still cause me pain and problems today, and I'm just hoping they don't get worse.

Joe DiMaggio on Mantle's 1951 World Series injury

I thought he had been shot.

Whitey Ford

Mickey had bad knees all the time he was with the Yankees. Once I was sitting at the bar in the Hotel Cleveland with Bill Kane, and he has this real bad leg—you know, it's a lot thinner than the other one and Bill walks with a limp. Anyway, we were having a few drinks there at the bar, and the way Bill had his legs crossed, his pants were up a little and you could see this tiny, thin ankle on his bad leg.

Then this drunk guy comes up to us at the bar and right away he recognizes me, but he thinks Bill Kane is Mickey Mantle. . . . Kane and

*"I know I could have set a lot of records that I didn't get a chance to because of my legs."
Mickey Mantle, June, 1963, after breaking a bone in his foot. In the foreground, offering a hand, is teammate and roommate Whitey Ford.*

I played along with him and didn't let on that Bill really wasn't Mantle, and this guy keeps talking away.

All of a sudden he looks down, and he sees this thin leg of Bill's and then looks straight up in his face and says, like he got struck with religion, "Mickey, I know you went through a lot of pain but, by God, I don't think the fans around the country realize how bad your legs really are." And after that I always pictured this guy going back to his home town and telling everybody that he met Mickey Mantle and what great courage Mick must've had to run on a leg like that one.

I'll tell you, though, he wasn't too far wrong. If I have any lasting picture of Mickey myself, it's probably a picture of a really strong, powerful guy with all these muscles—and with two of the worst knees you ever saw. Sometimes we'd be sitting and talking or having dinner, and he'd be there sort of rubbing his knees with his hand, and then when it came time to get up and leave, he'd take a long, long while just lifting up out of his chair. I think he was in pain all the time I knew him.[2]

Duke Snider

The great disruption of my career was when the Dodgers left Brooklyn. Baseball-wise, I was *born* in Ebbets Field. The same team was together there for ten years, and we felt like family and Ebbets felt like home. There's only one old ball park left in the National League today—Wrigley Field—so most fans never get to experience the kind of closeness you had in Ebbets. We could carry on running conversations with the fans. Hilda Chester would holler at you till you nodded to her. That sort of thing.

It was a hitter's park, and we were in most games until the final out because we were always a threat to score six or seven runs in any given inning. Mr. Rickey put together a ball club that was tailored to that ball park. The fans rarely left early, I can tell you that.

When Mr. O'Malley decided to move the team to Los Angeles, it hurt all of us to some degree. It was tough to leave those loyal fans and that ball park. Later, when I saw the picture of the steel ball knocking down the outfield wall, I felt like crying.

Then we showed up at the Coliseum, which was essentially a football field—with that spiky grass in the outfield and that long, long shot to right field (430 feet). It was a very frustrating year out there for me individually and for the team. We were already getting old, and the move took *something* from each of us. Our first year out there we dropped to seventh place.

"The move took something from each of us." Duke Snider in his new Los Angeles Dodgers road uniform.

To be fair and complete, though, I have to say that the move benefited the Dodgers in the long run. After Chavez Ravine was built and the team and the city adjusted to each other, Los Angeles proved to be a very fine city for big league baseball. But when the move was first decided on, that was sad.

Whitey Ford

If you were normal you could stay awake half the night worrying about a lot of things in baseball—the team getting old, the manager getting fired, yourself getting traded or even hit in the face by a line drive.

It got worse in 1960 because I was out half the season with a bad arm. But I pitched two shutouts in the Series against Pittsburgh and probably saved myself. My problem was that George Weiss didn't like me and Mickey. . . . Not Mickey—he wouldn't trade him—but me. I was a candidate, I thought.

I didn't worry about getting hit by a ball until one day in Kansas City when Bob Cerv lined one back at me. It was getting dark, and there were a lot of white shirts behind home plate that kept the ball hidden when it was hit.

Cerv belted this one, and the ball shot like a bullet through the middle. It ticked my ear and went into center field. I didn't even realize it *was* the ball until the catcher came out and told me. Then I really started to shake.

They had a lot of white shirts in the background in Vero Beach, too, where the Dodgers trained. So whenever big Frank Howard came up, I'd throw him big slow curves on the inside. I didn't care if he pulled the ball over the palm trees, as long as he didn't smash it back to me.

As for managers, they always lived dangerously. If you were a player you knew you might get traded; if you were a manager you knew you were sure to get fired. Maybe they blamed Casey when we lost the 1960 Series to the Pirates and retired him, but he was already seventy years old then, and you had to admit he'd had one hell of a career. But after Ralph Houk ran the ball club for the next three years, he was promoted to general manager, and they made Yogi the field manager.

I thought Yogi did a hell of a job. I was his pitching coach—both a pitcher and a coach, actually. But we lost the Series that year, it was 1964. I'd pitched only one game, the first of the seven we played. After that I was useless. My hand was getting numb. For that matter, I wasn't much help in the first game, either.

So flying home from St. Louis, Yogi came back to me in the airplane and said, "Will you be my coach again next year?" I said, "Sure, Yog." And he said, "Thanks." And he got fired the next day.

When things cooled down a few days later, I called him up and said, "Thanks for assuring me of my job, Yogi."[3]

Sandy Koufax

[In 1964 Sandy Koufax began experiencing serious arm trouble.]

Anyone could see that the elbow was no problem at all. My record had come up to nineteen and five, and I had won fifteen of my last sixteen decisions. I was actually one full start ahead of my 1963 record.

I never won the twentieth.

When I woke up in the morning I couldn't believe it. I had to drag my arm out of bed like a log. That's what it looked like, a log. A waterlogged log. Where it had been swollen outside the joint before, it was now swollen all the way from the shoulder down to the wrist—inside, outside, everywhere. For an elbow I had a knee; that's how thick it was.

I didn't have more than an inch's worth of movement in any direction. But, just moving it that tiny distance, I could actually hear the sound of liquid squishing around, as if I had a wet sponge in there.

Dr. Kerlan was at the park. He took one look at the arm and drove me down to his office for treatment and X rays.

He had taken other X rays of my elbow through the years, so he had a basis for comparison. After you've pitched for any length of time, the X rays show spurs and a general irregularity brought on by the accumulation of minor injuries to the protective cartilage covering the joint—all the nicks and chips and pulls and tears from the thousands upon

Mark "The Bird" Fidrych, Tiger Stadium, summer, 1976

thousands of times that the hinge has snapped, the sheer wear and tear of pitching.

Dr. Kerlan's test showed that it had passed over the line between temporary damage and permanent trouble. An arthritic change had taken place.[4]

[Faced with the prospect of permanent disability in his left arm, Koufax retired after the 1966 season. He was only thirty years old.]

Al Kaline

I guess the saddest things I've ever seen in baseball are the guys that are cut down in mid-career by freak accidents, and injuries. You may not know them personally, but as an athlete you can identify with them. Like a Roberto Clemente, who at the time of his death was playing the best game of baseball I'd ever seen, or a Harry Agganis or a Herb Score. Or a Mark Fidrych. I won't say he's all through, because he's still trying to come back. The whole team, even the other teams, are all pulling for him to make it, because he's a tremendous guy and he loves playing baseball. We'll just have to wait and see. But in the meantime, what he's gone through in the last four years is *tragic*. And a real loss for baseball too. "The Bird" just *electrified* the fans. It's hard to explain, but everyone in the stands was just so happy and emotional when he pitched. But all the poor kid had was just that one great season.

Hotel . . . taxi . . . train . . . taxi . . .
hotel . . . and then all over again.
—GOOSE GOSLIN in
The Glory of
Their Times, by
Lawrence Ritter

22.

On the Road

Connie Mack

[In the late 1880s, before spring training had become an institution of professional baseball, the Washington Senators worked themselves into shape by playing a series of preseason exhibition games in the Deep South.]

We arrived in Jacksonville, Florida, and went to a hotel to register. The proprietor received us cordially until he found out we were baseball players.

"Sorry," he said, "but we don't take baseball players."

The fact that we were the Washington Senators and came from the nation's capital made no impression whatsoever on hotel clerks.

We went from hotel to hotel, but we always got the same brush-off. Finally, the proprietor of a third-rate hotel agreed to take us, but with this reservation: "I'll take you in on one condition: We can't let baseball players mingle with the other guests."

We weren't even allowed to use the dining room, but were given our meals in a special room. Ted Sullivan, our manager, would put a silver dollar on the table when we sat down and say to the waiter:

"Now go ahead and feed my boys up right."

The waiter's eyes would bulge. He'd bring us fried chicken, corn on the cob, sweet potatoes, corn muffins. When the meal was over Sullivan would pick up the silver dollar and put it back in his pocket. I saw that same silver dollar the whole time we were in the South.

Other teams in those days apparently also ran into difficulties on the road. Once the Cleveland team was quartered in a hotel on a road trip. Ossie Schreck ordered a steak. When it came it was so tough that he couldn't cut it with a knife.

"Waiter," he said, "will you kindly bring me the porter?"

When the porter came hurrying in, Ossie smiled politely. "Porter," he said, "will you kindly bring me a hammer and nail?"

The porter, somewhat perplexed, brought Ossie the articles he had asked for. Ossie got up with considerable pomp, walked ceremoniously across the room, and nailed the steak to the door. It wasn't long before the hotel manager came rushing in and threw the whole team out of the hotel.[1]

Wahoo Sam Crawford

We were considered pretty crude. If we went into the hotel dining room—in a good hotel, that is—they'd quick shove us way back in the corner at the very end of the dining room so we wouldn't be too conspicuous. "Here come the ballplayers!" you know, and back in the corner we'd go.

I remember once—I think it was in 1903—I was with the Detroit club, and we all went into the dining room in this hotel, I believe in St. Louis. We sat there—way down at the end, as usual—for about twenty minutes and couldn't get any waiters. They wouldn't pay any attention to us at all. Remember Kid Elberfeld? He was playing shortstop for us then, a tough little guy. Kid Elberfeld says, "I'll get you some waiters, fellows."

Darned if he didn't take one of the plates and sail it way up in the air, and when it came down it smashed into a million pieces. In that quiet, refined dining room it sounded like The Charge of the Light Brigade. Sure enough, we had four or five waiters around there in no time.[2]

Ty Cobb in 1914

After each game the fan sees the last of the players rushing for the clubhouse no matter how tired they all may be. That's the habit of a big leaguer. But the dash doesn't stop when the threshold of the clubhouse is crossed. Not on your life. It's born into every big leaguer, after he's been in the fast society for a time, to rush at everything he does. Therefore, all the boys dress as rapidly as they can and dig for the hotel when on the road, where they hurtle themselves into the dining room and abuse the waiter if he doesn't rush on the food with the speed of a sprinter. It's the nervous energy wearing off. All through the game a player is keyed up to concert pitch, and this strain breaks after the battle.

The first relaxation comes after dinner, when you'll generally find the man who was hastening most to grab his meal loafing around the lobby doing nothing. But when a ballplayer has something on his mind to be done, he always wants to accomplish it with a rush. It's the same with boarding a train. They all dash into the coaches and rush for their berths as if the berths were going to move away if they didn't flop into them quick. They get sore if there's some hitch in the arrival of their baggage, but train wrecks don't faze veterans to any great extent.[3]

Babe Ruth in 1928

Laymen I know find something fascinating in the thought of a big league ball club traveling around the country. To the outsider those hours on the train together and the hours in the hotels are a sort of magic.

To us they're only routine.

What do we do while traveling?

Here's a typical scene. The club is en route on a long jump, say from St. Louis to New York.

In one section a card game is in session. Meusel and Bengough, Ruether, Koenig, and Lazzeri are playing blackjack. They have their coats off, their collars discarded, and their shirts open at the neck. They're kidding and laughing over the game. The colored porter stands by watching the fun.

Down the car a bit Hoyt sits reading a book. Further on the fussy foursome is busy at bridge. That's Gehrig, Miller, Gazella, and myself.

Shocker is reading the newspapers, and his berth is messed up with a dozen sports pages, torn from as many different papers. Now and then he makes some discovery and pauses to discuss baseball with Pennock, who's writing letters across the aisle.

In an adjoining section Jules Wera is giving the phonograph a workout, and occasionally Koenig pauses in the business of playing cards to lift his voice in the chorus of some song the phonograph is playing.

Pat Collins is busy over a crossword puzzle, and cusses Woodie out when the trainer pesters him about starting a pinochle game. There's the tapping of typewriters as a couple of the newspapermen pound out their yarns for early editions.

Through the open door of the drawing room you can see Huggins, smoking his pipe and talking with O'Leary and Fletcher, his assistants.

Thomas comes along and slaps Wera with a folded paper, and Wera in return smears him with a pillow.

We're all one big gang together. Baseball has had its share of wonderful friendships, and most of them have started aboard rattling old Pullman cars when the boys get a few hours to themselves and have a chance to act natural.[4]

Connie Mack

One of the greatest thrills in my career was when I was delegated to go with the American baseball team to Japan and the Philippines in 1934 to demonstrate our national game.

Babe Ruth managed the all-star team, . . . and Judge Landis asked me to go along as goodwill delegate.

The Japanese were literally crazy about baseball and walked miles to see the American athletes. Every game was sold out at least three weeks in advance. Ruth was their idol.

The Japanese even began to get up before daylight to play at sunrise. One day when we went out about twenty miles from the city to practice in a place where there were no houses, about twenty thousand came to watch us. Where they came from no one knew, but they seemed to spring up from all directions.

Whenever they wanted to address the umpire, the Japanese always took off their hats! On one occasion they had twelve cameras to record our plays, so that they could imitate them later. No Japanese women were permitted to attend the games, however; quite a contrast to this country.

We traveled to Manila. There we learned that the Filipinos were good fielders and good runners, but at that time they had not learned to hit.

They played the game differently than we do. When a pitcher went into the game, he had to show that he was in good condition, so he would stand on the sideline and pitch to the catcher until the crowd was satisfied that he could finish the game. They consider it a dishonor to take a pitcher out of the box.

The Philippine pitcher was an excellent contortionist—but we made twenty-four runs (including several home runs) to their lone one run. Nevertheless, we congratulated them on their remarkable feat of making one run against what we considered the greatest ballplayers in the world.[5]

Charlie Gehringer

Yeah, I was on that trip to Japan. Quite an experience. I liked the Japanese: They were real fans—knew us all from reading their sports pages, I guess. I remember going through the streets of Tokyo in a motorcade and having trouble getting the cars through, there were so many people. It was almost as bad as Detroit after the '35 Series. And they jammed into the ball parks too. It seemed like every day was sold out, and that stadium in Tokyo held sixty thousand people. That place would be filled by the time we were halfway through batting practice.

Ruth was the headliner on that tour, and they really loved the big guy. He'd hit these long home runs during batting practice, and the whole place would go "O-o-oh." He loved it. He liked to clown around a little bit during the games too. He used to play first base sometimes, and when one of their little guys would get on, Ruth would stand up on the bag to emphasize the difference in heights. That never failed to get a big laugh from the crowd. So there was a lot of goodwill. . . .

Cool Papa Bell

In the 1930s and 1940s we were always on the road barnstorming, and it was rough. We'd ride trains, or if it was a little town without no train station, we'd take a bus. They scheduled us as many games as they could fit in. Sometimes we'd play three different games in three different towns in one day. Never changed uniforms all day long.

On weekends, when we could, we'd play in big league parks when the home team was on the road. Other times we played on rough little diamonds in city parks or playgrounds, with hard rocky base paths. Course, I used to run the bases a lot, so I'd get pretty skinned up sliding.

We'd catch up on our napping on the bus between times. We were so tired half the time we could sleep standing up if we had to.

Why'd we do it? For the love of it.

Casey Stengel *retiring for a post-breakfast nap after a grueling overnight trip*
Anybody looking for me, tell 'em I'm being embalmed.

Cool Papa Bell

In the spring of 1937 I was down in New Orleans training with the Pittsburgh Crawfords, and these guys in dark glasses were coming around looking for Satchel. We didn't know nothing about no political thing, but Trujillo, the dictator of the Dominican Republic, was recruiting American boys for his baseball team so he could win the pennant down there and get stronger with his people 'cause the people down there *love* baseball. So they were looking for Satchel. *Everybody* wanted Satchel back in those days. But Satchel didn't want to go. He'd run into the hotel and slip out the side door, hiding from them. But finally they caught him. They blocked the street with their car, so he couldn't get past. They said, "We want you to come down to Santo Domingo."

Satchel said no, no thank you, until they offered him seven thousand dollars—that's what I *heard*—and all his expenses, even for

"Why'd we do it? For the love of it." Cool Papa Bell, August, 1980.

his wife and everything. *That* was a good *offer*, so Satchel, he and his wife, went on down there.

Now, we were having trouble with our owner, Gus Greenlee. He owed me money and wouldn't pay me, and he was even trying to charge the team for spring-training expenses. So we were all ready to quit. One of our boys, Sam Streeter, even put in an application for a factory job. We were all mad at Greenlee.

Meantime, Satchel was doing all right down in the Dominican Republic, and he told them down there about me and some of the other boys, and they called and offered me eight hundred dollars and all expenses for six weeks. I wanted one thousand dollars and they agreed, so I went on down and some of the others did too—[Josh] Gibson, Sam Bankhead, and others. We had to slip out of town. The Dominican Consul gave us half of our thousand when we got to Miami, and we flew from there to a town called San Pedro about forty miles outside of Santo Domingo. Then we had to ride in cars, about twenty-five cars in front of us and behind us, all the way into the city with the sirens going. And all around the streets of Santo Domingo.

Satchel was mighty glad to see us.

They put us up in a private club, with guards to keep the people out and keep us in. The first day we put on our uniforms and went out to practice, the stands were full of people—a big crowd just to watch us practice. The people seemed to like us, but Trujillo's men wouldn't let us go out in the streets but a couple of days a week. They were afraid someone was gonna hurt us. They said we were gonna have to win or it'd be Trujillo's life—and maybe ours. Well, we won that championship down there on the very last day of the season.

Satchel Paige

That was one day Paige was not free and easy.

All we could hear from them fans was warnings about we better win. The more they yelled the harder I threw.

No sooner was the game over than we was hustled back to our hotel, and the next morning when we got up, there was a plane waiting for us, and were we glad to get on board. We never did see President Trujillo again, although that night after the game we were taken to a picnic and showed a nice time.

I read in a newspaper that Dr. Aybar, our manager, says, "Baseball in Trujillo City is not commercial. Money makes no difference. Baseball is spiritual in every respect, as indulged in by Latin races."

I am saving the clipping because I am thinking that if he is right and baseball is spiritual as it is played there, old Satchel could be a spirit right now if we didn't win that big game.[6]

Ted Williams

I liked life on the road. What the hell? I hadn't traveled much, and I was excited to see St. Louis, Detroit, Cleveland, Philadelphia. Bobby Doerr and I used to take long walks all the time. I don't know how many miles we covered—we probably hold the league record—but we walked and talked. We walked everywhere in every American League city and talked about everything under the sun.

Eddie Mathews

The road can be very lonely. Baseball players are lucky, though. They usually have a roommate or a close friend on the team to get together with after the ball game.

Now, since I've gotten out of the playing end and I'm scouting, I travel by myself all the time. That's when I've noticed . . . my children are all grown and I have no one waiting for me back home. So it's become quite lonely.

You know, that's probably why a lot of the ballplayers drink. It's a companionship type of thing. I like to go to a bar and strike up a conversation with somebody. Passes the time.

Mickey Mantle

Me and Whitey made a deal with the Yankees where we'd get our expenses cashed with the club. Also, that we'd have adjoining rooms in the hotels. They'd let us be roommates with separate rooms, and we'd open the adjoining door and turn them into a kind of suite.

The way we worked it out was like I'd sign room service for both of us. I'd get up before Whitey and order breakfast from room service, and sign the check. Then he'd do it for dinner. Like we'd have a night game, say, and the next day would be a night game. I'd always wake up like at eight o'clock in the morning, and he didn't get up till eleven. So I'd order up a cup of coffee or something and a newspaper, and watch TV, and be real quiet till he woke up at eleven o'clock. And when I thought it was near the time for him to get up, why, I'd order breakfast and a paper for him. We'd eat breakfast and sit around and watch TV for a couple of hours, or go to a movie, and that would be our day. Maybe at five o'clock it'd be time to get on the bus and go to the ball game.

Mickey and Whitey, voted into the Hall of Fame together in 1974.

Well, then after the game, most of the time we'd go out and have a few drinks and a dinner.

What I really liked about Whitey, and what he liked about me, was we didn't talk baseball very much.

It bugged me more than it did him—the games did. If I had a bad day it really stayed on my mind.

I don't think I ever remember him worrying about his game. I mean, he always knew he was going to come back out and win the next one. Whereas, if I went into a slump, I imagine it got pretty quiet in the room. I'd worry about it a lot more, it seemed, than he did. And he was good to be around when you were going bad.

I guess my biggest fault in baseball was striking out too much, and that was because when I hit left-handed, I'd uppercut a little bit and swing too hard. He used to tell me, like just before we'd walk out of the room, he'd say, "Come on now, let's see a short, choppy stroke today." He wouldn't go into it too much, just, "Let me see that short choppy stroke."

He wasn't tense before he pitched, but he was maybe different then. He'd never go out the night before he pitched. Most of the time, if he was pitching the next day, he'd even leave the game a little early and go home and go to bed. I wouldn't bother him then. If he hadn't gone to bed when I got home, we might watch the late-night movie on TV or something. I didn't ever ask him to go out with me those nights, I just figured he didn't want to.

But when Whitey pitched he always felt like unwinding that night after the ball game. And that's when most of our breaking would come on. I always felt good, too, especially if he won the game. I was always ready to celebrate it with him. Lucky for both of us, he won like 236 games when he was pitching for the Yankees.[7]

It would be a relief if they'd cut off
the flow of these kids for a while.
They seem to be getting bigger and
stronger every season.
—MICKEY MANTLE
in 1967, *The
Education of a
Baseball Player*

23.

The Veteran

Burleigh Grimes

At the very end of my career I went over to the Yankees, and one of the best things about that was I had an opportunity to pitch to one of the greatest catchers of all time—Bill Dickey. Which brings to mind an incident that tickled me at the time. I'd been there just five days when they put me in for the first time in relief of Johnny Allen. There was a man on first base—Heinie Manush I believe—and no outs. I'd had five days rest, so I had pretty good stuff warming up.

I went into the game, and Bill signaled for the spitter. I broke off a good one, low and away, and it bounced off the edge of his mitt and rolled away. Manush advanced to second. Then Bill gave me that spitter sign again. Ball got away from him again, and Manush moved over to third. Still nobody out.

So I called Bill out to the mound and asked, "What're we gonna throw him now?"

Bill said, "Throw that same goddamn thing and cover the plate."

Bill Dickey

That was the first time I ever caught Burleigh, and he had the widest-breaking spitter I'd ever seen. Also, I'm not offering any alibis, but it was getting dark—I believe it was the ninth inning—and the ball was hard to see. But Burleigh didn't tell you the end of the story. We got the man out. And we won the ball game.

Paul Waner

The last full season that Lloyd and I played together on the Pirates was 1940. That was my fifteenth year with Pittsburgh, and Lloyd's fourteenth. Heck, I was thirty-seven by then, and Lloyd was thirty-four. Of course, we hung on in the big leagues with various teams for about five more years, but that was only on account of the war. . . .

I remember one day when I was with the Boston Braves in 1942. Casey Stengel was the manager. I was supposed to be just a pinch hitter, but in the middle of the summer, with a whole string of doubleheaders coming up, all the extra outfielders got hurt, and I had to go in and play center field every day. Oh, was that ever rough! One doubleheader after the other.

Well, that day—I think we were in Pittsburgh, of all places—in about the middle of the second game, one of the Pittsburgh players hit a long triple to right-center. I chased it down and came back with my tongue hanging out. I hardly got settled before the next guy hit a long triple to left-center, and off I went after *it*. Boy, after that I could hardly stand up.

And then the next guy popped a little blooper over second into real short center field. In I went, as fast as my legs would carry me. Which wasn't very fast, I'll tell you. At the last minute I dove for the ball, but I didn't quite make it, and the ball landed about two feet in front of me and just *stuck* in the ground there. And do you know, I just lay there. I *couldn't* get up to reach that ball to save my life! Finally, one of the other outfielders came over and threw it in.

That's like in 1944, when I was playing with the Yankees. I finished up my career with them. Some fan in the bleachers yelled at me, "Hey Paul, how come you're in the outfield for the Yankees?"

"Because," I said, "Joe DiMaggio's in the army."[1]

Lefty Grove in his last year as a player

I'm throwing the ball just as hard as I ever did. It's just not getting there as fast.

Lefty Gomez

It seemed to me those last years that someone had dug up home plate and moved it back about five yards.

Bob Feller

In my early years I never learned to "pitch," because I didn't think I had to. I figured that even if I walked a few batters, I could power pitch my way out of a jam. By the late forties things were different. I'd lost a lot of my steam, and I realized I had to be a "pitcher" out there, not just a thrower. I learned.

Lou Boudreau

[In 1948 Satchel Paige was finally signed by a big league team after a long, illustrious career in the Negro leagues. That season he contributed significantly to the stretch drive of the Cleveland Indians as they captured their first American League pennant since 1920.]

The legendary Satchel Paige became a member of the Cleveland organization on July 7 and promptly made headlines all over America.

He was a fairy tale in the flesh, a regular Paul Bunyan whose feats with a baseball were passed around the countryside by word of mouth as much as by the printed page. Every baseball writer in the land fell eagerly upon the dramatic story.

Naturally, the reaction to Paige's signing was not completely favorable. A lot of people complained that [Bill] Veeck was just up to his old publicity tricks, that he knew Paige was too old to be a winning major league pitcher, and that he was just bent on exploiting Satch's name for a few more dollars at the gate. Such was not the case. Bill signed Paige because we needed another pitcher, preferably one with sharp control who could be of service as a relief man and a spot starter. Satchel was signed for what he could do, not for what he could draw.[2]

Satchel Paige in 1948

Age is a question of mind over matter. If you don't mind, age don't matter.

Buck Leonard

In 1952 I was playing down in Mexico, and I got a call from Bill Veeck, who was owner of the St. Louis Browns at that time. He wanted to know would I like to play for his team. I said no thank you. I was forty-five years old, too old to play major league ball full time. It was all right to play in Mexico where we only had three games a week and the competition was not so rough. But not major league. He said, "I'm gonna call you back tomorrow evening," but I still told him no. He even wanted me to come up to L.A. for spring training.

I was supposed to ask Bill Veeck for a job, and he was going to give it to me. In that way, he wouldn't be accused of recruiting me for publicity. But I told him no. My *legs* were too old. You know, your legs will always tell your true age. He said, "You don't have to play the field. We just want you to pinch-hit." But I didn't want that—to bat just once in a game.

Now, if they'd had the DH back then, I might've gone. . . .

Satchel Paige in 1952

Man, I'm a hundred years old and I can still strike these guys out.

Al Kaline in 1969

Sometimes I wonder what I'm doing, if I've wasted my time all these years. And sometimes I think I have.

I would like to have more to contribute to society. I don't know, maybe a doctor. Something where you really play an important part in people's lives.

But I never had much education. I'd always wanted to be in the big leagues, since I was a kid. And boom—I was there before I knew it.

Once in a while I'll sit in the dugout and look out on the field and wonder what good is all this, thinking about me, me, me, my batting average, my fielding average. Oh, sure, you care about the team. You have to. But in the end you're worried about you.

"A fairy tale in the flesh." Satchel Paige in the early 1950s with the old St. Louis Browns.

·So I have to think of myself as an entertainer, really. Maybe kids can draw an inspiration from what I do. Maybe people who come out to the park can forget their problems for a while. . . .

But don't get me wrong. A ball game is never a bore to me. Oh, geez, it's great. I love it. Every day there's something new: a ground ball you just beat out, the throw from the outfield to catch a runner.

And for me, as an entertainer, I'd have to be classified as a straight actor. I've always made it on ability alone. No gimmicks. A player like Norm Cash does funny things on the field, talking to fans, catching throws behind his back between innings. It relieves tension for him. I've never needed that kind of outlet.

I'm there and I do the job. Nothing great. But there is no phase of the game I don't do well. I've never been a one-way player.

I was a very good outfielder. I'm still a good outfielder, but I don't run as fast as I used to and I don't throw as well. And I used to beat out twelve to fourteen hits a season in the hole at shortstop. Now I'm lucky to beat out one or two a season. But even though I've been a .300 hitter, I don't think I was too much with the bat. . . .

I feel great so far this season. But the hot weather is coming and that tires me some. I'll play next year for sure. After that, I don't know. I'll sure miss baseball and the people in it. And when I'm done and gone, I think I would like for people to say, "Al Kaline? He was a real good outfielder." [3]

[Kaline retired after the 1974 season.]

Stan Musial

The first few years of my career were my happiest because we were young and winning pennants. Beating the Yankees in the '42 Series, *that* was exciting. We had a good spirited club, happy-go-lucky. Red [Schoendienst] was a good roomie, very compatible, very easygoing. And he got a lot of hits and won a lot of games, and I did too. So that was a happy time being around Red and those guys. Those early years when you're going up the ladder in skill, and salary too, and you've got some youngsters at home, those are the happy days.

In the fifties it was very different, especially from '55 on. I was getting older, and our club went way down. So it was harder to play. It's easier and more fun to win. Everyone's relaxed. When you're losing you feel like you should be doing more than you are, and you press. So it's tougher mentally, and don't forget you spend more time out on the field, so it's tougher physically, too. Day in and day out, night games, hot, cold, all kinds of weather, it can get to be a *very* long season, especially, as I say, on a second division club. So I think I probably would've enjoyed baseball a whole lot more if the bad clubs had come in the forties and the pennants had come later. We won pennants my first three years. I guess it would've been preferable if they'd come when I was a veteran and could really appreciate them fully.

But don't misunderstand me, I'm not complaining. There were lots of compensations. When I was thirty-five, thirty-six, thirty-seven, thirty-eight, I was still winning some batting titles and fielding well and hitting more home runs than ever. That homer swing was something I learned with experience. When I was young I used to punch the ball around to left and left-center and not try to pull. I'd get a better look at the pitch, and also I'd beat out a lot of those bouncers and rollers to the left. As years passed, I gained confidence and learned to pull the ball when I wanted to go for power. Ralph Kiner came up in the late forties and started to hit home runs, more than anyone else, and pretty soon he was getting more money than anyone else. Well, that got me thinking. And after 1947, 1948, I started swinging for the fences. I guess I lost fifteen to twenty points on my average, but I developed a capability to help the team in certain situations. It wasn't that I got bigger and stronger. I was always around 175. I just gained the maturity to direct the ball to right field. The secret of hitting homers is just flipping the ball over to that general direction. You don't have to swing as hard as you can. Ebbets Field, the Polo Grounds, Philadelphia, St. Louis—they all had short right-field fences. I guess it's not as easy as it sounds, though.

Ernie Banks was another guy who learned the secret of hitting home runs. He learned to just drop them over the fence in left-center in Wrigley Field.

Aaron was another one. When he was young, he'd hit hard *liners* all over the lot. As he matured, he learned to pull those long fly balls to left. So, there are some compensations as you become a veteran.

Actually, I didn't begin to think of this game of baseball as work until I got to be about forty. Those last couple of years it was much harder to get in shape and stay in shape. After a doubleheader I'd be stiff for two days. My reflexes wouldn't bounce back like they used to, and I had a much harder time getting loose. The ball looked smaller, especially at night, and I had a harder time generating that good quick swing or that burst of speed in the field. So the last couple of years *were* work.

And I should mention this too: Mentally, my concentration wasn't quite as sharp. You should concentrate intensely on every single pitch, but after age forty, my mind would occasionally wander.

I'd swing at balls for no reason and then wonder why I had. Whereas when I was *really* concentrating I was hitting only the pitches I wanted to hit. So it's a mental problem.

This is hard to explain. When I was younger I would listen to my subconscious, and my subconscious would always tell me what the pitcher was trying to do. It was an amazing thing. In the field, too.

*The veteran: Stan Musial in the
early 1960s*

Depending on the exact situation, the weather, who the pitcher was, the inning, the number of outs, the count, my subconscious *knew* what was coming, and it *never* deceived me. So I believe in the subconscious mind in athletics.

After I turned forty my subconscious tried to tell me what was coming, but I'd lost that perfect concentration, and I'd doubt my subconscious. It was a sad thing, but I just couldn't keep that same concentration going forever.

> I'm getting out of the game before
> I'm carried out.
> —BABE RUTH in
> 1934

24.

Hanging It Up

Grover Cleveland Alexander

I lasted long in the big leagues—twenty seasons—and won more games than any other National League pitcher except Christy Mathewson. But I should have had more. I don't feel sorry for myself, or excuse my drinking. I guess I just had two strikes on me when I came into the world. My father back in Nebraska was a hard drinker before me, and so was my grandfather before him. Sure, I tried to stop—I just couldn't. But I'd still go on winning games until I was forty-two. That's when I was suspended by Bill McKechnie in August, 1929.

The next year St. Louis traded me back to Philadelphia, my first big league club. The Phillies, as usual in those days, had a bad club, and at forty-three I didn't have much stuff left on the ball. . . . By the time they released me in mid-season, I hadn't been able to pick up my 374th win. I was none and three and was still tied with Matty. I pitched a little for Dallas after that, and then I grew a beard and qualified to pitch for a House of David team. I still could get batters out, and it did bring in groceries for our table.[1]

Frank Frisch

There are games you remember happily and those you recall sadly. Many of the sad ones come in the twilight of a career, but there are ones you still can laugh about. There was the game in late May in Philadelphia when we were having our troubles and I wasn't in the lineup very often, largely on account of old Father Time. I was playing second base that afternoon, and I was on second, with Terry Moore on first, when one of our sluggers, Joe Medwick I suppose, lined one to the center-field corner of the park. Mike Gonzalez was coaching third, and after a fleeting glance to see if the ball might be caught, I took off for third and home. Mike, excited as usual, was giving me directions and giving them to Moore at the same time.

"You come, Frank," Mike yelled. "You come, he go."

Well, I didn't pay much attention to what "he" was doing. I was running with all I had, and it wasn't much at that late day, I must confess. I finally slid for the plate, made it safely, and before I was through with my slide I felt a foot against my bottom. It was Moore sliding in behind me. He had made up ninety feet on the Old Flash in the race for the plate. I knew then that it was time to do something about it. So I told Jimmy Brown he was our second baseman from there on in.

Then there was my last major league base hit.

It was August 4, 1937, and we weren't going very well. We were playing the Boston club, at that time nicknamed the Bees, at Sportsman's Park, and we were trailing by five runs in the ninth inning, with Terry Moore on first base. Johnny Mize singled and Joe Medwick doubled. Don Padgett singled, and when Don Gutteridge came through with another one-base hit, sending Padgett to third and taking second himself on the throw, we had the tying and winning runs in scoring position. I sent in Pepper Martin to bat for Leo Durocher, and naturally Pepper was walked intentionally, filling the bases.

Jim Turner replaced Guy Bush on the mound, and I started scanning my depleted bench for a pinch hitter to go to the plate for my pitcher. While I was looking, somebody in the stands—or it may have been in the Bees' dugout—yelled in a high falsetto, "Why don't you hit, Grandma?"

That burned me up. I grabbed a bat, went up to the plate, and when Turner's first pitch was in there I hit it over first baseman Elbie Fletcher's head for a game-winning, two-run single. And the Cardinals were so happy about it that they carried Grandma off the field. What a way to get your last base hit![2]

Goose Goslin

My last year was 1938. The Tigers released me in May, and Clark Griffith heard about it and called me up. He was a wonderful man, always helpful and kind. He wasn't like a boss, more like a father.

"You started with me eighteen years ago," he said, "why don't you come back to Washington and finish up with me?"

So I did. I went back to the Senators for the rest of that season. Didn't play too much, though. Couldn't gallop around in that pasture like I used to twenty years before. Fact is, I didn't even complete my last time at bat. Lefty Grove was pitching against us—he wasn't any spring chicken anymore, either—and I swung at a low outside pitch and wrenched my back.

Bucky Harris was back managing Washington again—Bucky had been my manager there from 1924 to 1928, the best manager I ever played for, and I played for quite a few. So Bucky had to send in a pinch hitter to finish out my turn at bat.

"Come on out, Goose," he said, "and rest up a bit."

That was the last time I ever picked up a bat in the big leagues. It was also the first and only time a pinch hitter was ever put in for the old Goose.[3]

Lou Gehrig in the clubhouse after he ended his record consecutive-game streak—May 2, 1939

I decided on it Sunday night. I knew after Sunday's game that I ought to get out of there. I got up four times with men on base. Once there were two on. A hit any of those times would have won us the ball game. But I left all five men on. . . . McCarthy's been swell about it. He'd let me go until the cows came home, he's that considerate of my feelings. Well, maybe a rest will do me good.[4]

Joe Cronin, player-manager of the Boston Red Sox in the early 1940s

Lefty Gomez to Lou Gehrig on May 2, 1939

Hell, Lou, it took them fifteen years to get you out of the ball game. Sometimes they get *me* out of there in fifteen minutes.

Lefty Grove

When I got to 275, I said, "By gosh, I'm gonna win three hundred or bust." And when I got number 300 in Boston in 1941—I beat Cleveland 10–5—then that was all. Never won another game.

I knew it was time to go. You know how your old body feels. I just couldn't do it anymore. I wouldn't even go to a ball game for a couple years after that. I didn't coach anywhere—had plenty of offers—just had nothing to do with baseball. Not a thing. I just stayed up in the mountains and went down to the river and fished.

If I had to do it all over, I'd do the same thing. If they said, "Come on, here's a steak dinner," and I had a chance to go out and play a game of ball, I'd go out and play the game and let the steak sit there. I would.[5]

Joe Cronin

My last year as a regular was 1941. I'd slowed way down, though I could still see the ball as clearly as ever when I was hitting. But [John] Pesky came up in '42, and it was time to step down. The only thing that prolonged my career really was the advent of the war. I hung on mainly as a pinch hitter. I used to send myself up to pinch-hit whenever the wind was blowing out from home plate.

But it's a strange thing, in the spring of 1945 I got myself into the best condition in years. We trained in Plainfield, New Jersey, that year out on a high school field, but in spite of the chilly conditions, I worked hard and followed a strict diet and felt very good. Until the second game of the season when I broke my leg sliding into second base. At that point, the fact that I was manager of the team came in quite handy. I never played another game, but I still had myself a pretty good job, managing from the bench.

Cool Papa Bell

After I retired, I went back to St. Louis, went to work for the city, first as a custodian and then as a night watchman. Even after I quit, people still were after me to play. The Browns in 1951 tried to get me to play. I went down there to see Satchel Paige. Bill Norman, who used to play against us before going to the major league, saw me, said, "You want to play ball?"

I said, "No."

The secretary for the Browns came over. Norman said, "Yeah, man, he plays better than anyone we got out there now in the outfield."

The secretary said, "Is that Bell you're talking about? Cool Papa Bell?"

Norman said, "Yes."

He said, "Come on over here and sign this contract, and I'll put you on the field right now."

I said, "I don't want to play."

He said, "Can you hit?"

That's all I *could* do then. My legs were bad, I had varicose veins, I couldn't run. He said, "What are you hitting?"

I said, "I'm hitting .700 there with this farm team. All I can do is hit now. I can't catch the ball the other fellow hits."

He tried to get me to play, but I couldn't. I mean, I couldn't run, I'd get tired. I was forty-eight years old! They said, "You mean you're older than Satchel Paige is?"

I said, "Yes, I'm older than he is."

People told me I should have tried for the job just for the money, but I couldn't. I never had any money, so I never worried about it. I just didn't want the fans to boo me, and if I had played at that age they sure would have. Sometimes pride is more important than money.[6]

Casey Stengel in 1960, the day he was fired as manager of the Yankees

I commenced winning pennants when I came here but I didn't commence getting any younger. . . .

They told me my services were no longer desired because they wanted to put in a youth program as an advance way of keeping the club going. I'll never make the mistake of being seventy years old again.

Robin Roberts

I stayed with the Phillies until 1961. I went to the Yankees in '62, but never pitched for them. They released me at the end of April, which is a bad time to get released, since everybody is pretty much set. So I came home. I didn't know what to do. I was thirty-four years old.

I got a phone call. It's Cy Perkins [former pitching coach at Philadelphia].

"What are they trying to do to you, kid?" he asks.

"What do you mean?"

"Don't you let them drive you out of this game. You'll be pitching shutouts when you're forty."

"Cy, you son of a gun," I said.

"I'm telling you, kid, don't you quit."

So I went to Baltimore and had some fine years there. My first year in the American League I was second in earned-run average. I pitched another five years in the big leagues—thanks to Cy's phone call.

Cy passed away a year later, but his encouragement had helped get me back into the big leagues.

Robin Roberts, the Phillies' pitching ace during the 1950s

I stayed with Baltimore until August of '65, when I went to Houston. I pitched well there, but found my arm swelling up when I threw curveballs. I had an operation that winter to correct the problem. The next year I tried to pitch but the arm wasn't right. So they released me, and I went to the Cubs and finished out the year as a pitching coach. They wanted me back the next year, but I didn't go.

After resting all winter my arm felt good. So I decided I'd go to Reading in the Eastern League and pitch until June 1, and if nobody picked me up, then I'd go home and pack it in. I was forty years old now. I did all right, won five, lost three, pitched a shutout. But June 1 came and nobody had picked me up. So I quit.

As I was driving home that night, I knew it was over. I thought about Cy. I thought, Well, Cy, you son of a gun, you said I'd pitch a shutout when I was forty, but you didn't tell me what league it was going to be in.

So I came home smiling.[7]

Eddie Mathews

In 1968 I was with Detroit, and hell, I was feeling great! I was in *good* shape, swinging the bat, and giving Norm Cash a good run for the first-base job. One night in Anaheim Stadium I hit 2 home runs, number 511 to tie Mel Ott and number 512 to break his record. Mayo

Smith, the Tiger manager, said, "OK, Mathews, you got the job. As long as you can hack it."

But the next morning I woke up in my hotel room and I could *not* straighten up. I don't know what the hell I did or how the hell I did it, but I was in the hospital in traction for twelve days, and then I started to lose all feeling in my leg, and they had to do a disc operation.

So I was out most of the rest of that season. I was a cheerleader on the bench until the last couple of weeks when I was well enough to play again. We won the pennant, and I pinch-hit once and played one game in the World Series.

After the Series, I said, "Well, I'm thirty-eight years old, and I think I'll go out on top." So I hung it up. I'd seen some of my friends like Warren Spahn play too long and embarrass themselves, and I didn't want that. But looking back on it now I wish I'd gone to spring training again the next year. I could've played another year or two, because the back has *never* bothered me since. But I was having some marital problems at the time and thought, Go out on top. You've got a nice job as a manufacturer's representative. Shit, the job turned out to be a real disappointment. It wasn't as good as playing ball, that's for sure. In fact, *nothing* is. And I believe that being home all the time cost me the marriage.

So if I'd known then what I know now, I'd've said, "Hey, I'm going to spring training. I'll see you in a year." And I'd probably still be married.

Mickey Mantle

One thing that disappointed me was that I lost my .300 lifetime average during my last four years. 'Cause I knew I was a .300 hitter. But my last four years I just tailed off. Actually I should have retired when I was thirty-three years old. I was through. My legs were shot. I couldn't run. I couldn't hit left-handed, because my leg would give way on me. I never hit over about .270 those last four years. I could still hit home runs, but otherwise I just couldn't play.

If I had it to do all over again, I would have trained harder and taken better care of myself, not drank and caroused so much. I'd have played better my last four years and probably lasted longer in the big leagues. I was only thirty-six years old when I had to quit—which is practically the prime of life. And that hurts—when you have to quit doing the work you love at an age where other men are just hitting their prime.

I'll tell you something. They examined all my organs. Some of them are quite remarkable, and others are not so good. A lot of museums are bidding for them.

> —CASEY STENGEL in 1960, meeting the press after a brief hospital sojourn

Just had a triple bypass operation. Only triple I ever got.

> —LEFTY GOMEZ in 1980, as reported in *The Hartford Courant*

Part Three

THE

OLD-TIMER

Joyless in Mudville

For each generation today's game
becomes tomorrow's nostalgia.
—MONTE IRVIN in
The Ball Parks,
by William
Shannon

AFTER THE DUST

HAS CLEARED

Hack Wilson, home run hitter

Youth is the life of baseball—and
we can't keep our youth forever.
—BABE RUTH in
1928, *Babe
Ruth's Own
Book of Baseball*

25.

Is There Life After
Baseball?

Babe Ruth

I wanted to stay in baseball more than I ever wanted anything in my
life.

But in 1935 there was no job for me, and that embittered me.

I felt completely lost at first. I thought I'd wake up and find it was a
bad dream, and when it became apparent that it wasn't a dream I felt
certain that the phone would ring telling me it was all a mistake. But
the phone didn't ring.

I went to a lot of games at the stadium at first, from habit I guess.
But it wasn't the same.

So after a while I began staying away from the stadium. I turned to
golf and played every possible hour of the day. Without it I would have

blown up to three hundred pounds. Without it, also, I would have gone nuts.

Instinctively, I returned to St. Pete in the late winter of 1935, as I had done for so many years before that. But, once again, sitting in the stands was a poor substitute for being a part of the Yankees. They'd call on me every once in a while, at a game, and I'd stand up in my box and wave. The people were kind and would cheer, and I'd sit down— wishing I could get out there and really give them something to cheer about.[1]

Fred Lindstrom

I'll always remember the time I saw Hack Wilson in a nightclub act in Chicago. Some friends and I had played handball together one evening on Madison Street, and afterwards we decided to go someplace for a drink and a bite to eat. So we went into a nightclub on the Near North Side on Rush Street. It was a great big barnlike place, and there weren't more than twenty couples in the whole establishment. Well, it seems Hack was the star performer that evening. He saw me and came over to the table and sat down with us for a drink. Finally, the drums started to roll, calling him up on stage, so he went up there and sang "Take Me Out to the Ball Game." Mercifully, they played the music quite loudly, so you couldn't hear much of Hack.

He'd only been out of baseball a couple of years, but he was going downhill. It was very sad, because he was such a fine fellow. I'd always liked Hack quite a bit—most people did—and what a hitter!

But after he lost his ability to hit home runs . . .

Dizzy Dean

[After Dean retired from the playing field, he became one of baseball's most popular early radio announcers in spite of criticism from some over his idiosyncratic use of the English language. The inventor of such immortal baseball terms as "slud," "overswang," and "slugger's fest" cheerfully dismissed his detractors pointing out that "a lot of folks that ain't saying 'ain't,' ain't eating." In 1948 he further elaborated upon his media philosophy.]

I've always said it pays to be a character, especially on radio. Since I was young people has tried to tell me that modesty is the best policy, and that a fellow of genuine ability don't have to show himself off. Don't ever believe it! I've seen plenty of people that gots lots on the ball but no fans in the bleachers. They don't get the pretty gal or the heavy dough. They don't get elected president or nothing. And do you know what their trouble is? They just don't have enough confidence in theirself.[2]

Joe Cronin

After I broke my leg and ended my days as a player, I continued as bench manager of the Red Sox. My first full year as a bench manager, 1946, was a real high point because we won the pennant that year. That was the first pennant in Boston since 1918, so we were the big heroes of the city that year.

Meanwhile, Eddie Collins, the Red Sox general manager, was having trouble with his heart, and I was gradually assuming more and more of his work, under his direction. Finally, at the end of 1947, Tom Yawkey asked me to come up to the front office to stay.

When I took over the general managership I found that I missed the field terribly, but I schooled myself to stay away from it. It was my idea to hire my old friend Joe McCarthy, who'd been such a great manager of the Cubs and Yankees. We knew that with Joe the ball club on the field was in great hands, and I just divorced myself completely from what took place during the ball games. I had to do it. . . .

There were many things I was proud of during my years as general manager. It's true that we didn't win any pennants, but we could easily have won a couple. In '48 we finished the season in a tie with Cleveland and lost the famous play-off game. And the next year, 1949, we went down to the final day of the season with New York. So you can't come much closer than we did those two years.

As general manager you have your farm director, but essentially you're the overseer of the whole shooting match—just a real tedious twenty-four hours a day, twelve months a year job. A lot of details. A lot of committee work. A great job, though, for a baseball team.

Tom Yawkey was a wonderful man to work for. From 1947 to 1958, when I was elected league president and left the Red Sox with Mr. Yawkey's blessing, we never signed a written contract. Everything was based on a handshake. We trusted each other completely. He was not only the team *owner*. He was the team's number one *fan*. He threw every pitch and swung at every ball for the Boston Red Sox. Even worked out with the team regularly. And he kept us on our toes in that front office, morning, noon, and night. He'd call you anytime, out of the blue, and ask you what was going on in Roanoke, Virginia. "Did you see where that second baseman on Roanoke got three hits? Is he a right-hand hitter or a lefty?" Quite a man. And those were good years.

They couldn't *compare* with playing on the field, though. After all, all the fun and excitement is on the field. When all is said and done the game begins and ends on the field.

Fred Lindstrom

I retired from the Dodgers in '36 and tried my hand in a few business ventures—developed a lake up in Wisconsin, invested in a new

Fred Lindstrom in 1980. INSET: *with the Cubs in 1935.*

improved light bulb—but they never amounted to as much as I'd anticipated. I kept coming back to baseball. I spent a couple of years in radio, sports announcer for WLS in Chicago, and then managed a minor league team for a year. And most importantly I coached the baseball team at Northwestern from 1948 to 1961, where I was lucky enough to have all my three sons with me.

My son Andy was signed by the Phillies in his third year at Northwestern, but the draft board grabbed him and then he got married, so he never pursued baseball professionally. He's been a teacher and writer down through the years. My son Chuck, who was my catcher at Northwestern, actually made it to the major leagues—for one game—and batted 1.000. What he did was, the first time up he hit a sacrifice fly, and then he walked and tripled. So officially he's one for one. That was at the end of the 1958 season. The White Sox had him up for a cup of coffee.

He never pursued it either, though. Like Andy, he got a girl, and he was more interested in getting married and being with her than in making the sacrifices necessary to pursue baseball. I thought he was a marvelous prospect, but once a boy loses interest . . .

But Chuck has become quite a successful college coach at Lincoln

College in Illinois, and he's connected with big league ball again in a completely different capacity. He has a product called Diamond Dry, which they use to dry athletic fields after rain. Eight of the major league teams are using the stuff now. He also represents a light company which specializes in lighting for ball parks, playgrounds, and so on. So baseball is still very important in our family.

To complete the story of my career after baseball—in 1958 I had an opportunity to become postmaster of Evanston, Illinois, and I took it. Held that position until 1972, when I retired with a pension and moved to Florida. We'd prepared for the move and the post office sweetened the pot, so it worked out quite well. My wife wanted to go back to Illinois at one point. She wanted to be near her sons and their families, but she eventually realized this was best. *They* have their own families and their own lives, and *we* have everything *we* need right here. I have everything *I* want anyway. We have so many nice friends around here, and they're all more or less in the same class and they all more or less want the same thing—a place to quietly pass their last days away. This is it, and we all try to help each other along.

Billy Herman

I missed the 1944 and 1945 seasons to World War II, and when I returned in 1946, I never could get back into decent shape again. So I played that year and that was it. I was thirty-eight.

The next year, 1947, I was managing the Pittsburgh Pirates. What a fiasco that was! I tried to treat my players the way I'd wanted to be treated as a player, and it wasn't until too late that I realized that was a complete mistake. I should've realized it long before, and I don't blame anybody but myself. I was a highly motivated player on teams that were usually in contention. These guys were okay, most of them, but there were a few foul balls and bad actors in the group, and the team was way down in the second division. So there was no morale. No discipline. And I got fired at the end of the season.

Next I managed Minneapolis in the American Association. Then I decided I'd try to play just a little bit longer and went out to the Coast League, where I played one season as a utility infielder.

Then I got an offer from the Dodgers to coach, and I came back up to the big leagues. Spent six years with that organization—the best organization in baseball—and then went over to Milwaukee, where I was a coach on those great teams of the late fifties. Then in 1960 I came to the Red Sox and coached for a few years until they asked me to replace Johnny Pesky as manager. I managed all of '65 and most of '66 up there, and even though they let me go, I'm satisfied in my own mind that I contributed quite a bit to the development of that team that surprised everybody and won the pennant in '67. I helped cultivate a lot of those kids. It was tough on the manager there though because Yawkey babied some of the players—like Yaz. He was Yawkey's boy; and if he was mad about something, he'd just go through the motions. Best player in the league—when he was in the mood. Nothing much the manager could do really. Yaz and Yawkey were buddy-buddies. Son of a gun messed me up a few times. I hear Yaz has changed now. Shame he didn't do it fifteen years ago. . . .

After I left the Sox I coached a year for the Angels and then became a scout. Did that until just recently. So I managed to stay in the game at the major league level right on through just about. It's been *very* interesting, and I guess I've picked up some knowledge that can provide some basis for comparisons.

As I said, the Dodgers have the best organization in baseball. The six years I was there we were fighting for the pennant every year—this was in the early fifties. Every so often somebody'd get hurt, and we'd have to bring up a replacement from the minors. All you had to do was show him the signs and he was ready to go out there and play like a ten-year veteran. The Dodgers drill on fundamentals at every level of their operation from Class D on up. Fundamentals, every day, every day, every day, until it's automatic. The kids get awful sick of it, but it pays off. They play good fundamental baseball. Another thing that helps—they have a standard book on fundamentals that *everyone* in their organization follows. So there's consistency as the player advances up the chain, and after three or four years he knows how to play baseball—the Dodgers way.

Now the Braves were a little different. They'd bring a kid up from the minors, and he didn't even know how to put his uniform on.

Then I went to the Red Sox, and they were even worse. *Nobody* knew the fundamentals—not even the veterans. They reminded me of that Pirate team, my first year managing, back in '47. Cutoffs, relays, they didn't know anything.

So I saw the best and the worst. During the years I was involved I kind of longed for the challenge of managing more than just the three seasons I did manage; but looking back if I had it to do again, I think I'd choose coaching. It's easier on you. And then, my thoughts on baseball are a lot different from most of the younger players—I think that happens in every walk of life—and there's a lot that goes on now that you just have to grit your teeth and turn your head and act like you don't see it. It's easier to do that when you're coaching than when you're the manager.

Luke Appling

I could've gone with the Yankees toward the end, but the White Sox wouldn't give me my release. Casey [Stengel] wanted me to come over and play for him—guaranteed me a raise and that he'd carry me through that year and the next.

"I hear Yaz has changed now."
Carl Yastrzemski in *1980*.

I talked it over with Paul Richards (White Sox general manager).
Told him that I knew they wanted to rebuild and that I was just holding a spot they could give to a young player. But they wouldn't release
me. I either had to stay in Chicago and play or go manage Memphis in
the Southern League. I chose Memphis.

Had three good years down there, but I guess I got spoiled. They let
me run the club without interference, which I never again found to be
the case with any of the clubs I managed later. The owner said to me,
"The only time you'll see me in your office is when I come down there
to congratulate you for winning the Dixie Series." Which I did the next
year. I loved it down there. All-day ball games and nice *hot* weather.
Good place for sore-arm pitchers to make their comebacks. We had our
share of *them*; but I loved it—for three years.

Why'd I leave? 'Cause young Comiskey, the kid, beat me out of a
five-thousand-dollar bonus he was supposed to pay me. We'd shaken
it, but he went back on his word, so I left and told him I'd never sign
another contract with him. I could've went to the commissioner and
got my money, but I just didn't want to have anything more to do with
it.

So I went over to manage Richmond. That was 1953. I won't go into all the details, but I had many good years in baseball from then on—mostly managing in the minors, coaching for the Tigers, Indians, and A's, and doing a lot of special-assignment scouting. Even *managed* the A's for a few weeks. Look it up in the baseball record book, you'll see I didn't make a very good record. Wasn't much I *could* do. There's a story behind that.

See, I worked for Charley Finley for six years as a coach and scout and instructor for minor league players. I loved the guy. He was good to me. Just don't lie to him.

But in '67 he slipped up on my blind side. I was working with the Peninsula Club in North Carolina. One night about 3:00 A.M. the phone rang. It was Charley. He said, "Luke, I've got a big favor to ask of you."

"What is it, Charley?"

"It's a *big* favor?"

"What is it, Charley?"

"A big *big* favor?

I said, "What bar are you in?"

He said darkly, "I'm in *no bar*." Then I knew he was serious. I asked him again. "What's the favor, Charley?"

He said, "I've seen fit to fire Alvin Dark. I want you to come out here and baby-sit the team for the rest of the season."

Well, I agreed, but believe me I was glad when that season was over. I was right in the middle of a *war*. See, I helped raise all those kids in the minor league system—[Sal] Bando, [Rick] Monday, [Bert] Campaneris, [Catfish] Hunter, [Reggie] Jackson, Blue Moon Odom—so I cared about them. But Charley made me promise not to help them. "Just baby-sit," he said. "I don't want you to even have a team meeting." See, he was *mad* at them, because they were bringing a lawsuit against him. Some silly thing . . .

Well, I called a meeting. Told them they didn't have a leg to stand on. They said they'd think about it. But they didn't. Then some stool pigeon told Charley about the meeting, and *he* gave me hell.

Then that damn Monday blasted me and said I was a horseshit manager. Twelve years later he told me he realized he should've listened to me. But at the time he was mad. And Jackson. You could put him in a cement block and he'd still find some way to get in trouble with his mouth. He was as good a ballplayer as anyone, but believe me, he could've been better. Monday too. If they'd stuck to baseball.

Oh, it was a mess. I was glad when that season ended. That was my last managing.

I'm pretty much retired today. Still work with the kids some, the kids in the Braves system. Go to spring training every year. I take my wife, and the club picks up all expenses. So it works out well. *I* enjoy it. Keeps me young.

Joe Cronin

It was February 1959 I took over from Mr. [Will] Harridge as president of the American League. I felt it was quite an honor and I thought I'd like the job. Served from '59 to '73. Since '73, I've been chairman of the board. That's largely a figurehead position, which suits me just fine.

The president's office is more or less a clearinghouse for the league. You're more of a coordinator than a boss. The one thing you always have to concern yourself with as president is to protect the rights of the players to unobstructed progress. The draft and waiver rules are all set up to prevent anyone from retarding the progress of the players. You keep track of every player's movements.

And then you're in charge of the umpires, and that's a real headache because *no one likes* the *umpires*. And there's so much rivalry among the clubs in the league, and you're always trying to help settle disputes. It can be a lot of pressure. And you have to be impartial.

The Chairman of the Board: Joe Cronin in 1980

In spite of my strong connections with the Washington and Boston clubs I had to treat them just like the rest, and I had to treat Griffith and Yawkey just like the other owners. Of course, Mr. Yawkey was vice-president of the league, so he certainly understood. We worked closely on *many* league matters.

The job had too many bosses, though—eight—and then after expansion—ten. Before they'd say "Hello" they'd say, "Why don't you do this?"

I was fortunate though to have much good counsel during the years—Mr. Yawkey, Mr. Harridge—my predecessor, and a few trusted newsmen. Sports editors. Whitman of the Boston *Herald*, John Kieran of *The New York Times*, Arthur Sampson, Dan Parker, and Fred Lieb. So even though I found myself up to my neck in controversy at times during those fourteen years in office, I never felt alone.

Roy Campanella

I had my car accident during the winter between the 1957 and 1958 seasons. I was planning on a big year out there in the Los Angeles Coliseum with that short left-field fence, and I'd promised Mr. O'Malley I was still gonna be with him in '61 when he opened the stadium at Chavez Ravine. He'd flown me over the site in a helicopter and showed me scale models. Gee, that's a pretty park! So I was happy about those things, and I was flying out to Los Angeles every couple of weeks to help Mr. O'Malley sell tickets. Until the accident.

At first, when I came to in the hospital, I thought I was still gonna be able to get better and get back to playing. But gradually it dawned on me that I was paralyzed. Oh, that was an awful feeling. The doctors told me my spinal cord had been damaged. All I could do was pray to the good Lord to help me accept my situation. I've been working on that for twenty years now. Rehabilitating.

I feel I've been pretty lucky. I received wonderful care in the hospital and in therapy, and I'm able to live a good life. I have to thank the O'Malleys as much as anybody. After my injury, gee, Mr. O'Malley stood right by my side, and in later years his son, Peter, stood by my side.

I'll never forget the night that Mr. O'Malley paid tribute to me in the Coliseum. This was before Dodger Stadium opened, and the Coliseum could hold a lot more people; and Mr. O'Malley got the Yankees to fly all the way to the Coast to play the Dodgers in the exhibition game. What a tribute that was. I had never played one game in Los Angeles, but 93,103 people paid tribute to me that night. Pee Wee Reese pushed my wheelchair out in the center of the field; and Vin Scully, our announcer, asked for the lights to be turned off, and when it was dark, he asked for everybody to strike a match or light a lighter. It was a beautiful sight, a tremendous tribute. Then they asked me to say

"All I could do was pray to the Good Lord . . ." Roy Campanella in 1980.

something, and I said, "Thank God that I was able to be alive to see it."
It was something that I'll never forget for the rest of my life.

So I always had a special attachment to the O'Malleys and the
Dodgers. I was able to join the team at Vero Beach in 1959 for spring
training, and every year since then I've been back.

During the years, I had other jobs, though. I ran my liquor store in
Harlem, and I worked in TV and radio for the Yankees and the Mets
and WINS. But like I say, I always felt connected with the Dodgers. I
don't fly very well, but I flew down to Vero Beach and out to Los
Angeles every year for a visit. And the O'Malleys used to always say,
"When are you gonna come out here to stay, Roy?"

Finally, in 1978, my wife and I decided to go. Peter O'Malley gave
me a job in community relations; and it has made me feel so tremendous, because, you know, how many people are lucky enough to have a
good job after suffering a broken neck? But I know baseball, and thank
goodness I can still talk and still use my brain. It makes me feel that
I'm still human as a man—and I'm a part of the Dodgers.

And I have a fine wife and five fine children—three boys and two
girls, and seven grandchildren. I was able to send them all through
college, and three of them has master's degrees. And I'm proud of them
all. So wouldn't you say that God has been pretty good to me?

Stan Musial

I never play baseball anymore . . . oh, maybe a game of catch in the
backyard with my grandchildren.

I used to play in old-timers games, but I saw too many fellows get
hurt out there. You're not in shape, and you're trying to extend yourself

to make a good appearance, and you overdo it. What was it Casey Stengel said about old-timers games? They're like airplane landings. If you can walk away from them, they're successful.

So the last five years I've passed them all up. The fans can remember me the way I was as a player.

I do enjoy golf. I play of lot of the celebrity tournaments around the country, and I do well enough not to embarrass myself. I have a set of lefty clubs, but you know it's a funny thing about left-handed golfers and left-handed baseball players. We look so graceful on a baseball field and so awkward on a golf course. It's almost as though baseball were designed for lefties, we look so natural out there.

I also play tennis, though I'm not very good, and I do enjoy swimming. I was chairman of Lyndon Johnson's physical-fitness program in the sixties, and I'm a strong fitness advocate. I still work to keep in shape, though naturally it's harder as the years pass.

The first few years after I quit as a player, I used to work out with the Cardinals, come to spring training every year, and so on. Red [Schoendienst] was manager of the club and I was vice-president, so I'd travel with the team and everything. Now, though, I've kind of faded it out and gotten away from it.

Traveling gets harder. It's not as easy as most people think. With a big league club you're traveling every third day and flying at night and getting into hotels at five in the morning and trying to get to sleep. . . . So I gradually cut down my involvement.

So what do I do with my free time now that I don't have to travel anymore? Travel! That's right. Funny, isn't it. My wife and I *love* to travel. See the world!

Joe DiMaggio

It's a funny thing about golf. I never played the game at all when I was playing baseball; I thought it would hurt my swing. Then I quit baseball, and my friend Lefty O'Doul got me interested. Now I play almost every day, as much as I can. I make a lot of tournaments. I enjoy the game, but I don't enjoy the travel to get there. That's why I quit baseball. I didn't want to travel anymore. Now look at me, I'm traveling just as much.[3]

Al Kaline

When I quit baseball I wasn't just leaving and hoping for a living. I had a good job waiting for me as a manufacturer's rep. Did that full time for three years.

Then I was offered a job in television, working the Detroit Tiger games as color man along with George Kell who does the play-by-play. I decided to give it just ten games as a trial because I'd never had *any* background in the field. Never had given it a *thought*. But after ten games, I knew I really liked it, although I was aware that I had a lot of rough edges. So—I've been doing it ever since.

And then I work with the Tiger outfielders and hitters at spring training. My job is with the network. But I work with the young Tigers because I enjoy it and feel like I'm repaying a debt. A lot of help was given me by older players when I was a young man just breaking into the big leagues. Now *I'm* trying to pass some of that along to the youngsters today. If I can help someone—whether it's with his playing skills or his attitude—that's a good feeling.

I love being back in the game, even if most of it is way upstairs in the broadcast booth. Nothing can beat being back with something you've geared your whole life for. Really, the only thing I know to any extent is baseball.

Ralph Kiner

I've been a TV broadcaster for the Mets since they began in '62. It's a *wonderful* way to extend a playing career. In fact, the main difference between being a player and a broadcaster is I don't have to keep in shape.

I love baseball as much as ever, and I've been traveling so long that I don't mind that much. I love to fly. . . .

So other than the dog days when you're in last place in September and trying to make a dull ball game sound exciting, it's really fun.

Eddie Mathews

I'm a special-assignment scout and batting instructor, and I'm very content with it. I don't have a wife or kids at home anymore, so I'm free to move anytime, and consequently I don't mind the traveling as much as some other guys might. And I really do like helping a hitter, and I do have a fairly good knack for detecting and correcting batting flaws. I don't care whether he's a millionaire or a rookie, if I can help him, that makes me feel good.

So if I can I'm gonna stay in baseball. I tried a couple of years outside and I did not care for it. This is the one thing I know well. I have no doubt, baseball is my bag.

Bob Gibson

I've been spoiled. When you've been an athlete there's no place for you to go. . . . But where I am right now is where the average person has been all along. I'm like millions of others now, and I'm finding out what that's like.[4]

Roberto Clemente in 1971

I would be lost without baseball. I don't think I could stand being away from it as long as I was alive.[5]

Buck Leonard and Billy Herman, Cooperstown, New York, August, 1980

Buck Leonard

My wife and I were married twenty-eight years. She died in February 1966. No kids. And I didn't never remarry so I've been living alone in Rocky Mount [North Carolina] ever since. I have a special room for baseball trophies, pictures, scrapbooks. Some nights when my mind starts to fret, especially when I'm feeling lonesome, I go in there, sit down, look over some of my mementos—remember.

I go to Cooperstown every year for the Hall of Fame induction, and I go to Florida every year for spring training and the governor's baseball banquet. Leave Rocky Mount at seven in the morning and get to Daytona at six that evening. Then visit a different training camp each day. I used to stay down there ten or twelve days, but that's a little too much for me now. But I still enjoy it. I have so many friends in baseball. . . .

When you're playing, awards don't
seem like much. Then you get
older and all of it becomes more
precious. It is nice to be
remembered. When you're sixty
maybe that's all you've got.
                    —HANK GREENBERG
                    in *Where Have
                    You Gone, Joe
                    DiMaggio?* by
                    Maury Allen

26.

The Hall of Fame

Connie Mack

[The Baseball Hall of Fame was opened in the summer of 1939 in Cooperstown, New York.]

I was invited to the dedication and considered it a great honor to be there. Taps were blown in honor of the living and the dead, and more than ten thousand people bowed their heads in silence.

The first players elected to the Hall of Fame numbered thirteen. But when the doors were officially opened that dedication day, only eleven passed through. Two were missing—Christy Mathewson and Wee Willie Keeler, who had passed away.

The ceremony of cutting the ribbons at the entrance gates was performed by Ford Frick. Beside him stood Judge Kenesaw Mountain Landis, Will Harridge, president of the American League, and the late W. G. Bramham, president of the minor leagues.

As the gates swung open the crowd of onlookers broke into cheers.

There stood the three greatest outfielders of all times: Ty Cobb, Babe Ruth, and Tris Speaker.

I was privileged to go through the open bronze doors first because I was the oldest, no doubt. Each of us, as we were presented to the throng, tried to express our gratitude in a few words. The records say that I "choked up and moved on with tear-filled eyes."

In the true American style photographers were on hand to snap our pictures. When we sat down Eddie Collins, the smiling Babe Ruth, Connie Mack (still stagestruck), and Cy Young were in the front row. Ty Cobb, however, failed to appear in time to have his photograph taken. Someone was heard to say, "Ty's late—just as he always was for spring training."

Standing behind us was a row of immortals: Hans Wagner, Grover Cleveland Alexander, Tris Speaker, Napoleon Lajoie, George Sisler, and Walter Johnson.

We then went to Doubleday Field, where three exhibition games were played during the day. The first game was old-fashioned "town ball," the kind I used to play as a boy in the old Brookfields.

The crowd was fascinated by a two-inning game of early baseball, the kind played by the New York Knickerbockers in the 1850s. The pitcher, called the thrower in those days, stood only forty-five feet from the batter, who was then called the striker. The catcher stood back at a safe distance, as was the custom in the days before masks and chest protectors and shin guards and catchers' mitts.

The centennial exhibitions closed with a modern nine-inning game between two major league mixed teams. Lefty Grove, Dizzy Dean, Ducky Medwick, Hank Greenberg, and Mel Ott were among the stars. This anniversary day brought back to me many happy memories.[1]

Wahoo Sam Crawford

When I got elected to the Hall of Fame, back in 1957, I was living in a little cabin at the edge of the Mojave Desert, near a little town called Pearblossom. Nobody around there even knew I'd been a ballplayer. I never talked about it. So there I was, sitting there in that cabin, with snow all around—it was February—and all of a sudden the place is surrounded with photographers and newspapermen and radio-TV reporters and all. I didn't know what in the world was going on.

"You've just been elected to the Hall of Fame," one of them said to me.

The people living around there—what few of them there were— were all excited. They couldn't figure out what was happening. And when they found out what it was all about, they couldn't believe it. "Gee, you mean old Sam? He used to be a ballplayer? We didn't even know it. Gee!"

STANDING: *Honus Wagner, Grover C. Alexander, Tris Speaker, Napoleon Lajoie, George Sisler, and Walter Johnson.* SITTING: *Eddie Collins, Babe Ruth, Connie Mack (still stagestruck), and Cy Young.*

BACK ROW: *Bowie Kuhn, B. Leonard, S. Koufax, Warren Spahn, W. Ford, A. Kaline, D. Snider, R. Roberts.* MIDDLE: *Chub Feeney, R. Kiner, Jocko Conlan, S. Musial, Bob Lemon, C. Gehringer, J. Cronin, B. Herman, Lee MacPhail, unidentified.* FRONT: *E. Averill, B. Dickey, C. P. Bell, Bob Feller, M. Irvin, A. Lopez, J. Sewell, B. Grimes, R. Campanella.*

From then on, of course, I've gotten thousands of letters. I still get a lot. Mostly from kids, wanting autographs. Sometimes they send a stamped envelope, and sometimes they don't. But I've answered every one by hand.[2]

Ted Williams in 1966, at his Hall of Fame induction speech

I hope that someday Satchel Paige and Josh Gibson will be voted into the Hall of Fame as symbols of the great Negro players who are not here only because they weren't given the chance. . . .

Buck Leonard in 1971

I was in Cooperstown the day Satchel Paige was inducted, and I stayed awake almost all night that night thinking about it. You know, a day like that stays with you a long time. It's something you never had any dream you'd ever see. Like men walking on the moon. I always wanted to go up there to Cooperstown. You felt like you had a reason because it's the home of baseball, but you didn't have a *special* reason. We never thought we'd get in the Hall of Fame. . . . I never had any dream it would come. But that night I felt like I was part of it at last.[3]

And in 1972, from his Hall of Fame induction speech

The greatest moment until the present time of my life was in February in New York City. Monte Irvin, who works in the commissioner's office, called and asked would I come from North Carolina to New York to select an all-star Negro team from the old Negro leagues. I told him yes, I would be happy to. I arrived in New York on a Monday morning. . . . He came over on Tuesday morning, and we went across the hall to the Americana Hotel to the meeting, and we saw the commissioner standing over there. I asked Monte, "What's he doing over here?" He said, "Well, he wants to sit in on the meeting." Then they opened the door and there was all those cameras, men, lights, and I asked Monte, "What they gonna do now?"

And he said, "They're going to name Josh Gibson for the Baseball Hall of Fame." Then they were arranging the platform, and after they got everything arranged, the commissioner, Campanella, Larry Doby, Irvin on the platform, they said, "Come up here, Buck. We want you to sit on the platform."

I said, "For what?"

"They're going to ask you some questions about Josh Gibson, you played with him nine years and you ought to know quite a few things about him."

I went up and sat on the rostrum, and the commissioner began to talk. He said, "We have met here today to make an announcement. The committee has seen fit to elect Josh Gibson to the Baseball Hall of Fame." Well, everybody clapped. Then he said, "The committee has also seen fit" and I started sweating . . . he said, "They have also seen fit to select Buck Leonard for the Hall of Fame." I was speechless. All the cameras started clicking and lights went on and I was already sweating enough. So they said, "Say something."

I said, "I don't have anything to say, somebody ask me a question, maybe I can answer that." So they began to ask questions. It was the greatest moment of my life.

Cool Papa Bell in 1974, from his Hall of Fame induction speech

There were a lot of great ones in the Negro leagues. We—Satchel, Irvin, Campy, Leonard, and myself—were the lucky ones. I'm thanking God for letting me smell the roses while I'm still living.

And in 1980

There are still a lot of fellows from the Negro leagues who are mostly forgotten who belong in the Hall of Fame. Pitchers just as good as Paige. Catchers just as good as Gibson and Campanella. We had a pitcher, Theodore Trent, used to beat Paige all the time. And the big leaguers couldn't hit him either when we played them in exhibitions. Or Smokey Joe Williams. He was in the same class with Satchel. The only thing is Satchel pitched in the big leagues, so they knew about him.

Or catching, we had a fellow named Biz Mackey. Gibson is in the Hall of Fame, but Mackey was our greatest all-around catcher.

Or Willie Wells, the greatest shortstop I ever saw.

I just hope some of those fellows make it. They deserve it as much as I ever did.

Monte Irvin

The Hall of Fame is the greatest thing that can happen to a baseball player. I was walking on cloud nine for quite a while after I was selected.

However, when I was a youngster, I knew that I was a super ballplayer. Didn't think *anybody* could play any better than I could. I could almost get base hits at will off *any* pitcher. I could throw like Mays or Furillo or DiMaggio and run like a deer. Had a lot of power to all fields and always hit for very high average. Rarely struck out. A DiMaggio type of hitter.

I'm sorry if it sounds like bragging. I'm just trying honestly to tell it like it was.

But I came up to the majors late. I was thirty years old. My only wish is that major league fans could've seen me when I was at my best—which was when I was in the Negro leagues. I'm talking about the late thirties and early forties. In 1942 in Mexico I hit .398 with a lot

"My only wish is that major league fans could've seen me when I was at my best." Monte Irvin with the New York Giants in the early 1950s.

of home runs. And I threw a lot of runners out. They *dared* not run on me after a while.

I sincerely believe that if I'd been able to play big league ball right from the start, I could've set some batting records, comparable to DiMaggio, Mays, Aaron, Williams—six or seven hundred home runs, that type of thing.

I was selected to the Hall of Fame by a special committee on the Negro leagues. But I wish that I could have made it on my major league record from the start.

Ralph Kiner

There are a lot of old-timers who should be in the Hall of Fame but aren't. Ernie Lombardi. Lefty O'Doul. *Babe Herman* has great statistics. Unfortunately for him he's always remembered as the guy who wound up on third base with two other runners. It wasn't his fault, but it just made a heck of a good story.

But I know from experience how hard it is to get in. I guess I was handicapped inasmuch as I never played in a World Series and didn't get that media attention, but other than Babe Ruth and maybe half a dozen others—maybe a dozen—I don't think anybody set as many batting records as I did. But it took me long *years* to get in. I think over the years I accumulated more votes than anyone else in the history of the Hall of Fame voting before I finally got in. Usually when you finish second that means you'll go in the next year, but I ran second and third for several years before I made it in 1975. It was not easy to take.

I think there's a lot of personality in it. Look at Ducky Medwick. A great player and he went in on his last ballot, but he was antagonistic and difficult with the reporters and that hurt his chances of getting in. It shouldn't have anything to do with it, but the fact is, it does.

Eddie Mathews

I wasn't surprised by my selection. I thought my record deserved consideration if anybody's did. I don't put myself in the same league with Willie Mays or Musial, but I certainly am equivalent to Ralph Kiner or Sandy Koufax, both of whom got in before I did. Koufax only played ten goddamn years, and only a few of them were outstanding. I couldn't understand that choice. It's like if they put Roger Maris in for his one great year. Other than that one year his career was mediocre. But the guys who have established themselves for fifteen to twenty years and have *maintained* that level of production, guys like Pete Rose, Brooks Robinson, Harmon Killebrew, Aaron, Frank Robinson— these are the type of guys who belong in the Hall. They've earned it, just like I feel that I earned it.

Billy Herman

Yaz'll be in the Hall of Fame. [Dave] Winfield. [Dave] Parker. [Jim] Palmer. There's a lot of names you could name that will be in the Hall of Fame, no doubt about it. But I'm trying to think of the guys who . . . See, my idea of baseball is not statistics, it's *winning*. Who's the guy who helps you win the most games? He can't be a .220 hitter or a poor fielder, but my ideal ballplayer doesn't necessarily have the most impressive record. I'm thinking of Pee Wee Reese type, the Dave Parker type. They go out and they can run, throw, field, and hit, and they also hustle like hell to try to win games. That's my idea of a Hall of Famer.

You know, back years ago—you don't hear much about it anymore—but back years ago they used to grade players as first division players or second division players. There were certain players, you'd put them on losing teams like the old Phillies or the old Reds from the thirties and they'd play good. As soon as you put them on a contender they didn't play so good. Chuck Klein, Babe Herman. This was common knowledge among the players and baseball people. Certain guys had a reputation that they couldn't play on a good ball club. When the pressure mounted, their abilities dropped.

So my idea of an ideal Hall of Famer is a Ruth, a DiMaggio, or an Ed Mathews or Warren Spahn. In other words, a player who knows how to *win*.

Duke Snider

The night after I was voted into the Hall of Fame in January 1980, I went out to dinner with some friends to the River Cafe in Brooklyn. We were dining quietly in a corner when some people recognized me, and pretty soon the whole place was applauding, and someone had a bottle of champagne sent to our table and toasted us.

Then a young man about thirty came over to the table and said he'd been carrying around my baseball card from the Brooklyn Dodgers ever since he was eight years old, and he asked me to sign it. Take it from me, it does feel good to be remembered.

Al Kaline in 1980, six months prior to his Hall of Fame induction

The players I've talked to who have been inducted tell me it was the most emotional day of their lives. And I am an emotional guy, although most people don't realize it. I learned from a very young age to keep my emotions under control, not to get too excited. I think that's going to be difficult at my induction.

And six months later, in Cooperstown on the day of his induction

I plan to return here when it's quiet, after the crowds have gone. I'm an old-time baseball buff, and I want to go through the museum at my own pace, carefully. I also intend to come back every summer for each new induction to welcome the "rookies."

If I were to write my own epitaph,
it would read: "He loved his God,
his home, his country, his fellow
men, and baseball."

> —CONNIE MACK at
> age eighty-eight,
> *My Sixty-six
> Years in the Big
> Leagues*

27.

Regrets, Confessions, and Proud Memories

Ty Cobb in 1925

If I hadn't been determined to outdo the other fellow at all cost, I doubt I would've hit .320. In other words, my lifetime batting average has been increased at least fifty points by qualities that I'd call purely mental.[1]

In 1960

Sure I fought. I had to fight all my life to survive. They were all against me . . . tried every dirty trick to cut me down. But I beat the bastards and left them in the ditch.

I fought so hard for my father, who was the greatest man I ever knew. He was a scholar, state senator, editor, and philosopher, and I worshipped him. . . . He was the only man who ever made me do his bidding.

My father had his head blown off with a shotgun when I was eighteen years old—by *a member of my own family*. I didn't get over that. I've never gotten over it. It happened the same week I became a major leaguer. He never got to see me play. But I knew he was watching me, and I never let him down.[2]

Finally in 1961, a few months before he died

I've had a lot of time to think things over and meditate on things of the past. I think if I had my life to live over again, I'd do things a little different. I was aggressive, perhaps too aggressive. Maybe I went too far. I always had to be right in any argument I was in, and I always had to be first in everything. I do indeed think I would have done some things different. And if I had I believe I would have had more friends.[3]

Stanley Coveleski

It's a tough racket. There's always someone sitting on the bench just itching to get in there in your place. Wants your job in the worst way: back to the coal mines for you, pal.

The pressure never lets up. Doesn't matter what you did yesterday. That's history. It's tomorrow that counts. So you worry all the time. It never ends. Lord, baseball is a worrying thing.[4]

Rogers Hornsby

I've always played hard. If that's rough and tough, I can't help it. I don't believe there's any such thing as a good loser. I wouldn't sit down and play a game of cards with you right now without wanting to win. If I hadn't felt that way I wouldn't have got very far in baseball.[6]

Babe Ruth

If it wasn't for baseball I'd be in either the penitentiary or the cemetery. I have the same temper my father and older brother had. Both died of injuries from street fights in Baltimore, fights begun by flare-ups of their tempers.[5]

Burleigh Grimes

Compared to farming or working in the lumber woods or in a steel mill, baseball was a picnic.

Goose Goslin

Heck, let's face it, I was just a big old country boy having the time of his life. It was all a lark to me, just a joy ride. Never feared a thing, never got nervous, just a big country kid from south Jersey, too dumb to know better. In those days I'd go out and fight a bull without a sword and never know the difference.

Why, I never even realized it was supposed to be big doings. It was just a game, that's all it was. They didn't have to pay me. I'd have paid *them* to let me play. Listen, the truth is it was *more* than fun. It was heaven.[7]

Lou Gehrig on July 4, 1939, "Lou Gehrig Day" in Yankee Stadium

I have a wonderful wife. I have a wonderful mother and father, and wonderful friends. I have been privileged to play many years with the famous Yankees, the greatest team of all time. What young man wouldn't give anything to mingle with such men for a day, as I have all these years? You've been reading about my bad break for the past two weeks now. But today I can say that I consider myself the luckiest man on the face of the earth.

Joe DiMaggio

Baseball was my life. I was six years old when I started playing baseball. It was all I knew. It was all I ever wanted to know. . . . I was always a conservative-type fellow. I shied away from things having to do with the limelight. I just enjoyed playing the game.[8]

Connie Mack

Nothing can equal in value my lifetime of memories from baseball:

That day in 1884 when I signed up with the Meriden, Connecticut, team at ninety dollars a month as a catcher.

My debut with the Washington Senators, then in the National League, September 11, 1886, against the Phillies. . . .

My first major league managership, that of the Pittsburgh Pirates, in 1894. . . .

The first time I saw Rube Waddell pitching for Detroit in 1898. I signed him up in 1900. . . .

Taking over the managership of the newly set-up Athletics in the fall of 1900.

The famous court battle over Larry Lajoie.

My first major league pennant in 1902, my second in 1905. . . .

Eddie Collins's first day as a member of the Athletics, September 17, 1906.

Winning the World Series against the Cubs in 1910—repeating against the Giants in 1911, and again in 1913.

Taking the American League pennant in 1914.

Signing up Ty Cobb for the Athletics in 1927.

The World's Championship again in 1929 and 1930; the American League pennant in 1931.

Memories? Yes . . . [9]

Ted Williams in 1971 accepting a brotherhood award at
   Howard University

As I look back on my career I'm thankful that I was given the chance to play baseball: It's about the only thing I could do—and I've thought many a time, what would have happened to me if I hadn't had a chance. A chill goes up my back when I think I might have been denied this if I had been black.

Monte Irvin

The first question most people ask the old-time Negro League players is "Are you bitter?" And most of them'll answer, "No. That was just the way it was." But I don't think that's really their feeling about it. They might not be burning with bitterness, but they're sure *sorry*—sorry that they didn't get a chance. It's easy to just say no and hide the feelings . . . but most of these men would've played without pay—just to have proved that they were good enough to play in the major leagues. And they were denied.

Most of the white players they barnstormed against said, "You guys play ball well enough to play in our league. It's a shame you can't. Maybe someday." We'd say, "I hope that someday comes soon, 'cause I'm not getting any younger."

Cadet Ted Williams, left fielder for the Cloudbusters at the U. S. Navy Pre-Flight School, Chapel Hill, North Carolina, 1943

Bob Feller

At the time I entered the navy the winter after the '41 season, I was running ahead of the great pitchers of the modern era in most statistical categories, including wins and strikeouts. My last three years there I'd won seventy-six games.

When I received my discharge toward the end of the '45 season, I'd missed almost four full years. Nineteen forty-six, my first full year back, I won twenty-six games. Based on the statistics and the way I felt physically, I think it's reasonable to assume that I'd have won another hundred games anyway and probably accumulated another one thousand to twelve hundred strikeouts. But after the war I knew those greatest lifetime records were out of my reach. So I just concentrated on doing a good job for the Cleveland Indians. Sure, I was disappointed, but I certainly didn't feel sorry for myself. I came home from the war in one piece. A lot of fellows didn't. So I'd say I was one of the lucky ones.

Ted Williams

I guess my main regret was that I missed the five years to war, but I don't feel as badly about the World War II years as I do about the two years in Korea. Hell, everybody and their uncle was going into World War II, but I still don't think the Korean thing was quite right, and I think a lot of people realize that. But I guess I should be thankful I got out of it with my ass.

My other regret is that in my early years, before the World War, I didn't take my outfielding seriously enough. 'Cause I wasn't that bad an outfielder at all, but I was sloppy and careless and didn't work on it enough. What I did at the plate was all-important to me those first five or six years, and I was just going through the motions in the field.

But after I got out of the service, and we won the pennant in '46, I realized that it was really my life's *work*, and I said, "Boy, this fielding is pretty damn important. This is my bread and butter." And I was a better outfielder from then on. Of course, it was too late for my reputation. Whatever you do *early* in your career determines whether you're judged real good or just ordinary. But that was nobody's fault but my own. I just regret I didn't see the light earlier.

Robin Roberts

I felt very fortunate to be able to throw a baseball the way I could. If I have a regret it's probably that I didn't get quite as much out of my arm as was there. I had a fine right arm and a great delivery, but I pitched too much and wore myself down. I wasn't quite selfish enough or smart enough.

You've got to take care of *yourself*. You really do. You can act like you're really loyal and all that, but maybe you're being a little stupid if you don't take care of yourself.

There were times when my arm was tired and stiff and I would've been better off telling the manager "no." But really when you look back you don't know whether it was that stubbornness was what made you the winner you were. So it's a thin line.

But there are certain responsibilities you have with something that's a gift like that. You've got to learn how to take care of it. And it's such a thin line between being smart and babying yourself. I never had any thin line there, though. I just kept bulling ahead. I never realized that wasn't smart till I got older.

But that was my makeup. I really had the temperament of a catcher or a shortstop. I would've much preferred playing one of those positions because I wanted to play every day. The sitting around between starts used to drive me buggy. Which is another reason I often *wasted* the tremendous ability I had to throw a baseball. I used to throw it all the time between games just for the sheer fun of it.

Eddie Mathews

As I get older I find that I regret things that I never thought that much about when I was younger. For instance, I keep coming back to my father.

He was a big baseball fan, played semipro when he was young, and really got me started in the game, playing catch, hitting me grounders, pitching to me, and the whole runaround. And he encouraged me right along. Later on, I believe his main desire in life was for me to make the big leagues, and he was proud as punch when I did make it. I was glad that he was able to see that I made it and lived to see me have my first good year in Milwaukee. But what I regret—and I regret more as the years pass—is that he never saw me play in person. He died in '54 after a long illness of tuberculosis, and he never saw me play the big leagues. In fact, he never saw me play in a pro ball game. He'd been sick the whole time.

I was playing in Pittsburgh the day he died, and I flew home for the funeral. You get over it . . . but now I wish I'd spent more time with him. I look back and say, "Goddammit, I should have flown him back east to some games when he was able to do it." But, he always said, "Well, I'm just not up to it quite yet." And we never did do it.

At that time I was involved . . . I got married right after he passed away—at the end of that season—and my wife got pregnant. And I was playing baseball, and I really didn't have time to stop and think about all the things. But now I do have more time to think about them, with the kids grown and everything. But you can't go back.

But the sad thing is now I wish I could spend more time with *my* kids. My oldest son I see maybe once or twice a year because he's in med school up at the University of Wisconsin. My daughter's up that way too, living in Milwaukee, so I only see her and her family once or twice a year. And my youngest son I see more often because he lives and works in San Diego, near me. But hell, I'm on the road so much that I don't see that much even of him. So it's not the ideal arrangement.

Yogi Berra in 1963
I'd rather be the Yankees' catcher than the president, and that makes me pretty lucky, I guess, because I could never be the president. . . .

Casey Stengel in 1974
I'm just glad I had baseball knuckles and couldn't become a dentist.

Mickey Mantle
I have my regrets and I have a lot of things I'm proud of—hitting over five hundred home runs, playing more games than any other Yankee. And I've got about four or five World Series records and I'm proud of all those. And I'm not worried about anyone breaking them soon either because I doubt you'll see anyone else playing in thirteen World Series in his first fifteen years, which is another thing I'm proud of. I guess the won-and-lost records of the teams I played on are better than anyone else, except maybe Yogi. Yeah, Yogi's would be better because he didn't play on those losing teams after 1964.

But when you talk about individual moments . . . it's hard for me to remember them very clearly. . . . People come up to me and tell me about some great thing they saw me do in some game in 1957. They tell me every last detail about it. . . . It's like the whole thing happened to them instead of to me.

Whitey Ford
I think I could tell you just about every pitch I threw in the 3,170 innings I pitched. . . . Most guys have this total recall about the things they saw or did in ball games.

As for the things I saw or did *after* the games, I have pretty good recall there, too. And it's probably a good thing it's not total. There's a lot of those things I'd just as soon not remember.[10]

Casey Stengel
There comes a time in every man's life and I've had plenty of them.

Joe DiMaggio and Mickey Mantle in 1951

The big parade of famous players
and teams is endless, for every year
new players are coming over the
horizon, as those before march on.
—CONNIE MACK,
My Sixty-six
Years in the Big
Leagues

SPECULATIONS AND

CONCLUSIONS

Pete Rose in action

I think one of the most difficult
things for anyone who's played
baseball is to accept the fact that
maybe the players today are
playing just as well as ever.

—RALPH KINER

28.

Changing Times

Connie Mack

The first bases were not bags at all, but wooden posts standing four feet high. In 1876, the year the National League was organized, F. W. Thayer, of the Harvard Club, constructed the contraption of wires and leather that we call the catcher's mask. Allison, a catcher for the Cincinnati Reds in 1869, had the first glove or mitt made by a saddle maker.

Before 1886, when a ball was lost, the umpire called a recess of five minutes while everybody searched for it. If, after five minutes, the lost ball was not found, the umpire was allowed to put a new ball into play.

When I was catcher of the Washington Senators, the rule for major league batters was seven balls and three strikes. One year [1887] it was four strikes to make an out. Pitchers were using underhand delivery, fifty feet from the batting box. We were catching the ball on the bounce. Infielders and outfielders were catching them bare-handed.

A batter was allowed to tell the pitcher what kind of ball he wanted pitched to him. A foul ball caught on the bounce was out until 1880. Back in 1887 we players were assessed thirty dollars for our uniforms and had to pay half a dollar a day for our board when away from home. A dollar a day was the usual for both room and board.

If you were injured there were no extra players to take your place. You had to play as long as you could stand up.

The game was played with but one official, the umpire. He stood a safe distance behind the batter. When there was a man on base, the umpire walked out to the middle of the diamond and stood behind the pitcher.

These were the "good old days" before we had to worry about the cost of living. You could get a suit of clothes for ten dollars and a good dinner at a hotel for fifty cents. For twenty-five cents you could go to the ball game and sit in the bleachers. You could sit in the grandstand for fifty cents.

If there were three thousand to four thousand fans at a game in those days, we considered it a big crowd. A score of seventy to eighty runs was merely a "good game . . ."[1]

Albert G. Spalding in 1908

The future of baseball is without limit. The time is coming when there will be great amphitheaters throughout the United States in which citizens shall be able to see the teams take part in the finest athletic struggles of the world.[2]

John McGraw in 1923

In thirty years I have seen much baseball. My greatest asset has been a good memory.

There is no question in my mind but that present-day baseball is better. Also there are more good ballplayers today than there ever were before, simply because there are more people playing ball.

While we have more good ballplayers today and while the game itself has improved, I do not mean to say that baseball spirit has improved. Rather I would be inclined to say that team spirit was even better thirty years ago. Today the baseball player is more of a businessman. He looks out for himself.[3]

Babe Ruth in 1928

Baseball has changed a lot in the last ten or fifteen years.

When I first broke in baseball was a defensive game. The pitchers and fielders had all the best of the argument.

Walter Johnson was in his prime then, and Alexander and Rube Marquard and Eddie Plank. And those boys could pitch, believe me.

They had everything it takes to make a great pitcher, and in addition they were permitted to rough the ball and use trick deliveries. And besides that the ball in those days was dead.

I guess that period is what you would call baseball's defensive age.

And naturally with the big leagues playing defensive ball the sand-lotters and the amateurs took it up too. Kids in those days dreamed of becoming great pitchers. Even hitters like Wagner and Lajoie had to play second fiddle to the Mattys and the Browns.

The change from defensive to offensive play came gradually. John McGraw was one of the men most responsible. He's always just a couple of jumps ahead of the other fellow, and he's always looking for something new. I've had my run-ins with John, but he's a baseball wizard just the same.

And while all the other managers were going nutty over defensive play and making themselves bald trying to dope out ways to develop their pitchers, John decided that what baseball needed was more action. So he went in for hitting and base stealing, and the first thing the rest of the managers knew John was winning the pennant.

And how the fans liked it!

They began to yell for more hitting and more action.

Other managers began to copy McGraw's style, too, and it wasn't long before they passed rules limiting pitchers on trick stuff. They did away with the spitball and the emery ball and the other freaks. They built a little more life into the ball, and they ordered umpires to use new and clean balls as much as possible.

The boys began smacking the fences with long drives, outfielders began playing with their backs to the wall. And that's the story of how baseball's era of defensive play passed into history. At least that's the way it seems to me—and most of the changes have taken place since I first put on a big league uniform.[4]

Al Lopez

It hurt the hitters, especially the home-run hitters, when the National League deadened the ball after 1930. In 1930 I hit .309; the next year my average dropped to .269. Balls that I had been hitting up against the walls or even into the stands were all of a sudden just easy lazy fly balls. The fellows that hit the ball up into the air got hurt the most. Hack Wilson, for instance, dropped from fifty-six to twenty-five home runs because he didn't pull the ball and he hit *high* fly balls. In 1931 they were being caught by the right and center fielders. But *all* the hitters were complaining. The league batting average on the whole dropped a good twenty-five points.

Now this ball they're using today is even livelier than the balls we had in 1930. I really believe that. The livelier ball combined with the smaller bats these kids are using results in more home runs and more strikeouts than ever. They get a faster swing but they miss the ball more. I guess that's the trade-off.

Ralph Kiner

In 1930 the *League* batting average was over .300. They had to have some kind of a rocket going at that time. Then they got it down to where it was almost a dead ball during the war, and now it's back alive again. It's a question that's hard to argue, but for anybody to do what they did in 1930. . . . I mean Hack Wilson knocked in 190 runs in 1930. One hundred and *ninety!* That ball had to be juiced!

Ty Cobb in 1952

Baseball has degenerated into a slugging match. The way they play today, it's as if two golfers decided to forget all about the course—with its doglegs, sand traps, roughs, and putting greens—and instead just went out to see who could hit the ball the farthest at a driving range. . . . Phil Rizzuto and Stan Musial are the only two players nowadays who can stand comparison with the old-timers.[5]

Ralph Kiner

I believe that the postwar years up until expansion in 1961 were the golden years of major league baseball. You had more outstanding athletes in the game than any time before or since. I'm sure you couldn't prove it, but you can look at it logically. You had the advent of the black player, especially in the National League. Before Jackie Robinson there were no blacks in the majors. Now that *had* to detract from the quality of *prewar* play. Another thing, you didn't have competition from other pro sports for the young superathlete. Pro football started that in the sixties and then pro baseball got big and now *everything*— golf, tennis, soccer, you name it. We still get our share, but we used to get them *all*. And they were all loaded on the rosters of just sixteen teams. But the expansion of 1961 turned it around.

You've got 650 players on big league rosters now as opposed to 400 when I was playing. True, the population of the country has grown, but counterbalancing that, as I pointed out, is the fact that we don't have our former monopoly on recruiting young athletes. A guy like Dave Winfield coming out of college gets lucrative offers from teams in *several* pro sports.

Of course, counterbalancing *that* is the fact that you're bringing big league baseball to more cities where you reach a wider and wider audience of young kids who might be attracted into the game. So it's been a tremendous advantage when you look at the overall picture of national popularity, attendance, and profits; and I think the future is bright. The young talent will keep coming. But from the short-term perspective, I have to maintain that the postwar years saw the highest-quality baseball.

Ty Cobb in 1960
These days, any tax-dodging mugwump with a bankroll can buy a franchise, field some semipros, and get away with it. Where's our integrity? Where's Baseball?[6]

Frank Frisch in 1964
Today's ballplayers are spoiled. They get big bonuses to sign, they draw big salaries, they have fancy pensions to look forward to, they wear big gloves on their hands to make sure they catch the ball, they play on manicured fields, they live in the finest hotels and eat in restaurants that charge more for dinner than I used to make in a week.

Take the way these boys suffer through spring training. They live in country-club surroundings. They swim, play golf, lounge on the beach, and about two or three hours a day play a little ball. Nothing strenuous, mind you. . . . After all, they have all that money in the bank.[7]

Burleigh Grimes
I have to say most of it is improved for the ballplayers today. Just take the clubhouses. I can remember some of the clubhouses used to have one or two light bulbs in the whole place, and they smelled like old socks. Little bitty stalls. You didn't have room enough to hang your clothes. I was in a big league clubhouse last year, and each player had a great big locker and the room was air conditioned and the floor was carpeted and there were leather-upholstered chairs all around. There was music playing, and half the fellows were blow-drying their hair. And I said, "Boy, this is the life."

Bob Feller in 1968
I'm too busy to go to many games, and frankly, when I do I find them rather dull. The owners are just interested in filling the stands by having close games and tight pennant races. They couldn't care less about the caliber of play.[8]

And in 1980
There are some fine players today—Rod Carew, Tom Seaver, Dave Parker—but not as many as thirty years ago. The reason is they don't get the proper training. This is not really their fault. Maybe some of them could work harder on fundamentals, but the real problem is that there aren't enough minor leagues to train them. Many of them play college ball, but that's no substitute. They have to learn a lot of their baseball while playing in the big leagues.

Stan Musial

Years ago we players wouldn't get out of line because no matter what club we were on, that organization had someone down in Triple A waiting to take over our positions. There were only eight teams in each league back then and we had thirty minor leagues, so there were plenty of hungry young guys ready to take over those eight second-base spots or those eight catcher's spots.

Today we don't have so many ballplayers in the minors, and there are twenty-six starting jobs at every position on the major league level. So it's kind of switched around.

Duke Snider

The American League has gone one expansion beyond the National League—from twelve teams to fourteen. I guess the talent's pretty watered down over there. The problem is mainly one of team depth. It'll improve with time, though. It just takes the new teams time to catch up.

Other than that baseball's the same game. Maybe there's a little more speed nowadays, which has tended to liven things up a little. And the kids are bigger and stronger than ever—though I won't say necessarily smarter.

Luke Appling

They're milking the cow dry. The major leaguers are getting all the money, and the minor league kids can't even make enough to eat right. Inflation in the last few years has put them in a very rough situation.

Of course, the older boys on the big clubs, they just say, "You gotta pay your dues. Pay your dues." They're twenty-eight, twenty-nine, thirty, or older, and they might get cut short anytime; so they're trying to accumulate money and get it in deferred payments.

One thing I *can* say for the boys in the minors—they're not down there very long. But that's bad too in a way. It's hard on youngsters, especially if they're signed with a bad ball club. They escalate them so fast that they're in the major leagues before they have a chance to get their feet on the ground. They all *want* to go fast, or at least they say they do; but it would be better for them if they could stay in the minors until they're ready.

But like I say, the big clubs don't have enough good players, and anyway, there aren't enough minor leagues to keep them in. They used to have thirty or forty minor leagues, now they got five or six, with a very small number of loyal fans.

Every player wants a Cadillac, and every fan wants to see *major* league baseball.

Billy Herman

The kid who gets hurt is the one who has the potential but struggles for a few years trying to develop it. See, some kids develop slower than others. I know *I* did. Some of them are still developing when they're in their mid-twenties. But since they don't have as many minor leagues as they used to, they don't have any place to send that slow-developing kid where he can play every day. So I'd assume they release a lot of good ballplayers before they can reach their potential.

And the sad thing is the minors might have to contract even more for the simple reason that the major leagues are spending so much money on salaries and travel that they don't have enough left over to subsidize the farm clubs as well as they maybe should.

On the other side of the coin, they do provide *instruction*, and I guess that's the next best thing to actual experience. Back in my day they'd give you the ball and say, "Go out and play." If you couldn't do it—tough! So I assume that back *then* a lot of good ballplayers were lost for lack of proper instruction.

Ralph Kiner

My son Mike played pro ball for a year and a half until he was released. He played catcher, first base, and outfield, and swung a pretty good bat, and he probably could've been a good player if he'd had a chance to play longer. I thought he had fine potential. But today because of the economics of the situation it's "make good right away or forget it."

Robin Roberts

I've been coaching the University of South Florida baseball team since 1977 and I love it. We play about a fifty-game schedule from March 1 to May 15.

I don't think the day will ever come when big league baseball teams will let colleges train their players the way it's done in football and basketball. It might not be a bad idea, though . . . although baseball generally requires a little more training than those other sports.

As it is now the pros draft the top 15 percent directly from high school, which of course adversely affects the quality of college ball. So they have all these kids in the minor leagues, most of whom are never gonna make it. There are maybe three or four on each farm club who will probably make it at some point. The rest are just there to give them somebody to play with. But they're paying them anyway. It's a cost that so far they've been willing to bear. At some point they may decide it's too expensive. Let somebody else train them. Just pay the twenty-five to forty guys on the squad rather than the hundred to hundred and fifty they have under contract under the present setup.

I think that could be done if they had just two minor leagues just for polishing the kids up. They could keep twenty-five on the big club and fifteen others on their minor league squad. Maybe they could even run three minor leagues, each with nine or ten clubs, that's twenty-seven to thirty farm clubs, roughly one for each big club.

They could sign a boy, assign him to a league, and then draft from that league. If the farm system was a cooperative thing run by baseball, and the draft was drafting those boys each year, then I think you'd have the answer quality-wise and you'd also keep it pretty even competitively. It would also upgrade your college and semipro baseball.

I don't think the individual owners are thinking cooperatively, though. Which is a *good* thing but a dumb thing business-wise. But that's baseball, I guess.

Luke Appling

On the field the game is the same. The main changes have been in speed and equipment. These kids today can fly. And you need that speed on the Astroturf. Golly, that ball's fast moving! You can't get away with slow-footed fielders like you could on the grass.

Gloves are bigger and better. In my day the first baseman's mitt wasn't as big as the fielders' gloves are now. Bats, lighter. Balls, faster. Fields, better, and better kept. Astroturf. Anybody misses a ground ball on Astroturf oughta have his head examined.

Pitching's a little different. You don't see as many curveballs. They all throw that slider ball, cause those home-run hitters to lunge and jump. We used to call it the "two bit curve," but it's become a good pitch because the boys overswing. Even the smallest boys out there want to hit the ball out of the park. They have a saying, "You hit singles, you drive a Ford. Hit home runs, you drive a Cadillac."

Charlie Gehringer

Naturally, the batting averages have dropped. The hitters are going for distance, and when you do that you start the bat quicker and swing at more bad balls. And you're fooled more easily. I know about it from personal experience. In 1932 I went for distance. Got off to a great start. I remember I had eight homers when Ruth had only three or four. I believe I still had eight when he hit his thirty-fourth. But I kept going for distance. Wound up under .300.

[Nineteen thirty-two was one of the three years Gehringer failed to reach .300 during his sixteen years as a regular. He finished the season with nineteen home runs though, one short of his single-season high of twenty. Ruth finished with forty-one.]

Stan Musial

Astroturf can give a fast guy twenty to thirty hits a season. For a while there I thought Rod Carew might hit .400. He was having some great years out there in Minnesota, and they didn't even have turf.

But I think one of these days, some guy who's a line-drive hitter with good speed and Astroturf in his home park might go over .400 for a season. Those guys come around once in a lifetime.

Al Lopez

You see more home runs today and more strikeouts. The home runs are okay, but the strikeouts are bad for the game 'cause I think the public would like to see more of the ball in play—the good fielding plays and the runners running. What do you see when a guy strikes out? He just walks back to the bench. Maybe he throws his helmet.

When Babe Ruth struck out, he was such a giant, the fans of the other team always got a big kick out of it. But nowadays they strike out everybody. It's nothing special.

I think my White Sox, the Go Go Sox, were the first part of another change that was a *good* change, an increased emphasis on running and stealing. I think the game overall is moving in that direction now, and I think it's very exciting. In fact, Mr. Allen, the owner of the White Sox when I was managing there, asked me one time, "Al, if you had a chance to get someone in the league who you feel would be exciting for our fans, who would you get?"

I said, "I want the [Luis] Aparicio type. Someone who when he gets on base, they don't know what he's gonna do." I think he expected me to say the big home-run-hitter type, but I honestly believe the public goes for the little guy who's quick and daring.

Eddie Mathews

Yeah, Maury Wills, and [Lou] Brock, and Aparicio kind of started something. I think part of it too stems from the weak catching. A lot of the catchers today can't throw anybody out. You better believe there's a shortage of good catchers. I'd say half the first-string catchers in the majors can't throw worth a shit. Del Crandall, Campy, Yogi—these guys could *throw*. Still, base stealing *has* become more of an art, I guess the one baseball art that's in better shape than ever.

Johnny Evers in 1910

There are not ten really first-class catchers in America, and the team which lacks one of these ten, no matter how strong in other departments, is doomed to failure before it starts.[9]

Al Kaline

Here's something that's changed from my day. Relief pitching has become so much a bigger part of the game today. It's the most important factor of all now. Twenty years ago there were very few relief specialists. Now every team has at least one. I mean really outstanding pitchers—as good as any of the starters.

I think this is one reason the hitters aren't making such impressive numbers anymore. It used to be you could get the starter out of there and fatten up on the second-line pitchers. That's when you'd really get your hits and home runs and RBIs. But now they bring in a guy better than the one you just knocked out.

Stan Musial

Nowadays the relief pitchers are even specialized within their specialty. We have long men who can step in there early in the game, and then we have short-relief specialists who come in to nail down the close ones. Naturally, this fact, plus the advent of the slider, affected batting averages. Old-timers, the generation before mine, used to say the slider was just a "nickel curve," but it wasn't that simple. It gave many pitchers a fourth pitch, and because of the fast break I found it much more difficult to pick up than the fastball, curve, or change-up.

Bob Feller

It used to be expected that a starting pitcher would pace himself and make it through the complete game if he possibly could. Nowadays the manager tells him, "Go out and give it everything on every pitch! That's why we have a bull pen." So, after say six innings, the pitcher's looking over his shoulder for some relief, whether he really needs it or not. In addition, my personal view is that the pitchers don't have as much stamina as they used to. In my case, I built myself up working on a farm from a very young age and eating good farm food. Not many kids today come up that way, which I feel is a loss to the game.

Joe Sewell

It seems like the pitcher *wants* to get taken out of the ball game—that is if he's ahead. . . .

I get a kick out of these little fellows playing today. I set there and watch them on the TV. . . .

There are a *few* good players today—you can count them on the fingers of one hand. But generally they're just out there going through the motions, just playing for the money. I get a kick out of . . . they have to get ready "mentally" for the ball game. Shucks, when I crawled out of bed in the morning, I was ready to play. Nobody had to pamper me around.

Take Bill Dickey. Shucks, these pitchers out there made the mistakes they make when Dickey was catching them, he'd run right out to the mound and grab them and shake them. That man was *serious*.

Take some of these modern fellows. They'll hit a fly to the outfield, look at it, run three-quarters of the way to first, and then run back to the bench. These guys are drawing *big* money. There's guys drawing six-figure paychecks who'd be in Class C ball in my day.

We had *hitters* back then. Take the Detroit Tigers when they had Cobb, [Bobby] Veach, and [Harry] Heilmann in the outfield. They used to knock that ball *flat*. Oh, good gracious! If Cobb were hitting today with this Astroturf and these little fellows they got pitching now, he'd hit closer to .500 than .400.

Or Ruth . . . if the pitchers back in 1927 had pitched to him the way they pitched to Roger Maris and Hank Aaron, he'd've hit *one hundred and sixty* homers. Ain't no question about it. I saw Hank Aaron hit two home runs in Atlanta off Al Downing one day. You could've hit them yourself. Little bitty fastballs right down through the middle of the plate. As old as I am I could've hit them *myself*.

Robin Roberts

They asked Willie Mays about the big salaries today and did he resent them? He said no he didn't resent the big money at all, but it did piss him off when they didn't run to first base. I think that's a hell of a summary of how we all feel.

I think Roger Maris really started it when everybody was getting on him in New York. He'd hit a ground ball to second base and run to the dugout. And a lot of guys do that now. I guess when you're making half a million bucks it seems like a waste of time and energy to run unless you really hit one.

I think if you have a leader like a Willie Stargell on your team you're all right. Or if your club is fighting for the pennant. Where the problem is usually is with the bad clubs. No one *ever* enjoyed being in the cellar, but I think there used to be a certain pride in showing up and doing your best. Nowadays, it's scary. It's bordering on anarchy in some cases.

Luke Appling

Nowadays the players get everything handed to them on a silver platter, and they don't take advantage of it. See, I had to learn everything myself; and maybe because I had to work for it, I remembered it better. Teaching these kids, you got to tell them over and over and over.

And a lot of them won't work as hard as they should. . . . I don't know why. They get a little heavy and lazy and always worried about money. They all want to play in the big city so they can do TV commercials. When I signed a contract I got as much money as I figured I

"If you have a leader like Willie Stargell on your team, you're alright."

could, and then I threw the contract away and forgot about it. Went to playing baseball.

Mickey Mantle

I used to make one hundred thousand dollars a year. Now the benchwarmers make more than that. I think these kind of salaries are gonna ruin baseball. As far as I'm concerned they're gonna have to get the reserve clause back.

Of course they draw more people every year, so I guess people are going for it.

I think the *players* nowadays are as good or better than they used to be. They're bigger, stronger, hit the ball, throw the ball, run. They're getting faster all the time.

I don't think they practice the fundamentals as much. You know, we used to drill on fundamentals *all spring*. These guys today just come out and get loose and take batting practice and go back to the clubhouse to take care of their business.

Al Kaline

The big bucks and the long-term contracts do tend to undermine incentive, I believe. You don't see the extra effort, the extra fire, from the players who've been well taken care of by their teams. Not that it's a picnic. In fact, the pressure from fans is *greater* than it used to be. They seem to be more vocal in their criticisms than ever before. I think there's a lot of resentment.

Another effect of the changed business climate with free agency and all is that players are more individual today. They don't look at the team concept as much as they used to; and I can understand why, because the negotiations are based on your performance, which is mostly measured by statistics. So it's very important to have a good year. Management used to preach that winning was everything, and it's still very important; but a player can go out now and have a good year and demand a contract so lucrative that he can insure his future and his family's future right then and there. So I think the players do tend to be more oriented to individual rather than team performance.

But all in all, I'd argue that the players are getting exactly what they deserve, simply because the owners obviously are willing to pay them. You'd have to almost be out of your mind not to take advantage of the situation. And I don't think that it all means they're playing just for the money.

I loved the game and felt very fortunate to be able to do it for a living. I'm sure there are many players today who feel exactly the same way.

Billy Herman

You talk to the modern-day player and he'll tell you about his individual accomplishments. Back when I played you didn't talk about how much you hit, you talked about how many games you won. Generally, I think that old-time attitude has escaped the modern player.

There *are* exceptions, from individual to individual and from team to team. Now, the Orioles are the best-run and best-disciplined team in the American League. They get more results with less individual talent than anyone else. There isn't a real solid all-around player on the whole club except their pitching; but they *win*.

Earl Weaver deserves a lot of the credit. You may not like the man, a lot of people don't, but you've got to respect his results. On the ball field he's the boss, and the players do it his way. And he's smart enough so that his way is usually right.

Unfortunately though, as I say, Baltimore is the exception rather than the rule.

Eddie Mathews

I've been involved with big league baseball for thirty years now, and the biggest changes I've seen have been in two areas—the *money* that's available to the players and the *attitude* of the players.

I'm no psychologist, and I couldn't say if the two things are related, but . . .

It was really noticeable to me when I first had to manage them back in '72. I'd ask them to do something and they'd want to know why. Hell, when I played it never *occurred* to me to ask why. Bunt, hit, and run—whatever the manager told me to do I did to the best of my ability. And I tried to hustle all the time. I ran full speed down to first base whether I hit the ball back to the pitcher or between the outfielders.

You know, a bunch of us were talking recently about this, and Pete Rose came up. Now Pete's a good player and a real hustler, but why is it that they always make such a big deal about his hustle? Because he's a rarity today. Hell, the guys I played with hustled like that every day. They didn't slide headfirst, but they hustled like hell at all times. That was just the way the game was played. I admire Pete for doing it because that's the way he *should* do it. But my point is that everybody else should too.

Most of them do what they *have* to do, but no more. In other words, if a guy hits a high pop fly to the infield, you show me one modern player who ends up on second if the ball's dropped. Rose would, I'll guarantee you. The rest of them'd be standing on first base. Sure there are other ball-busters besides Rose, but not many.

I'm not saying they're not good hitters. They have more ability than ever. But it's all hitting. That's what they want to be known for. The money's in hitting, and the hell with the rest of it. Money's fine, but if you've got any personal pride in your performance, there's a lot more to baseball than just hitting.

Money. That's the other thing that's changed. These guys seem to be very, very concerned with money. They've got financial advisers and are interested in a whole bunch of other things beyond baseball. I never was. I lived and breathed baseball. I had investments, but they were not a major part of my life. I'd go to a bank—not an agent—and say, "Here's my money. Please invest it for me."

I guess it's just the changing times. I think you'd find a lot of these changes in other areas besides sports.

When I was playing, nobody knew the other guy's salary. It wasn't even discussed. That's the way everybody wanted it. I didn't want anybody to know what I was making. Of course, maybe if I signed a million dollar contract, I'd want everyone to know. But . . . I made a damn good living. And was *happy*. That's all I can say. I was happy. These guys aren't even happy with what they're getting. They have a million dollar contract, and they want to renegotiate after two years. I just don't think they're having as much fun. I had a *ball*, Christ! Mantle, did you talk to Mickey? He's the same type of guy. He had fun both on and off the field. And he *always* played hard—the way baseball is supposed to be played.

Billy Herman

The thing that hurts the game more today than anything else is those long-term contracts. No way that you can take a twenty-five-year-old man and give him all that financial security and have him go out and give you 100 percent every minute. He's got a five-year contract, those first three years he's not gonna strain himself. Why should he?

Now, the Pete Roses and the Fred Lynns it doesn't bother. I don't care whether you give them ten thousand dollars a year or a million a year, they're gonna go out and try and beat you every way they know how. That's their natural character. Nobody's gonna change Pete Rose. You give him a fifty-year contract, it won't make any difference. But there's not many like that.

Most of them sign that contract and then sit back and say, "Well, I'm all set till 1985. . . ." These guys are not gonna risk running into a wall to catch a fly ball. If they have a little muscle pull, it's "I can't play, I have a sore muscle." They're like the average person. When you're comfortable and secure you get more cautious. You start thinking about protecting your investments.

Robin Roberts

Baseball's popularity comeback over the last six years has been phenomenal. There was a period there in the sixties and early seventies when baseball was losing fans to other sports, but I think people are coming again to appreciate more and more the commonsense sport baseball really is. The players don't beat the hell out of one another, and you don't have to be six feet five inches tall to play. And it requires a lot of brains. Little League may be training more fans than players, and expanded TV coverage has helped as well.

Bob Skinner and Robin Roberts. In background—Bobby Winkles and Al Kaline.

To give you an indication of what I'm saying—when we won the pennant in Philadelphia in 1950 we drew 1.2 million fans. Last year they drew more than twice that.

[The 1980 Phillies drew 2,651,650 in paid attendance.]

Joe Cronin

Baseball has a powerful hold on the public. I foresee a bright future for the game. When radio first came in we thought radio was gonna hurt. Well, contrary to our fears, it enhanced our attendance. Then here comes TV, and we feared the same thing. But the exposure's been tremendous. Baseball's a great date game. The young fellow can take his date to the ball game and have a great night for ten dollars. You can't go to the theater for less than ten dollars apiece. I hope baseball doesn't price itself out of this position. I hope the owners are smart enough to keep it within range.

Ted Williams in 1980

Ted Williams

Baseball's future? Bigger and bigger! Better and better! No question about it—it's the greatest game there is!

[Author's note: The interviews quoted in this chapter were all conducted before the disastrous major league baseball strike of 1981. Obviously, millions of fans are still angry and disgusted with the whole business. The questions now anxiously being asked in baseball circles are how much damage was done to baseball's reputation, to what extent can it be repaired, and how long will it take? When, if ever, will baseball regain its place of honor in the American mythological firmament?]

The clouds that gather round the
   setting sun
Do take a sober coloring from an
   eye
That hath kept watch o'er man's
   mortality
                        —WILLIAM
                        WORDSWORTH
                        "Intimations of
                        Immortality"

29.

Wisdom for Rookies
and Other Young

King Kelly in 1888

Now, to my boy friends, and I hope I have many, I will give a few
simple rules . . . : First, study hard, go to school regularly, . . . and obey
your teachers. When school is over, go out and begin a ball game. Do
not play with a soft ball. It is just as well to have a good hard one. When
you see it coming to you hard, do not go out of the way, but rather go
towards it. If you make an error do not feel badly about it. Just make up
your mind that you are going to do better the next time. Never close
your eyes when you see a ball coming. Just keep them open, and say to
yourself, "Well, here's a friend of mine coming; I'll stop him before he
can do any harm." When you go to bat swing the bat gently. If the ball
is coming quick it won't require a great amount of strength to send it
far. Then run for your life, and don't be afraid to slide. The bones in

your body are more limber than they will be half a dozen years hence. You can stand knocks as a boy that would almost kill you as a man. Never run into another player with the intention of hurting him. Never get angry, and never fight. Be manly, and only resort to fighting when you must do it to protect yourself. . . . Make up your mind that it's much better to run than fight. But if you run hard, and the other fellow is a better runner than you are, stop. Stop suddenly. Don't lose any wind. Just turn around and give him a good sound thrashing. When it's all over say that you are willing to shake hands with him. Then go home and tell your mother and father all about it.

Boys, just one more word. If you want to be successful in life, remember this:

Never do anything that you wouldn't have your mother know.

Now a word to parents. If your boys become interested in outdoor sports, do not crush them. If they love ball playing do not put them to bed without supper because they have a few bruises on their person. Try and remember that they are as proud of those bruises as you are of a new dress or a new suit of clothes. If you can afford it, buy them balls, and bats, and gloves, and masks, even uniforms. Put a baseball uniform on a boy, and you can starve him for a week afterwards. But while you are starving him allow him to keep the clothes in the room with him. The moment he puts that uniform on, he's the proudest bit of human-ity in this world. Go and see him play ball if you can. Encourage him in the sport.[1]

Yogi Berra

I don't like Little League—never did. Kids only get up to bat twice a game, and most of them either walk or strike out. Too much pressure too. My three boys played Little League, but they also played together all the time on their own. You don't need Little League. You don't even need nine kids. Four is plenty—a pitcher, a batter, and a couple of shaggers. You can play ball all day long.

My boys used to try to get me out there, but I'd just say, "Go play with your brothers." If kids want to do something, they'll do it. They don't need adults to do it for them.

Robin Roberts

I have four sons, and when my wife asked me about Little League, I told her, "No way in the world." And most professional athletes feel that way about kids under fourteen. If you try to make it serious before they're physically able to handle what they're doing, you run into all sorts of problems.

Generally in the Little League you're up against a good pitcher who throws like hell. What does the coach say? Get a walk. Isn't that a

LEFT: *Yogi Berra and sons in the 1950s.* RIGHT: *Dale Berra, Pirate third baseman, 1980.*

beautiful way to learn to hit? For four years you stand up there looking for a walk.

Baseball at that age should be a softball thrown overhand where a boy can hit fifteen times a game, with no walks and strikeouts. They should be running and sliding into bases. The score should be 42–38.

I certainly would never let my boys enter a league where they'd be throwing curves at eight- or nine-year-olds. And I wouldn't want them all steamed up, heading for a pennant play-off at eleven, or a World Series at twelve. My father encouraged me to take it easy, and at eighteen I had an arm prepared for the strain of real pitching.[2]

Willie Mays

Youngsters of Little League age can survive undercoaching a lot better than overcoaching.[3]

John Montgomery Ward in 1888

No one will ever become an expert ballplayer who is not passionately fond of the sport. Baseball cannot be learned as a trade. It begins with the sport of the schoolboy, and though it may end in the professional, I am sure there is not a single one of these who learned the game with the expectation of making it a business. There have been years in the life of each during which he must have ate and drank and dreamed baseball. It is not a calculation but an inspiration.[4]

Christy Mathewson in 1908

You must not go at baseball as you would seat yourself at an office desk at nine o'clock in the morning and then keep your eye on the clock until five in the evening. You must love it.

If you've ever been around a group of actors, you've noticed, no doubt, that they can talk of nothing else under the sun but acting. . . . It's exactly the same way with baseball players. Your heart must be in the work.[5]

Roy Campanella

You got to be a man to play baseball for a living, but you got to have a lot of little boy in you, too.

Cy Young in 1908, "Rules for Pitching Success"

1. Pitchers like poets are born, not made.
2. Cultivate good habits: Let liquor severely alone, fight shy of cigarettes, and be moderate in indulgence of tobacco, coffee, and tea. . . . A player should try to get along without any stimulants at all: Water, pure cool water is good enough for any man.
3. A man who is not willing to work from dewy morn until weary eve should not think about becoming a pitcher.
4. Learn to be patient and cool. These traits can be cultivated.
5. Take the slumps that come your way, ride over them, and look forward.
6. Until you can put the ball over the pan whenever you choose, you have not acquired the command necessary to make a first-class pitcher. Therefore, start in to acquire command.[6]

John McGraw in 1923

With the same amount of natural common sense behind him, the college boy has a full two years' jump on the town-lot boy.

The difference is simply this—the college boy, or anyone with even a partially trained mind, immediately tries to find his faults; the unschooled fellow usually tries to hide his. The moment a man locates his faults he can quickly correct them. The man who thinks he is keeping his mistakes undercover will never advance a single step until he sees the light.

That in a nutshell is the difference, and it may explain why I have steadfastly tried to get college boys with natural ability on my many ball clubs. Usually they arrive quicker and last longer.[7]

Connie Mack

I cannot emphasize too strongly my feelings about the importance of education. And there's only one time in your life to obtain a solid education; that is while you're young. Don't go into professional baseball with the idea that you'll play the game for a few years, make enough money, and then go back to finish your college education. It just isn't done.[8]

Satchel Paige
[Paige held strong and definite opinions on physical conditioning.]

I don't generally like running. I believe in training by rising gently up and down from the bench.

Mickey Mantle in 1964
Nothing is easy except when you work hard at it. Nobody worked harder at learning everything there is to know about hitting than Ted Williams, and nobody works harder on pitching than Whitey Ford.

Or take Willie Mays. . . . He so seldom makes a bad play that he makes playing baseball seem like a breeze. But don't think it's easy. I can't forget that Willie collapsed and passed out on the bench during ball games a couple of times a season or two back. When the doctors examined him they said he was suffering from utter exhaustion. Willie had been driving himself so hard that he had literally worn himself out. But figure it out. You have to work hard to be able to make things look as easy as Willie makes them look.[9]

Al Kaline
There are no shortcuts. To be a great player you've got to give it that *extra* effort. Nothing can beat working. You can use that philosophy in any phase of your life.

Bill Dickey
Work hard! Work on your weaknesses so as to become a complete ballplayer. Your strong points will develop naturally.

Be competitive! If you haven't got that competitive fire, you may stay in the big leagues for a few years, but you're not going too far. That competitive spirit means the difference between great and mediocre. I'll give you two examples. Pete Rose and Enos Slaughter. There are plenty of players around with more ability who'll be forgotten long before those two fellows. They're both bear-down guys. Rose'll make the Hall of Fame, and I sincerely hope Slaughter does. Any young player could take those two as models.

Eddie Mathews
They're very conscious today at management level of player attitude. So go out there and show them you're trying. It can't substitute for talent, but it'll sure as hell help.

Ted Williams

If you want to be a hitter, remember this. The best hitters that ever lived were the guys that practiced the most. And it's hard because you've got to get somebody to pitch and somebody to shag. It's not as easy as golf, where you just bring a bucket of balls down to the playground and bam, bam, bam. Christ, if a player hits twenty balls a day he's luckier'n hell. But I say this, if you can't hit against pitching at least swing the damn bat. And I don't see any of them doing it, and that's something I have to criticize about the youngsters. They don't swing the bat enough.

If there's one thing I advise it's swing the bat, even in the off-season, at least three or four hundred times a week.

Bob Feller

No smoking. No drinking. Go to bed early, work hard. Work at holding men on base and fielding your position. And keep the ice off your arm and in your soda pop.[10] . . .

Burleigh Grimes

Save it for the ball game. I think I've could've lasted longer if the managers had given me more rest instead of putting me in the bull pen between starts. *They* don't care that much. They've got plenty of younger fellows to put in your place when you're through. Don't go disobeying orders, but you don't need to volunteer all the time. And you *can* avoid wasting your energy when you're *not* pitching.

So spread it out if you can. Now, Ted Lyons pitched for the White Sox once a week, every Sunday, and I forget how many ball games in a row he finished. But he had that six days of rest, see. And he lasted till he was forty-six.

Satchel Paige, "How to Stay Young"
1. Avoid fried meats, which angry up the blood.
2. If your stomach disputes you, lie down and pacify it with cool thoughts.
3. Keep the juices flowing by jangling around gently as you move.
4. Go very light on the vices, such as carrying on in society. The social ramble ain't restful.
5. Avoid running at all times.
6. Don't look back. Something might be gaining on you.

Stan Musial

I believe there's still a lot of great opportunity in this country, whether it be in sports or in business. It may be harder to find, but it's there. So I say, set your sights high when you're young; and when you've chosen your profession, make sure you start by mastering the basic fundamentals. This is true of athletics and I think it's true of any field. If you want to be a writer, make sure you learn the rules of grammar. If you decide to be a photographer, make sure you begin by mastering your camera.

Mainly, in today's world, I think our youngsters ought to get a college education. I think that's more important then ever—to broaden your mind.

I also think it's important just to listen to older people. They can give you good advice. I've seen it through the years. Seems like I was always with older people when I was growing up and even when I was playing ball. Like when I was sixteen, I was playing with guys in their twenties. I've always valued my older friends and respected their experience. When Ty Cobb came around to offer advice, I took it—and profited by it. Still do.

Al Kaline

I always remember some advice my dad gave me. When I was young I used to get mad on the field and throw helmets and bats until my dad taught me, "Never get too high or too low. Anything you do, you're gonna have days where you do great, but don't think *too* great of it. And you're gonna have times when you fail, but don't get *too* down about it." So I always tried to follow that philosophy and follow a good happy medium. I didn't bring my problems home with me or brood on them, and I tried to keep from getting too excited. And I think that philosophy was one of the things that enabled me to play so long in the big leagues.

Ralph Kiner

I predict that you'll see more young athletes than ever turning to baseball in the future because of the money being poured into salaries and benefits and also because of the longevity potential. You can play longer and with less chance of injury than in football, say.

The biggest problem as I foresee it, though, will be keeping their incentive and their values. It's extremely difficult for *anybody*—I don't care who—to receive a whole lot of money and still keep their head on straight. That's a real challenge for the young players coming up in the game. Because the way baseball is structured now, you can jump straight from high school or college, where you may have no money at all, and become rich overnight.

I'm not just talking about baseball alone. You see it happen whenever people, especially young kids, inherit a fortune. There's the danger of going off the deep end. Leon Spinks is a perfect example.

So the young athlete beginning this type of career should have his beliefs and values as intact as possible—easier said than done—and he's gonna have to work very hard to maintain his perspective.

Wisdom for the young. Charlie Gehringer in 1980.

Charlie Gehringer

It seems like I've been in every church basement in the city of Detroit over the last fifty years giving talks to father and son dinners. One thing I've always tried to get the kids to listen to is the fact that, as far as we know, we only pass this way once. Therefore—don't blow it. Don't clown your life away.

It *seems* like more and more kids all the time are wasting their lives on drugs and whiskey and cheap thrills. They don't seem to be going anywhere. They've had a tough life, I think. The Vietnam War started them off badly. In fact, I don't think I'd want to be a kid today, although many of them do turn out beautifully. But anyway, this is what I recommend to any young kid of this generation or any generation— don't waste your life. Don't blow it.

Al Lopez

This is going to sound simple, and maybe it's obvious, but it's the best advice I can give to a young person. Do what you love to do—and give it your very best. Whether it's business, or baseball, or the theater, or any field. If you don't love what you're doing and you can't give it your best, get out of it! Life is too short! You'll be an old man before you know it. And that's the truth—take it from an old man. You'll be an old man before you know it.

Notes

For certain quotes which many fans will immediately recognize, I was unable to credit a primary source, having encountered them undocumented in numerous secondary sources. In fact, these stories and sayings have been passed down through generations of fans and sportswriters and have accumulated in a common treasury of baseball wisdom and wit.

Chapter 1

1. Willie Mays (as told to Charles Einstein), *Willie Mays: My Life In and Out of Baseball* (New York: E. P. Dutton, 1966).

2. Michael J. "King" Kelly, *Play Ball!* (Boston: Emery & Hughes, 1888).

3. Sanford Koufax (with Ed Linn), *Koufax* (New York: The Viking Press, 1966).

4. Tyrus R. Cobb (with Al Stump) *My Life In Baseball: The True Record* (Garden City, NY: Doubleday & Co., 1961).

5. Connie Mack, *My Sixty-six Years in the Big Leagues* (Philadelphia: John C. Winston & Co., 1950).

6. Lawrence Ritter, *The Glory of Their Times* (New York: Macmillan Publishing Co., 1966).

7. Donald Honig, *The Man in the Dugout* (Chicago: Follett Publishers, 1977).

8. Stan Musial (as told to Bob Broeg), *Stan Musial* (Garden City, NY: Doubleday & Co., 1964).

Chapter 2

1. Babe Ruth (with Bob Considine), *The Babe Ruth Story* (New York: E. P. Dutton, 1948).
2. Donald Honig, *The October Heroes: Great World Series Games Remembered by the Men Who Played Them* (New York: Simon & Schuster, 1979).

Chapter 3

1. Mack, *My Sixty-six Years in the Big Leagues.*
2. Tyrus R. Cobb, *Bustin' Em and Other Big League Stories* (New York: E. J. Clode, 1914).
3. Cobb, *My Life In Baseball.*
4. Ritter, *The Glory of Their Times.*
5. Ritter, *The Glory of Their Times.*
6. Babe Ruth, *Babe Ruth's Own Book of Baseball* (New York: A. L. Burt Co., 1928).
7. Ritter, *The Glory of Their Times.*
8. Louisville (Kentucky) *Courier-Journal*, March 1955.
9. Jackie Robinson (as told to Wendell Smith), *Jackie Robinson: My Own Story* (New York: Greenberg, 1948).

Chapter 4

1. Cobb, *My Life in Baseball.*
2. Ritter, *The Glory of Their Times.*
3. John Carmichael, ed., *My Greatest Day in Baseball* (New York: A. S. Barnes, 1945).
4. Frank Graham and Dick Hyman, *Baseball Wit and Wisdom* (New York: David McKay Co., 1962).
5. Christopher Mathewson, *Pitching in a Pinch: Baseball from the Inside* (New York, Grosset & Dunlap, 1912; copyright renewed New York: Stein & Day, 1955).
6. Adapted from accounts in *My Greatest Day in Baseball* and *Casey at the Bat.*
7. Gordon C. "Mickey" Cochrane, *Baseball: The Fan's Game* (New York: Funk & Wagnalls, 1939).
8. Edward W. Ford, Mickey Mantle, and Joseph Durso, *Whitey and Mickey: A Joint Autobiography of the Yankee Years* (New York: The Viking Press, 1977).

Chapter 5

1. F. C. Lane, *Batting* (New York: Baseball Magazine, 1925).
2. Jackie Robinson (as told to Alfred Duckett), *I Never Had It Made* (New York: G. P. Putnam's Sons, 1972).

Chapter 6

1. Ruth, *Babe Ruth's Own Book of Baseball.*
2. Ritter, *The Glory of Their Times.*
3. Willie Mays (as told to Charles Einstein), *Born to Play Ball* (New York: G. P. Putnam's Sons, 1955).
4. Mantle, *Whitey and Mickey.*

Chapter 7

1. Cobb, *Bustin' Em.*
2. Ritter, *The Glory of Their Times.*
3. Ruth, *Babe Ruth's Own Book of Baseball.*
4. *New York Magazine*, 21 April 1980.

Chapter 8

1. John Evers (with Hugh Fullerton), *Touching Second: The Science of Baseball* (Chicago: Reilly & Britten Co., 1910).
2. Quoted from newspaper article in clipping file; paper unidentified.
3. Ritter, *The Glory of Their Times*.
4. Lane, *Batting*.

Chapter 9

1. Albert G. Spalding, *America's National Game* (New York: American Sports Publishing Co., 1911).
2. *Cosmopolitan Magazine*, October 1888.
3. Kelly, *Play Ball!*
4. John McGraw, *My Thirty Years in Baseball* (New York: Boni and Liveright, 1923).
5. Lane, *Batting*.
6. Cobb, *Bustin' Em*.
7. Cobb, *My Life in Baseball*.
8. McGraw, *My Thirty Years in Baseball*.
9. Ritter, *The Glory of Their Times*.
10. Koufax, *Koufax*.
11. Phil Musick, *Who Was Roberto?* (Garden City, NY: Doubleday & Co., 1974).
12. Mantle, *Whitey and Mickey*.

Chapter 10

1. Mack, *My Sixty-six Years in the Big Legues*.
2. Cobb, *Bustin' Em*.
3. Mathewson, *Pitching in a Pitch*.
4. Cobb, *Bustin' Em*.
5. Mathewson, *Pitching in a Pinch*.
6. Evers, *Touching Second*.
7. Lane, *Batting*.
8. McGraw, *My Thirty Years in Baseball*.
9. Ritter, *The Glory of Their Times*.
10. Mickey Mantle, *The Quality of Courage* (Garden City, NY: Doubleday & Co., 1964).

Chapter 11

1. Spalding, *America's National Game*.
2. Mack, *My Sixty-six Years in the Big Leagues*.
3. Lane, *Batting*.
4. Lane, *Batting*.
5. Mickey Mantle, *The Education of a Baseball Player* (Simon & Schuster, 1967).
6. Lou Boudreau (with Ed Fitzgerald), *Player-Manager* (Boston: Little-Brown, 1949).
7. Ford, *Whitey and Mickey*.
8. Mantle, *Whitey and Mickey*.
9. Charles Dillon "Casey" Stengel (and Harry T. Paxton), *Casey at the Bat: The Story of My Life in Baseball* (New York: Random House, 1962).

Chapter 12

1. McGraw, *My Thirty Years in Baseball*.
2. Robinson, *Jackie Robinson*.
3. *Look* magazine, January 1957.
4. Roger Kahn, *The Boys of Summer* (New York: Harper & Row, 1971).
5. Lawrence "Yogi" Berra (and Ed Fitzgerald), *Yogi* (Garden City, NY: Doubleday & Co., 1961).
6. Stengel, *Casey at the Bat*.
7. Ford, *Whitey and Mickey*.
8. Musick, *Who Was Roberto?*

Chapter 13

1. Cobb, *Bustin' Em.*
2. Al Silverman, ed., *Best of Sport: An Anthology of Fifteen Years of Sport Magazine* (New York: Bartholomew House, 1961).
3. Cobb, *My Life in Baseball.*
4. Lane, *Batting.*
5. Lane, *Batting.*
6. Ruth, *Babe Ruth's Own Book of Baseball.*
7. Donald Honig, *Baseball When the Grass Was Real* (New York: Coward, McCann, & Geoghegan, 1975).
8. Kahn, *The Boys of Summer.*

Chapter 14

1. Stengel, *Casey at the Bat.*
2. Carmichael, ed., *My Greatest Day in Baseball.*
3. *Hartford Courant,* 12 October 1979.
4. Ford, *Whitey and Mickey.*
5. Mantle, *Whitey and Mickey.*
6. Stengel, *Casey at the Bat.*
7. Ford, *Whitey and Mickey.*

Chapter 15

1. *Cosmopolitan Magazine,* October 1888.
2. Cobb, *Bustin' Em.*
3. Ritter, *The Glory of Their Times.*
4. Berra, *Yogi.*

Chapter 16

1. Ritter, *The Glory of Their Times.*
2. Mack, *My Sixty-six Years in the Big Leagues.*
3. Mays, *My Life In and Out of Baseball.*
4. Ford, *Whitey and Mickey.*
5. Musial, *Stan Musial.*

Chapter 17

1. Evers, *Touching Second.*
2. Ruth, *Babe Ruth's Own Book of Baseball.*
3. McGraw, *My Thirty Years in Baseball.*
4. Mack, *My Sixty-six Years in the Big Leagues.*
5. Ritter, *The Glory of Their Times.*
6. Spoken to Les Biederman in 1938.
7. Jimmy Breslin, *Can't Anybody Here Play This Game?* (New York: The Viking Press, 1963).

Chapter 18

1. Ritter, *The Glory of Their Times.*
2. Ruth, *Babe Ruth's Own Book of Baseball.*
3. Carmichael, ed., *My Greatest Day in Baseball.*
4. Rogers Hornsby (J. Roy Stockton, ed.), *My Kind of Baseball* (New York: David McKay, 1953).
5. Cochrane, *Baseball.*
6. Carmichael, ed., *My Greatest Day in Baseball.*
7. Quoted from unidentified article in clipping file.
8. Leroy "Satchel" Paige (as told to David Lipman), *Maybe I'll Pitch Forever* (Garden City, NY: Doubleday & Co., 1962).

9. *Baseball Bulletin*, February 1980.
10. Mantle, *The Quality of Courage*.
11. Roy Campanella, *It's Good to Be Alive* (Boston: Little, Brown & Co., 1959).

Chapter 19

1. *Saturday Evening Post*, 27 January 1962.
2. Ted Williams (with John Underwood), *My Turn at Bat: The Story of My Life* (New York: Simon & Schuster, 1969).
3. Art Rust, Jr., *Get That Nigger Off the Field* (New York: Delacorte, 1976).
4. Mays, *My Life in Baseball*.
5. *New Yorker*, 22 September 1980.
6. Jackie Robinson (with Charles Dexter), *Baseball Has Done It* (Philadelphia and New York: J. B. Lippincott, 1964).

Chapter 20

1. Mack, *My Sixty-six Years in the Big Leagues*.
2. Spalding, *America's National Game*.
3. John Holway, *Voices from the Great Black Baseball Leagues* (New York: Dodd, Mead, and Co., 1975).
4. Koufax, *Koufax*.
5. Evers, *Touching Second*.
6. Kelly, *Play Ball!*.

Chapter 21

1. Ritter, *The Glory of Their Times*.
2. Ford, *Whitey and Mickey*.
3. Ford, *Whitey and Mickey*.
4. Koufax, *Koufax*.

Chapter 22

1. Mack, *My Sixty-six Years in the Big Leagues*.
2. Ritter, *The Glory of Their Times*.
3. Cobb, *Bustin' Em*.
4. Ruth, *Babe Ruth's Own Book of Baseball*.
5. Mack, *My Sixty-six Years in the Big Leagues*.
6. Carmichael, ed., *My Greatest Day in Baseball*.
7. Mantle, *Whitey and Mickey*.

Chapter 23

1. Ritter, *The Glory of Their Times*.
2. Boudreau, *Player-Manager*.
3. Ira Berkow, *Beyond the Dream: Occasional Heroes of Sport* (New York: Atheneum, 1975).

Chapter 24

1. Fred Lieb, *Baseball As I Have Known It* (New York: Coward, McCann, & Geoghegan, 1977).
2. Frank Frisch (with J. Roy Stockton), *Frankie Frisch: The Fordham Flash* (Garden City, NY: Doubleday & Co., 1962).
3. Ritter, *The Glory of Their Times*.
4. Mel Allen, *You Can't Beat the Hours* (New York: Harper & Row, 1964).
5. Honig, *Baseball When the Grass Was Real*.
6. Holway, *Voices from the Great Black Baseball Leagues*.
7. Donald Honig, *Baseball Between the Lines* (Coward, McCann, & Geoghegan, 1976).

Chapter 25

1. Ruth, *The Babe Ruth Story*.
2. Curt Smith, *America's Dizzy Dean* (St. Louis: Bethany, 1978).
3. Maury Allen, *Where Have You Gone, Joe DiMaggio? The Story of America's Last Hero* (New York: E. P. Dutton, 1975).
4. *New Yorker*, 22 September 1980.
5. Musick, *Who Was Roberto?*

Chapter 26

1. Mack, *My Sixty-six Years in the Big Leagues*.
2. Ritter, *The Glory of Their Times*.
3. Holway, *Voices from the Great Black Baseball Leagues*.

Chapter 27

1. Lane, *Batting*.
2. "Ty Cobb's Wild Ten-Month Fight to Live," *True Magazine*, 1961.
3. "Ty Cobb's Wild Ten-Month Fight to Live," *True Magazine*, 1961.
4. Ritter, *The Glory of Their Times*.
5. Lieb, *Baseball As I Have Known It*.
6. Rogers Hornsby, "I Always Kept My Bags Packed," *Sport Magazine*. August 1955.
7. Ritter, *The Glory of Their Times*.
8. Allen, *Where Have You Gone, Joe DiMaggio?*
9. Connie Mack, *From Sandlot to Big League: Connie Mack's Baseball Book* (New York: Alfred A. Knopf, 1960).
10. Ford, *Whitey and Mickey*.

Chapter 28

1. Mack, *My Sixty-six Years in the Big Leagues*.
2. *Sporting Life*, 19 December 1908.
3. McGraw, *My Thirty Years in Baseball*.
4. Ruth, *Babe Ruth's Own Book of Baseball*.
5. Ty Cobb, "They Don't Play Baseball Anymore," *Life*, 19 July 1952.
6. "Ty Cobb's Wild Ten-Month Fight to Live," *True Magazine*, 1961.
7. From Frank Frisch's foreword to William Reilly Burnett's *The Roar of the Crowd* (New York: Clarkson & Potter, 1964).
8. Robert Liston, *The Pros* (New York: Platt & Munk, 1968).
9. Evers, *Touching Second*.

Chapter 29

1. Kelly, *Play Ball!*.
2. James Michener, *Sports in America* (New York: Random House, 1976).
3. Mays, *My Life in Baseball*.
4. John Montgomery Ward, *Baseball* (New York: Penn Publishing Co., 1888).
5. Christopher Mathewson, "Baseball in Its Worthier Aspects," *Baseball Magazine*, 1908.
6. Cy Young, "How I learned to Pitch," *Baseball Magazine*, 1908.
7. McGraw, *My Thirty Years in Baseball*.
8. Mack, *From Sandlot to Big Leagues*.
9. Mantle, *The Quality of Courage*.
10. *Baseball Bulletin*, January 1980.

Recommended Readings

Allen, Maury. *You Could Look It Up*. New York: Times Books, 1979.

Angell, Roger. *The Summer Game*. New York: The Viking Press, 1972.

Angell, Roger. *Five Seasons*. New York: Simon and Schuster, 1977.

Appel, Martin, and Goldblatt, Burt. *Baseball's Best: The Hall of Fame Gallery*. New York: McGraw-Hill, 1976.

Asinof, Eliot. *Eight Men Out*. New York: Holt, Rinehart, and Winston, 1963.

Bouton, Jim, with Shector, Leonard. *Ball Four*, Cleveland: World Publishing Company, 1970.

Brosnan, Jim. *The Long Season*. New York: Harper and Row, 1960.

Coffin, Tristam. *The Old Ball Game*. New York: Herder and Herder, 1971.

Coffin, Tristam. *The Illustrated Book of Baseball Folklore*. New York: The Seabury Press, 1975.

Holway, John. *Voices From the Great Black Baseball Leagues*. New York: Dodd, Mead, and Co., 1975.

Honig, Donald. *Baseball When the Grass Was Real*. New York: Coward, McCann, and Geoghegan, 1975.

Honig, Donald. *Baseball Between the Lines*. New York: Coward, McCann, and Geoghegan, 1976.

Honig, Donald. *The Man in the Dugout*. Chicago: Follett Publishing Co., 1977.

Honig, Donald. *The October Heroes*. New York: Simon and Schuster, 1979.

Kahn, Roger. *The Boys of Summer*. New York: Harper and Row, 1971.

Kahn, Roger, *A Season in the Sun*. New York: Harper and Row, 1977.

Lewine, Harris, and Okrent, Daniel. *The Ultimate Baseball Book*. Boston: Houghton Mifflin Co., 1981.

Lieb, Fred. *Baseball As I Have Known It*. New York: Coward, McCann, and Geoghegan, 1977.

McGraw, John. *My Thirty Years in Baseball*. New York: Boni and Liveright Publishers, 1923.

Reichler, Joseph. *The Baseball Encyclopedia*. New York: Macmillan Publishing Co., 1979.

Ritter, Lawrence. *The Glory Of Their Times*. New York: Macmillan Publishing Co., 1966.

Seymour, Harold. *Baseball: The Early Years*. New York: Oxford University Press, 1960.

Seymour, Harold. *Baseball: The Golden Years*. New York: Oxford University Press, 1971.

	Playing Years	Batted	Threw	Height	Weight	H	2B	3B	HR	R	RBI	BB	SO	SB	Batting Average	Slugging Average
FIRST BASEMEN																
Gehrig, Lou	1923-39	L	L	6'	200	2721	535	162	493	1888	1991	1508	789	102	.340	.632
Greenberg, Hank	1930-47	R	R	6'4"	218	1628	379	71	331	1057	1276	852	844	58	.313	.605
Buck, Leonard[1]																
SECOND BASEMEN																
Evers, Johnny	1902-17	L	R	5'9"	140	1658	216	70	12	919	538	778	142	324	.270	.334
Frisch, Frank	1919-37	Both	R	5'10"	185	2880	466	138	105	1532	1244	728	272	419	.316	.432
Gehringer, Charlie	1924-42	L	R	5'11"	185	2839	574	146	184	1774	1427	1185	372	182	.320	.480
Herman, Billy	1931-47	R	R	5'11"	185	2345	486	82	47	1163	839	737	428	67	.304	.407
Hornsby, Rogers	1915-37	R	R	5'11"	175	2930	541	168	302	1579	1584	1038	679	135	.358	.577
Robinson, Jackie	1947-56	R	R	6'	215	1518	273	54	137	947	734	740	291	197	.311	.474
SHORTSTOPS																
Appling, Luke	1930-50	R	R	5'11"	185	2749	440	102	45	1319	1116	1302	528	179	.310	.398
Boudreau, Lou	1938-52	R	R	5'11"	175	1779	385	66	68	861	789	796	309	51	.295	.415
Cronin, Joe	1926-45	R	R	5'11"	180	2285	515	118	170	1233	1424	1059	700	87	.301	.468
Wagner, Honus	1897-1917	R	R	5'11"	200	3430	651	252	101	1740	1732	963	327	722	.328	.468
Ward, Monte[2]	1878-94	L	R	5'9"	165	2123	232	97	26	1408	686	420	326	504	.278	.344
THIRD BASEMEN																
Lindstrom, Fred	1924-36	R	R	5'11"	160	1747	301	81	103	895	779	334	276	84	.311	.449
Mathews, Eddie	1952-68	L	R	6'1"	200	2315	354	72	512	1509	1453	1444	1487	68	.271	.509
McGraw, John	1891-1906	L	R	5'7"	155	1309	127	68	13	1024	462	836	74	436	.334	.411
Sewell, Joe	1920-33	L	R	5'8"	160	2226	436	68	49	1141	1051	844	114	74	.312	.413
LEFT FIELDERS																
Goslin, Goose	1921-38	L	R	5'10"	170	2735	500	173	248	1483	1609	949	585	175	.316	.500
Kiner, Ralph	1946-55	R	R	6'2"	195	1451	216	39	369	971	1015	1011	749	22	.279	.548
Musial, Stan	1941-63	L	L	6'	180	3630	725	177	475	1949	1951	1599	696	78	.331	.559
Williams, Ted	1939-60	L	R	6'4"	198	2654	525	71	521	1798	1839	2019	709	24	.344	.634
CENTER FIELDERS																
Bell, Cool Papa[3]																
Cobb, Ty	1905-28	L	R	6'1"	175	4192	724	297	118	2245	1954	1249	357	892	.367	.513
DiMaggio, Joe	1936-51	R	R	6'1"	195	2214	389	131	361	1390	1537	790	369	30	.325	.579
Mantle, Mickey	1951-68	Both	R	6'	200	2415	344	72	536	1677	1509	1734	1710	153	.298	.557
Mays, Willie	1951-73	R	R	5'10"	170	3283	523	40	660	2062	1903	1463	1526	338	.302	.557
Roush, Edd	1913-31	L	L	5'11"	175	2376	339	183	67	1099	981	484	215	268	.323	.446
Snider, Duke	1947-64	L	R	6'	180	2116	358	85	407	1259	1333	971	1237	99	.295	.540
Waner, Lloyd	1927-45	L	R	5'9"	150	2459	281	118	28	1201	598	420	173	67	.316	.394
RIGHT FIELDERS																
Clemente, Roberto	1955-72	R	R	5'11"	182	3000	440	166	240	1416	1305	621	1230	83	.317	.475
Crawford, Sam	1899-1917	L	L	5'11"	190	2964	455	312	97	1393	1525	760	104	366	.309	.452
Hooper, Harry	1909-25	L	R	5'10"	170	2466	389	160	75	1429	817	1136	412	375	.281	.387
Irvin, Monte[4]	1949-56	R	R	6'1"	195	731	97	31	99	366	443	351	220	28	.293	.475
Kaline, Al	1953-74	R	R	6'1"	175	3007	498	75	399	1622	1583	1277	1020	137	.297	.480
Ruth, Babe[5]	1914-35	L	L	6'2"	215	2873	506	136	714	2174	2204	2056	1330	123	.342	.690
Stengel, Casey	1912-25	L	L	5'11"	175	1219	182	89	60	575	535	437	453	131	.284	.410
Waner, Paul	1926-45	L	L	5'8"	155	3152	603	190	112	1626	1309	1091	376	104	.333	.473

[1]Buck Leonard played in the Negro Leagues from 1933 to 1950, but complete and accurate statistics are unavailable.

[2]Monte Ward also has pitching statistics.

[3]Cool Papa Bell played in the Negro Leagues from 1922 to 1950, but statistics are unavailable.

[4]Monte Irwin also played in the Negro Leagues from 1937 to 1948, but statistics are unavailable.

CATCHERS	Playing Years	Batted	Threw	Height	Weight	H	2B	3B	HR	R	RBI	BB	SO	SB	Slugging Average	Batting Average
Berra, Yogi	1946-65	L	R	5'7"	190	2150	321	49	358	1175	1430	704	415	30	.285	.482
Campanella, Roy[6]	1948-57	R	R	5'9"	190	1161	178	18	242	627	856	533	501	25	.276	.500
Cochrane, Mickey	1925-37	L	R	5'10"	180	1652	333	64	119	1041	832	857	217	64	.320	.478
Dickey, Bill	1928-46	L	R	6'1"	185	1969	343	72	202	930	1209	678	289	36	.313	.486
Hartnett, Gabby	1922-41	R	R	6'2"	190	1912	396	64	236	867	1179	703	697	28	.297	.489
Kelly, King	1878-93	R	R	5'11"	180	1820	360	102	69	1363	794	550	420	315	.307	.437
Lopez, Al	1928-47	R	R	5'11"	165	1547	206	42	52	613	652	561	538	46	.261	.337
Mack, Connie	1886-96	R	R	6'1"	150	667	79	28	5	391	265	169	127	127	.247	.302

PITCHERS	Playing Years	Batted	Threw	Height	Weight	IP	W	L	Pctg.	H	SO	BB	ERA
Alexander, Grover	1911-30	R	R	6'1"	185	5189	373	208	.642	4868	2198	951	2.56
Coveleski, Stanley	1912-28	R	R	5'9"	175	3083	216	142	.603	3055	981	802	2.87
Dean, Dizzy	1930-47	R	R	6'3"	185	1966	150	83	.644	1921	1155	458	3.04
Feller, Bob	1936-56	R	R	6'	185	3828	266	162	.621	3271	2581	1764	3.25
Ford, Whitey	1950-67	L	L	5'10"	180	3171	236	106	.690	2766	1956	1086	2.74
Gibson, Bob	1959-75	R	R	6'1"	190	3885	251	174	.591	3279	3117	1336	2.91
Gomez, Lefty	1930-43	L	L	6'2"	175	2503	189	102	.649	2290	1468	1095	3.34
Grimes, Burleigh	1916-34	R	R	5'10"	185	4178	270	212	.560	4406	1512	1295	3.52
Grove, Lefty	1925-41	L	L	6'3"	190	3940	300	141	.680	3849	2266	1187	3.06
Hoyt, Waite	1918-38	R	R	5'11"	185	3762	237	182	.566	4037	1206	1003	3.59
Johnson, Walter	1907-27	R	R	6'1"	200	5924	416	279	.599	4920	3508	1353	2.17
Koufax, Sandy	1955-66	R	L	6'2"	200	2325	165	87	.655	1754	2396	817	2.76
Marquard, Rube	1908-25	Both	L	6'3"	175	3307	201	177	.532	3233	1593	858	3.08
Mathewson, Christy	1900-16	R	R	6'1"	195	4781	373	188	.665	4203	2505	837	2.13
Paige, Satchel[7]	1948-53	R	R	6'3"	180	476	28	31	.475	429	290	183	3.29
Roberts, Robin	1948-66	Both	R	6'1"	200	4689	286	245	.539	4582	2357	902	3.40
Ruth, Babe[8]	1914-34	L	L	6'2"	215	1221	94	46	.671	974	488	441	2.28
Spalding, Albert[9]	1876-77	R	R	6'1"	170	540	47	12	.797	559	41	26	1.78
Ward, Monte[10]	1878-94	L	R	5'9"	165	2462	158	102	.608	2317	920	253	2.10
Wynn, Early	1939-63	Both	R	6'	220	4566	300	244	.551	4291	2334	1775	3.54
Young, Cy	1890-1911	R	R	6'2"	210	7377	511	313	.620	7078	2819	1209	2.63

[6] Roy Campanella also played in the Negro Leagues from 1936 to 1947, but statistics are unavailable.

[7] Satchel Paige pitched from 1926 to 1947 in the Negro Leagues, but statistics are unavailable.

[8] Babe Ruth also has batting statistics.

[9] The National League was organized in 1876 at the end of Spalding's pitching career, so statistics are available only for his last two years.

Index

| 1875 | 1885 | 1895 | 1900 | 1905 | 1910 | 1915 | 1920 | 1925 |

Albert G. Spalding

Pitchers

Cy Young

Burleigh Grimes

Christy Mathewson

Lefty (

Walter Johnson

Rube Marquard

Grover C. Alexander

Stan Coveleski

Waite Hoyt

Satch

Sam Crawford

Frankie Frisch

Ty Cobb

John McGraw

Babe Ruth

Connie Mack

Goose Goslir

King Kelly

Gabby Hartr

Monte Ward

Honus Wagner

Lou Gehri

Johnny Evers

Fred Lin

Edd Roush

Hitters

Harry Hooper

E

Casey Stengel

Paul

Rogers Hornsby

Llo

Mickey

Joe (

Cool Papa E

Joe Sewell

Charlie (